Black Woman's Burden

Black Woman's Burden

Commodifying Black Reproduction

Nicole Rousseau

BLACK WOMAN'S BURDEN
Copyright © Nicole Rousseau, 2009.

First published in 2009 by
PALGRAVE MACMILLAN®
in the United States—a division of St. Martin's Press LLC,
175 Fifth Avenue, New York, NY 10010.

Where this book is distributed in the UK, Europe and the rest of the world,
this is by Palgrave Macmillan, a division of Macmillan Publishers Limited,
registered in England, company number 785998, of Houndmills,
Basingstoke, Hampshire RG21 6XS.

Palgrave Macmillan is the global academic imprint of the above companies
and has companies and representatives throughout the world.

Palgrave® and Macmillan® are registered trademarks in the United States,
the United Kingdom, Europe and other countries.

ISBN: 978–0–230–61530–4

Library of Congress Cataloging-in-Publication Data

Rousseau, Nicole.
    Black woman's burden : commodifying black reproduction /
    Nicole Rousseau.
        p. cm.
    Includes bibliographical references and index.
    ISBN 978–0–230–61530–4
    1. Human reproduction—Government policy—United States—
History. 2. African American women—Abuse of—United States—
History. 3. United States—Social policy. I. Title.

HQ766.5.U5R68 2009
305.896′073—dc22   2009004006

A catalogue record of the book is available from the British Library.

Design by Newgen Imaging Systems (P) Ltd., Chennai, India.

First edition: October 2009

D 10 9 8 7 6 5 4 3 2

Printed in the United States of America.

For my mother, Mrs. Lynn Rousseau McDaniel, who taught me the true value of education and to always believe that I would succeed at anything I tried.

And to Black girls and women everywhere who continue the struggle for liberation, autonomy, and agency.

I love you for your brownness,
And the rounded darkness of your breast,
I love you for the breaking sadness in your voice
And shadows where your wayward eyelids rest.

Something of old forgotten queens
Lurks in the lithe abandon of your walk
And something of the shackled slave
Sobs in the rhythm of your talk.

Oh, little brown girl, born for sorrow's mate,
Keep all you have of queenliness,
Forgetting that you once were slave.
And let your full lips laugh at Fate!

Gwendolyn B. Bennett, To a Dark Girl, 1902

CONTENTS

TABLES

ACKNOWLEDGMENTS

I would like to acknowledge so many who helped make first this dissertation and later this manuscript possible. First and foremost I would like to acknowledge my committee members, Dr. Ralph Gomes, Dr. Walda Katz-Fishman, Dr. Ivor Livingston, Dr. Ron Manuel, and Dr. Moses Olobatuyi, who offered me support and guidance, not just in completing this research, but in my development as an academic throughout my time at Howard University.

I would especially like to thank Dr. Gomes for being my teacher, my advisor, my counselor, and my surrogate father when necessary. Working with Dr. Gomes has been an education in self-discipline, collegiality, and commitment.

My academic advisor, Walda Katz-Fishman also holds a special place in my heart as she embraced me when I first arrived at Howard, offering me much needed academic and personal guidance and encouragement. Her support has helped lead me to my life's fulfillment and I will forever appreciate her for that.

I am blessed for the time I have spent in Howard University's truly hallowed halls and appreciate the hard work and commitment each of us put forth in our cohort. I would like to acknowledge two of my dearest Howard University colleagues. My dear friend and study partner, Dr. Michelle Street, without whom none of this would be possible. And my colleague, my classmate, my writing partner, and my friend, Dr. Vernese Edghill-Walden, who reminded me daily that failure is not an option and that Dr. Rousseau lives inside of me.

I would like to acknowledge a strong and powerful collective of Black women based in the DC metropolitan area, who continue to offer me the support, guidance, and mutual respect necessary for academic and personal success. I would like to offer praise and gratitude to

Dr. Bette J. Dickerson for her ongoing mentorship, love, and support of myself as well as countless other sisters in the struggle.

I would like to thank my colleague and dear friend Dr. Alexander Benitez for his friendship, collegiality, and ongoing support, but most of all for the long afternoons at Mayorga and Panera.

I would like to acknowledge my colleagues in the department of Sociology at Kent State University whose support; guidance; and understanding made the completion of this manuscript possible. Particularly Dr. André Christie-Mizell and Dr. Richard Serpe, whose respect and mentorship have proven essential in my success.

I would like to acknowledge my two oldest and dearest friends, Phylisa Carter, J.D., and Brigitte Swenson for continually motivating me to strive for excellence.

I would like to acknowledge my stepfather, Tyrone McDaniel, for his unending support and respect of my work and for the vigilant devotion he continues to offer my mother. Ty is an inspirational Black man that I appreciate more and more the longer I know him.

Finally, I would like to acknowledge Michael H. Mease, for listening to every draft of this work, from idea, to proposal, to dissertation, to manuscript. I thank Michael for listening as I read it aloud, almost nightly, for encouraging me to keep writing, especially when I did not feel like it, for not judging me when I just couldn't write any more, and for patting me on the back when I found my inner reserve. Most importantly, I thank Michael for always having faith in me.

Cover Art Photo By Laurin Rinder www.rinderart.com
Cover Model Nakela Mitchell

PART 1

Why Black Reproduction?

Introduction

Several years ago, I gave a talk at the annual meeting of the Association of Black Sociologists. Though over the years I have given many talks at these summer conferences, I recall this event as special. It was one of my very first solo efforts. No student colleagues, no faculty to fall back on. It was just me and my work on a panel of other young scholars presenting their work. I was a bit anxious. I had never discussed my dissertation topic in front of anyone beyond my university community and my family. In truth, I wasn't sure anyone would get it, and even if they got it, I wasn't sure they'd care.

I stood up and offered up a brief talk, making every effort to synopsize nearly four hundred years of history into a fifteen minute spiel. As my eyes moved around the room, I realized that people were really listening. I don't mean they were being polite or professional or somewhat interested; they were fully and quite personally committed. Some actually had tears in their eyes. Heads were nodding all around the room, people were bursting with response. At one point I asked the audience, which by now had grown so large people were standing in the aisles and in the back of the room, if they had ever known anyone who had "had her tubes tied." Hands pop up throughout the room. It is in this moment that that I am faced with a startling epiphany. My historical research _really_ is culturally significant and relevant to today's lived experience. This community of Black intellectuals begins to invoke heartbreaking narrative after narrative of how their mothers, sisters, aunts, cousins, neighbors, and friends had been sterilized. Some voluntarily, many without their knowledge; consent; or desire.

One woman in particular shares the story of her older sister's birth in Chicago in 1955. She recalls her parents' struggle to find a hospital to accept her mother for the delivery as she went into labor unexpectedly. After having been turned away from one _Whites only_ facility, she and her husband made their way to a second major Chicago hospital. They agreed to accept her, but only if her husband would sign a consent form. Reportedly this form consisted of a significant amount of small print, giving the husband enough pause to insist that he read it before signing. Upon closer examination, he discovers that this is a sterilization consent form. He absolutely refuses to sign the form and this second hospital attempts to turn him and his wife away. She is in such agony at this point that she is literally on the floor screaming. A doctor is passing and insists that he will deliver the child without the aforementioned sterilization consent. Had her father not taken the time, this woman, now a sociologist and university professor would never have been born. What's more, without her here to tell us, none of us would ever have known this history.

This is why I have chosen to write my first book on Black women's reproduction. This nation has a history to be told, and save the few courageous Black feminists and even fewer White feminists who have insisted on telling the story; Black women's sexual and reproductive histories have gone virtually ignored by the majority for hundreds and hundreds of years. It is time that we not only tell this story, but that we offer an analysis of how and why it has historically been socially desirable to legislate the morality of Black women; especially given the inhumane fashion with which this so-called morality has been conveyed.

In exploring the varied and complex histories of Black women's reproduction, my primary point of departure is the political economy. As Black women's relationship with the United States begins with her role in a forced labor pool, it stands to reason that her continued position in society, even in the years following slavery, would remain connected with her labor location.[2] Even as this role is transformed from one period to the next and Black women experience various levels of oppression. As with all other elements of the structure, oppression, evolves as society's needs change. As you read this book, you will learn that the needs of the various stages of the U.S. political economy dictate social life on a number of levels in both personal and private spheres.[3] It is clear that Black women's historical relations with the capitalist State have been challenging in more ways than can be described in any one text. However, through careful historical analysis, contextualized in theory that perceives the nuances of race, class, and gender oppressions, the links between the needs of the political economy and the ever-intensifying regulation of Black women's reproduction can be discerned.

This book explores the relationship between shifts in instruments of production—tools and technology—and shifts in the demand for Black labor in the United States, and how that impacts the vital contributions of Black women's various forms of labor: productive; reproductive; and biological.[4] This book further examines the various ways in which Black women's sexuality and reproduction are affected by policy during stages of economic expansion and contraction.[5] This exploration links the economic wants of the State and the development of social rhetoric surrounding Black women's reproduction and the construction of social policies.[6] These policies more often than not, encourage regulation that both exploits and restricts Black reproduction, thereby constructing and cultivating a system of disproportionate control over Black women in the United States.[7]

Though analyses of Black women's sexuality, reproduction, and relationship to policies—specifically welfare—have been offered in the past by researchers of various disciplines, such as Shulamith Firestone, Maria Mies, Rickie Solinger, Dorothy E. Roberts, and Loretta J. Ross, no current comprehensive historical, political, and economic analysis of the commodification of Black women's reproduction exists.[8] This level of analysis is needed in order to fully explore the ways in which White supremacy, racism, and misogyny are exploited to perpetuate the patriarchal domination inherent in capitalist structure. To that end, the primary objective of this book is to illustrate the clear links between historical policies and practices that have exploited, restricted, and controlled Black reproduction as well as current assaults on Black womanhood that have resulted in coercive policies and programming.

Employing this historical political and economic analysis, I want this book to eradicate the myth of the "angry Black woman." I want us to realize that we have not simply come to the collective conclusion, as a nation, that Black women are controlling and aggressive and angry, on our own. Rather this perception has been built over generations, through clever and purposeful social rhetoric; oppressive social policy; and reactive masses. This book illustrates the ways in which various means of social rhetoric have been employed as hegemonic tools to direct national opinion as well as control Black women in the United States.

Reading this Book

Much of the research on Black women in the United States has been limited by not linking the various analyses of exploitation, manipulation, control, and coercion to the shifts in the demands of the national economy. As such, this book challenges these limitations by applying a unique historical analysis to research on Black women. This analysis, referred to herein as *historical womanism*, explores the transitions of the United States national economy and its impact on various forms of Black women's labor. At its root, an analysis of the political economy, historical womanist theory is derived heavily from Karl Marx and Friedrich Engels' dialectical and historical materialism.[9] However, due to the unique nature of the role of Black women's labor in the United States capitalist structure, historical womanist theory draws from several other perspectives rooted in race, class, and gender analysis which are well suited for examining the processes of marginalization and exploitation specific to Black women, including womanist theory; material feminism; Black feminism; and critical race theory.

Applying an historical womanist analysis, this text highlights shifts in the United States national economy over four key policy periods between 1845 and 2009.[10] Given the breadth of data collected and the unwillingness of some to accept the personal impact of the State, historical analyses analogous to historical materialism often go unemployed. This text goes forward with the understanding that every distinct element attached to personal life cannot be solely attributed to the political economy; however, it is safe to assume that much of our private realities directly correlate to the status of the social, political, and economic needs of the State. By revealing this economic history, this book exposes both direct and indirect relationships between the national economy and shifts in Black women's reproduction that indicate a long lasting and significant impact on Black women in the United States.

In exploring these relationships this book addresses literature that contextualizes the history of Black women and regulatory reproductive policies in the United States from slavery to the present day, with particular emphasis on four key policy periods that highlight reproductive policies that impact Black women's reproduction through: exploitation; control; restriction; and coercion. The analysis of this historical data is achieved through the collection of historical documents and a review of related literature. The review of previous and related literature is a significant element of this research and is infused into this text within three major themes: literature examining the national economy and Black labor in the United States; literature investigating regulatory reproductive policies in the United States; and, literature researching social rhetoric related to Black women's sexuality and reproduction in the United States.

Because the topics discussed within this book are so delicately nuanced and complex, no one text could ever cover every intricacy that has erupted over the course of the past two hundred years. With that understanding, it would still be ill-advised to attempt to explore the current status of Black women's reproductive rights with a callous disregard for these histories that have propelled the issue to its current location. That said, whenever possible, this text makes every effort to focus on the key policy periods, while simultaneously maintaining an attentiveness to the social, political, and economic trends of the previous periods that inform each of these historical policy moments. In an effort to address as much of this relevant history as possible without straying too far from the topic at hand, I have also included a Further Readings section that follows each part of the book. These readings are intended to augment the information provided in this text as well as offer interdisciplinary and divergent perspectives on the topics discussed here.

Part 1

Part 1 of this book, *Why Black Reproduction?* (chapters one–three), lays the theoretical foundation for the analysis. Chapter one examines the ways in which the historical womanist analysis employed in this research has been informed by dialectical and historical materialism; womanist theory; material feminism; Black feminism; and critical race theory. This chapter further explores the application of historical womanist theory—contextualized within historical race, class, and gender perspectives—to the topic of Black women's reproduction. Chapter two elucidates the role of historical materialist method in this research. And finally, chapter three elucidates the role of social rhetoric in developing a national image.

Part 2

Parts 2–5 of this book present a discussion of the findings of this research. In responding to the fundamental questions that guide this work, these chapters analyze the following variables: (a) the nature of the economy in the specified era; (b) the societal depiction of (and reaction to) Black reproduction in each period; and (c) the ensuing reproductive policies that disproportionately affect Black reproduction in each period. Each subsection is followed by an overall summary analysis of the effects of the nature of the economy and the ensuing social rhetoric on the reproductive policies of the era.

Part 2 of this book, *Slavery Matters!* (chapters four–six), contextualizes Black labor and reproduction in the historic slave era by examining the first policy period, which occurs under the agricultural force of production (1845–1865). Some of the literature discussed within part 2 that interrogates the reproductive policies and social rhetoric of the agricultural slave era include: bell hooks, Loretta J. Ross, as well as Darlene Clark Hine and Kathleen Thompson. Hooks examines the role of the enslaved Black woman as breeder.[11] While other literature examining the slave era, such as Ross as well as Hine and Thompson, respectively, explore ways in which enslaved Black women manage to resist forced reproduction in the agricultural era.[12]

Chapter four investigates how Blacks are transformed into instruments of production under capitalism, highlighting how Black women's reproduction in the United States has been manipulated for profit since the arrival of the first enslaved Blacks in the country in 1619.

Chapter five stresses the significance of social rhetoric as it examines the depiction of enslaved Black women as lascivious wild "jungle bunnies," painted as overtly sexual, amoral animals, with natural inclinations for both domestic and field labor.[13] Chapter six examines the exploitative reproductive policy period that arises from the economic needs of this era, when Black women's reproduction is exploited to its fullest—as it becomes common practice or *policy* to force slaves to breed for profit.

Part 3

Part 3 of this book, *Emancipated . . . Not liberated* (chapters seven–nine), explores the second policy stage, a critical period in Black women's history, that sees legally regulated sterilization that occurs under industrial forces of production (1929–1954).[14] Prime examples of literature that explore reproduction, social rhetoric, and reproductive policies in the second policy period are works by Wendy Kline and Kristin Luker. Each of these authors examines the rise of eugenics ideology in the United States and how it has historically been fundamentally attached to Black women's reproduction.[15]

Chapter seven looks at the United States as the nation's economy suffers the loss of the booming southern agricultural industry and the painstaking rebuilding of the South's infrastructure and economy in the wake of the Civil War. The public image of Black women's role in the national labor force changes as the economy's needs change. The nation experiences an across-the-board loss of profit caused by the end of slave-labor. The South finds itself with a scarcity of capable and available workers due to the significant exodus of Blacks to northern and urban cities in the Great Migration. The South further suffers the onset of sophisticated farming technologies that no longer demand an abundance of human labor, skilled or unskilled. Leaving a plantocracy that, having previously needed the Black woman to reproduce his labor pool, is now a displaced White male planter class requiring new labor opportunities for himself. In efforts to reserve employment for this White male class, the nation collectively problematizes Black labor, and in turn Black reproduction, for the first time.

With these economic, population, and technological changes, chapter eight describes how the image of the Black woman as the able-bodied subservient workhorse, capable of *reproducing* each successive generation of the labor force while simultaneously *producing* a profit for the planting class, now becomes obsolete. Instead, Black women's reproduction becomes the source of public controversy—frowned upon as irresponsible and crafted into a social problem.

Chapter nine illustrates how, already a concern throughout the post–Civil War years, Black reproduction becomes a serious policy issue during the Great Depression of the 1930s. This period sees the institutionalization of policies fashioned to dictate Black women's lives by unnaturally suppressing Black reproduction through forced (and coerced) sterilization.[16]

Part 4

Part 4 of this book, *A Brand New Day* (chapters ten–fourteen), examines the final two policy periods leading to the current era. The third policy period is the time of Black women's sexual and reproductive repression that occurs under global capitalism in the electronic age at the peak of White women's sexual liberation (1975–1995). If the transition from the agricultural to the industrial era is complex for the nation, the move from industrial to computerized is categorically difficult. Needs arise during this transition that had heretofore never existed. Literature exploring the third and fourth policy periods examines the current economic era, analyzing the post–Civil Rights period through the present day. Authors, such as Leslie J. Reagan and Bernard Asbell, respectively, examine the journey from reproductive freedoms to fertility control and how that has historically related to Black women in the United States.[17] While other authors such as Rickie Solinger; Angela Y. Davis; and Dorothy E. Roberts analyze the advent of population control policies from the turn of the twentieth century through present day.[18]

Chapter ten discusses the emergence and rise of technologies in the late twentieth and twenty-first centuries that revolutionize the concept of skilled labor. The notion of skilled labor takes on a new meaning during the technological boom of the mid-1970s. Thus, ushering in a period which sees, more so than ever before, the obsolescence of Black labor.[19]

Highlighting the extent to which Black women's reproduction is manipulated and curbed when no longer needed for labor; chapter eleven interrogates the creation of the image of the antagonistic emasculating Black woman, who is portrayed as the root of the "pathology" of the Black race.[20] This chapter goes on to explore the clear ties between the conceptualization of a sick Black community; the expansion of the prison industrial complex; and the launch of the wars on poverty and drugs, the asserted goals of which are to reform the urban poor.

Chapter twelve highlights how pathologizing Black women results in Black women's reproduction being regulated more and more heavily while simultaneously White women are discovering sexual and reproductive freedoms. This third policy period (1975–1995) occurs in the early period of the current stage of global capitalism in the electronic age. This period, developing in the aftermath of the "sexual liberation" of the previous era and witnessing the growing degradation of the social contract that will take hold in the next period, sees the infusion of powerful social rhetoric that will establish, not only control of Black reproduction in the period, but lay the foundation for the ideological hegemony that will follow in the next.

Chapter thirteen describes the ways in which this current economic stage paints Black women as "welfare queens" and carriers of "crack babies."[21] Accused of being public enemies in the wars on both poverty and drugs, Black women have found themselves at the center of several "moral" debates.

Chapter fourteen goes on to describe the final period (1996–2009) occurring in the current stage that has witnessed the dissolution of the social contract. The chapter analyzes previously restrictive and controlling policies that become proactively coercive, as the neoliberal period cultivates a culture of punishment that strictly regulates Black reproduction and motherhood; leading to shockingly high rates of female surgical sterilization among Black women in the United States and appalling trends in the child welfare industry.[22] Revealing that, ironically, the policies that encourage the stemming of Black reproduction in this era have been—arguably, for the first time in history, embraced by Black women themselves. This is evidenced by the high numbers of Black women who are voluntarily sterilizing themselves at a higher rate than any other group in the United States.[23]

Part 5

Part 5, *Commodifying Black Reproduction* (chapters fifteen–eighteen), advances a theory on this topic.

Chapter fifteen explores previous theoretical analyses of Black, feminist, and Black feminist thought that have already begun to supply building blocks for historically and economically grounded theories of Black women's reproduction.

Chapter sixteen explores the ways in which social rhetoric has been employed as a hegemonic tool to control Black women in the United States. This chapter further reiterates that there is a significant relationship between key reproductive policies that have disproportionately affected Black women in the United States and the status of the national economy.

Chapter seventeen contextualizes the historic and material forces that have affected Black women's labor in the United States within the framework of the development of historical womanist theory that explores the ongoing commodification of Black women's reproduction.

Part 6

Part 6, of this book, *Liberation,* explores the ways in which we will find freedom in this new era that has seen the democratic election of a bi-racial president in the United States, yet still has politicians lobbying to sterilize undesirables. An era suffering incongruities today as profound as those of a century and a half ago that saw the onset of Civil War as the nation battled over the first emancipation.

CHAPTER ONE

On Historical Womanist Theory

The fundamental basis of scientific research is theory. A solid theory offers a three-dimensional systematic view of social life by examining the relationships between and among variables in order to explore and predict social phenomena.[1] The research presented in this book is the continuation of work originated in a dissertation.[2] The initial project tests historical materialist theory as much as it addresses the research questions that explore the ways in which Black women's reproduction is reduced to an exploitable and controllable commodity by capitalist structure. Upon completion of the initial project it became clear that, though clearly relevant, historical materialist theory falls short of the analysis needed for research on this topic.

Rather than examining to what extent historical materialist theory can explain the commodification of Black women's reproduction; this book applies dialectical and historical materialism to several other appropriate schools of thought, including womanist theory; material feminism; Black feminism; and critical race theory. The resultant theoretical perspective, referred to herein as historical womanism, offers a more pointed in depth analysis of the social, political, and economic location of Black women as a unique laboring class. In applying this perspective of Black women as a distinct class, this work is able to develop a theory of the commodification of Black women's reproduction that takes into account her position as: a person of African descent in a nation fundamentally rooted in a racialized slave economy; her role as a woman in a profoundly patriarchal structure; and her position as laborer: productive; reproductive; and biological, within a capitalist system.

In order to apply historical womanist theory to the commodification of Black women's reproduction, we must also draw from a number of related theories, including the historical economic foundation of dialectical and historical materialism, as well as the race, class, and gender analyses inherent in: womanist theory; material feminism; Black feminism; and critical race theory respectively. This research locates the commodification of Black women's reproduction within this multitudinous context. In examining Black women's reproduction, this research uncovers Black women's historic relationships to the capitalist mode of production as well as the critical roles of Black women's production and reproduction in the success of U.S. capitalism.[3] In exploring these relations to the U.S. political economy, this research further elucidates the role of dominance within capitalist structure and the ongoing relationship between the continued commodification of Black women's reproduction and hegemonic domination by the state.

This chapter discusses the theoretical perspectives that guide this analysis. In doing this, the chapter examines the meanings of dialectical and historical materialism, including its relevant assumptions and its limitations when applied to Black women's reproduction. This chapter further explores the fundamentals of capitalist structure and the contributions of womanist theory; material feminism; Black feminism; and critical race theory to the development and application of historical womanist theory.

Why Rooted in Dialectical and Historical Materialism?

Some scholars analyze Black women's reproduction in the United States without regard for social, political, and economic considerations. These approaches present us with crucial theoretical and methodological problems. It is the conclusion of this researcher that the analysis of Black women's reproduction in the United States should be undertaken within some larger structural and institutional framework, notably, the economic, political, and social framework, that is, dialectical and historical materialist theory. Such a perspective helps reveal the structural factors affecting Black women's reproduction.

The historical materialist perspective, rooted in Karl Marx's theoretical philosophies of dialectical and historical analysis, is by no means original. Such views can be traced back to the early years of modern sociology.[4] In a celebrated passage from the *Introduction to the Grundrisse*, Marx states,

> It would seem to be the proper thing to start with the real and concrete elements, with the actual pre-conditions, e.g., to start in the sphere of economy with population, which forms the basis and the subject of the whole social process of production. Closer consideration shows, however, that this is wrong. Population is an abstraction if, for instance, one disregards the classes of which it is composed. These classes in turn remain empty terms if one does not know the factors on which they depend, e.g., wage-labour capital, and so on. These presuppose exchange, division of labour, prices, etc. For example, capital is nothing without wage-labour, without value, money, price, etc. If one were to take population as the point of departure, it would be a very vague notion of a complex whole and through closer definition one would arrive analytically at increasingly simple concepts; from imaginary concrete terms one would move to more and more tenuous abstractions until one reached the most simple definitions. From there it would be necessary to make the journey again in the opposite direction until one arrived once more at the concept of population, which is this time not a vague notion of a whole, but a totality comprising many determinations and relations.[5]

Assumptions of Dialectical and Historical Materialism

This study asserts that though the relationship changes as the forces of production (i.e., the farm, the factory, etc.) do, Black women's labor—biological, manual, and reproductive—has historically been fundamental to the development and maintenance of capitalism in the United States. This study, addressing the influence of shifts in the forces of production on the commodification of Black women's reproduction in the United States, is fundamentally rooted in dialectical and historical materialism because the paradigm considers six key assumptions that directly complement the analysis herein: inequality; exploitation; technology; bureaucracy; ideological hegemony; and revolution.

Dialectical and historical materialist theory assumes first and foremost that, capitalist structure, by its very definition, causes a bifurcation within a given society; with the *bourgeois* owners of the *means of production* on one side as a dominating or ruling class and the *proletariat* on the other side as the oppressed working class. The *bourgeois* control the means of production and capital, own the land, and dictate the distribution of resources within the capitalist society. While, the *proletariat* are forced to trade their only source of power—their labor—in order to survive.[6] This structured system of inequality is inextricably linked to the capitalist system.

As this commodification of the working class alienates the *proletariat* from both the product of their labor and control of their own *means of production*, they are objectified by the market and become alienated from their very humanity. Thus, a second assumption is that capitalism presupposes the ongoing exploitation of the working class by those who control the *means of production*.[7]

Further, social, political, and economic condition of the masses is related to shifts in the productive forces: *modes of production, means of production, and relations of production.*[8] Therefore, a third assumption is that, "The bourgeoisie cannot exist without constantly revolutionising the instruments of production, and thereby the relations of production, and with them the whole relations of society."[9] As evidenced in the twenty-first century, just as technological advancements can bring us closer together, creating what is often called a global village or a global society, it can and often does widen the gap that separates the working classes from the ruling classes.[10]

A fourth assumption is that within a capitalist system, the state and its "political and ideological institutions that serve the interests of the propertied classes" are used to maintain the ruling class' power over the working class.[11] This occurs through a complex system of institutions that subjugate the working classes through a maze of bureaucratic regulations.

Gramsci "stresses that it is not enough for the capitalist class simply to take control of the state machine and rule society directly through force, misinformation, and coercion; it must also convince the oppressed classes of the legitimacy of its rule."[12] Thus, a fifth assumption is that, "*ideological hegemony* of the ruling class, operating through the state itself, prolongs bourgeois class rule and institutionalizes and legitimizes exploitation."[13]

Due to this *ideological hegemony*, the oppressed working class will not only accept, but facilitate and encourage its own oppression until a higher level of class consciousness is achieved. Leading to the final key assumption of dialectical and historical materialism, only when "a social class has attained full consciousness of its interests and goals and engages in common political activity in pursuit of its class interests" can the oppressed class achieve sociopolitical liberation.[14] In other words, the only escape from such a structured system of inequality, exploitation, and abuse is through class consciousness and revolution.

Hegemonic Domination by the State

While Marx presents an analysis of the invention of the state as an assertion of the power of the ruling class and an ongoing method of controlling the masses, Gramsci offers an elaboration of this analysis that examines the varying depths of control employed by the ruling class—*ideological hegemony.* Gramsci, like Marx, asserts that the state aims to rule the subordinated classes, initially through dominance and active measures of control. However, according to Gramsci, true domination only occurs when the state no longer needs to employ complex apparatuses to maintain power. Instead, after consistent indoctrination and bureaucratic conditioning, the subordinated population, not only acquiesces to the powers that be, but, embracing a false consciousness, assists in their own domination.

Achieving this level of domination is a key to the survival of the ruling class' capitalist control:

> Although the dialectics of the accumulation process, which involves first and foremost the exploitation of labor, ultimately results in class struggle, civil war, and revolution to seize power, the *ideological hegemony* of the ruling class, operating through itself, prolongs bourgeois class rule and institutionalizes and legitimizes exploitation.[15]

Therefore, if the subordinated class believes in: (a) the strength of the ruling class, (b) the rights of the ruling class to control them, and (c) their location as a subordinate population, who deserve to be dominated by the ruling class, then the ruling class will continue to maintain power over the working class, with little fear of reprisal as well as with the consent of the very population being oppressed, exploited, and dominated:

> Gramsci argued that "the system's real strength does not lie in the violence of the ruling class or the coercive power of its state apparatus, but in the acceptance by the ruled of a 'conception of the world' which belongs to the rulers."[16]

Gramsci further asserts that by "buying in" to the hegemonic control of the ruling class, the working class further prolongs their exploitation as their collective false consciousness prohibits them from developing the class consciousness critical in moving toward inevitable class struggle and revolution evoked by Marx and Engels.[17] This condition of the working classes is known as *false consciousness.*

> False consciousness—or lack of working-class consciousness and adoption of bourgeois ideas by the laboring masses—Gramsci argued, was the result of a complex process of bourgeois ideological hegemony that, operating through the superstructural (i.e., cultural, ideological, religious, and political institutions of capitalist society, above all the bourgeois state, came to obtain the consent of the masses in convincing them of the correctness and superiority of the bourgeois world view.[18]

The concepts of consensual domination and false consciousness are particularly relevant to the theoretical framework of this research, as this study seeks to examine the ways in which Black women, as well as the rest of working-class society have accepted, embraced, and internalized the ruling class' image of Black women's reproduction with little collective organization and resistance. The working classes see themselves in the very images painted of them by the ruling class, and seem to have "bought in" to the notion that they need to be ruled; thereby forfeiting their own liberation.

> The oppressed, having internalized the image of the oppressor and adopted his guidelines, are fearful of freedom. Freedom would require them to eject this image and replace it with autonomy and responsibility. Freedom is acquired by conquest, not by gift. It must be pursued constantly and responsibly.[19]

Instead of banding together as a collective proletariat class, and taking an active role, as a collective, to revolutionize the structure, workers in the United States have allowed themselves to be divided, by race, nationality, gender, and so forth. As a result, oppressive policies have been ratified and accepted by the masses.

This research asserts that social rhetoric, stemming from propaganda (media) in all forms (film, television, radio, literature, advertisements, news reports [print and television]), has historically fed into this

[handwritten margin notes: "I would agree more w/ Foucault & Scott" / "not entirely"; "more to Freire than that"; "→ Not necessarily 'workers' first"]

national acceptance and the concept of Black women's reproduction. This national image has further lead to support of oppressive regulatory reproductive policies that disproportionately affect Black women's reproduction. This volume explores the ways in which media in its various forms has been employed by the state as tools of oppression aiding in the establishment of social rhetoric in the development of ideological hegemony.

Fundamentals of Capitalism

Keeping the key assumptions of dialectical and historical materialist theory in mind, it is clear that a capitalist system is based upon a social competition for the accumulation of wealth, which by its very nature is exploitative and dehumanizing to both classes.[20]

In the move from communal to capitalist societies, surplus product emerges for the first time in history. No longer working for survival alone, people could now accumulate product, and therefore wealth and status and power—thus classed societies replace the primitive communal systems. With the emergence of these classes also comes inequality, as the ruling classes claim ownership of the surplus product, while the working class producing it, has no authority. Instead the worker receives a wage as compensation for her/his labor.[21] The state, created as an instrument of the ruling class, protects its ownership of the newly attainable surplus product and its control over the working class:

> Ensuing struggles over the control of this surplus led to the development of the state; once captured by the dominant classes in society, the state became an instrument of force to maintain the rule of wealth and privilege against the laboring masses, to maintain exploitation and domination by the few over the many. Without the development of such a powerful instrument of force, there could be no assurance of protection of the privileges of a ruling class, who clearly lived off the labor of the masses...thus the state developed as an institution as a result of the growth of wealth and social classes.[22]

The worker must then trade this wage for goods and services for both survival and entry into the culture of the society in which s/he lives. The worker, needing capital to survive and thrive, now a consumer and a laborer, is both commodified and exploited as s/he upholds the circular structure of the capitalist system, by paying into the state with both his/her production and his/her wages. According to Marx and Engels,

> In proportion as the bourgeoisie, i.e., capital, is developed, in the same proportion is the proletariat, the modern working class, developed—a class of labourers, who live only so long as their labour increases capital. These labourers, who must sell themselves piece-meal, are a commodity, like every other article of commerce, and are consequently exposed to all vicissitudes of competition, to all the fluctuations of the market.[23]

The relationship between the owners of the means of production and the workers is inherently oppressive, as the goal of the ruling class is to accumulate wealth through profits from the labor of the working class and co-opting their production. According to Marx's historical analysis, this final fundamental element of capitalism is the root cause of the alienated working class's constant struggle for survival rather than flourishing in the system that their labor keeps afloat.[24]

Sernau asserts that this is the incongruity of the capitalist structure, the more industrious, prolific, and dynamic the capitalist system becomes, the less autonomy, agency, and freedom for the working classes. As production increases, so do the demands on the laborers. And further, as technological advancements bring new machinery that in theory should lessen the pressures on the worker, now fewer workers are expected to produce even more. The labor force is now trapped in a new phase of labor exploitation that they cannot challenge, because now more than ever, a constant supply of now unemployed, but willing laborers exists to replace them at the whim of the ruling class.[25]

Consider the current trend in automatic checkout counters cropping up in such varied locations as: grocery stores; banking centers; department stores; warehouse stores; movie theaters; even fast food restaurants. The consumer is expected to: scan sale items; input coupon information; provide sufficient payment; and bag said items—in some cases, the consumer is even expected to provide his/her own bags. However, this new trend also expects the consumer to pay the same prices, if not higher, in order to offset the costs for the new machinery. The business in question is employing fewer laborers, providing less benefit coverage, for example: health care or retirement, and is now employing the labor of the consumer. Further, the laborers that are employed are now required to assist consumers at as many as three, five, even seven times the rate they had been expected to work previously, as they are now responsible for multiple lines, registers, and checkouts. Just as no adjustments have been made to offer recompense to the consumer for her or his labor, no compensation will be offered the wage laborer for this significant increase in work.

Material Feminism

Material feminism perceives the inherent inequalities associated with the capitalist structure and relates them to the experience of a female laboring class. Beginning with Marx and Engels' description of the relations of society at the start of humanity, in which they contend that a vital element of our nature is wrapped up in our role as primary agents of material production. This forms the foundations of production and the reproduction of the existence of humanity. They further contend that working classes experience an assault on their humanity as laborers within a capitalist system.[26]

Alexandra Kollontai contends that women experience an oppression, distinct from that of the general *working class*, as women, both produce as laborers within the capitalist structure and reproduce the wage labor force that perpetuates the capitalist structure.[27] The indispensable nature of their dual roles, as both producers and reproducers, is considered particularly acrimonious to Kollontai as women's labor is the fundamental element that perpetuates the success of the system that so oppresses them. In her analysis of the oppression of women's labor, Kollontai asserts that women will never fully achieve liberation from this cycle of oppression as long as they continue to be located in a system centered on the notions of private property and ownership.[28]

Just as Kollontai perceives *women* as located in a distinct class of workers, who have suffered a historical exploitation and oppression within the capitalist structure, specific to their class, I assert that Black women occupy an equally distinct position as a *Black* working class of women. Taking a note from theorists such as Angela Davis and bell hooks, this text analyzes the effects of the demands of the capitalist owning class on this Black female laboring class. Though clearly tied to the oppression of women described by Kollontai, it seems evident that the intersection of race within an already complex web of labor, gender, and sexual oppressions creates yet another distinct laboring class. Further, as the

sexual & reproductive labor

working-class women described by Kollontai are relegated to positions of both producers, as workers within the wage labor system, and reproducers of the wage labor force; Black women's labor exploitation, interlaced with race, gender, and sexual exploitation, is further exacerbated by forced labor within the slave labor system and sexual and reproductive labor exploitation and abuse both during and after slavery.

Davis and hooks each examine these evolving relationships of Black women's reproduction to the capitalist mode of production. Davis, for example, examines the connection between sterilization of Black women and institutionalized racism in the United States.[29] While hooks examines the persistence of misogynistic ideologies that transcend Black and White, but are instead distinctly American—that justify the regulation of Black reproduction in the United States.[30]

Reproductive labor paradigm

The exploitation of these various forms of women's labor have been unique in regards to Black women as biological and reproductive labor have historically been reserved for White women's own families, while Black women's various forms of labor have been regulated for profit since their arrival in the United States.[31] Even in the periods following the end of slave labor, Black women are relegated to *Black* women's work. Now beginning ongoing campaigns to restrict Black women's biological labor, productive and reproductive labor is even further exploited. Black women continue to respond to the economic imperative that forces them to trade productive labor for survival, even when White middle class women struggle for their rights *to* work. Further, though White women have historically experienced a noteworthy feminization of work, that is, nursing, teaching, secretarial, et cetera; Black women remain relegated to positions firmly entrenched in a reproductive labor paradigm, that is: housekeeping; hospitality; and social work, leaving Black women superexploited by the capitalist system.

Much of the previous literature fails to analyze the status of the Black female laboring class within a historic and material framework and therefore fails to provide sufficient context to the role of Black reproduction and its commodification in the United States.[32] The application of material feminist theory, illustrates the ways in which all forms of Black women's labor have been controlled by the state since the inception of the U.S. nation. First through government sanctioned policies that exploit biological, productive, and reproductive labor during the slave era. Then, during the industrial era, while restricting Black women's reproduction through compulsory sterilization programs, the capitalist structure continues to grow itself through the exploitation of Black (and other) wage labor. Later Black women's labor is controlled through propaganda imagery that vilifies Black motherhood. In the following period, the current era, now nationally perceived as a problem, Black women are no longer forced or manipulated into compliance in order to control her labor and reproduction. Instead, she has been coerced into acquiescence by centuries of terror attacks and hostile media campaigns that place her at odds with the national agenda.[33]

Womanist Perspective

A term most often attributed to Alice Walker, womanism is typically employed in Black women's literary analysis; however, the conceptualization of womanism has been adopted in various interdisciplinary forms.[34] Womanist theory asserts that, as Black women are profoundly rooted in a complex history of racial oppressions, they can neither ignore nor marginalize race matters, as some assert that other forms of feminism would demand. Womanism asserts that Black women's identities as oppressed people of color causes Black women to be unable or unwilling to disentangle gender issues from racial issues.

Unlike White women, Black women have historically struggled for the rights to be connected to Black men, not to gain independence from them. This is not to insert a heteronormative view of Black men and women, nor to imply that Black women cannot seek independence. It is instead to acknowledge that Black men and Black women, though biologically and communally connected as parents, children, siblings, neighbors, co-workers, and friends; have historically not been free to maintain those ties in a manner of their own choosing. This historic repression of the organic bond between men and women within Black communities logically leads Black women to seek the freedom to connect with male members of their communities, rather than the freedom from men, as so many historically White feminist agendas have sought.

Further, having survived the battles in the trenches, as it were, one could liken the experiences of Black men and women to that of war buddies. Given the depth of the bond of shared racial oppression, there is no way to separate the Black man from the Black woman. Again, not to imply that this connection is, must be, or even should be a sexual or romantic bond. Having the shared experience of the ongoing and tumultuous realities of life within a racially stratified system, Black women have historically occupied the role of sympathetic partner to Black men. As in any *family*, Black male female relationships are not without their own complexities. What's more, the relationship continues to be significantly challenged by the patriarchy of the American system. Still, Black men and women remain well-informed allies in the ongoing struggles with racial oppressions.

As the historical oppressions suffered by Black women have been rooted in abusing both their race and their gender. Having been forced for so many years to choose to pursue either a Black consciousness or a so-called feminist agenda, Black women have essentially been challenged to choose—race or gender. This historic conundrum reared its ugly head during the 2008 presidential election. Would Black women support Hillary Clinton as the first woman candidate or would Black women choose race and support the Black presidential hopeful—a man. Constantly asked to choose, womanist theory asserts that the reality for Black women is that both her race and her gender are socially perceived at all times. As such, she is unable to make a decision where choice does not exist. Furthermore, womanist theory asserts that given her positions as both female within a patriarchy and Black in a racist system, she should not have to attempt to bifurcate and compartmentalize her identity, and essentially privilege one oppression above another. Demanding this of Black women would be antithetical to the subversive nature of the feminist agenda.

Though revolutionary by design, the so-called feminist agenda is fundamentally insensitive to the needs of Black women as their histories and their goals remain cataclysmically disparate. In a nation that has propelled White women from near-property status to women's liberation; Black women have not fared as well in regards to race or gender. Still assaulted by racial discrimination and never fully accepted as women, Black women exist in a unique space somewhat removed from White women's feminism.

I am, however, hesitant to reference a *feminist agenda* as the term is misleading, implying that there is one specific agenda that speaks to all feminists the world over. Instead, there are a series of perspectives from diverse and varied schools of thought that speak to myriad issues related to various feminist ideologies. As such, womanism was never meant to be mutually exclusive of feminism. Rather, womanist theory places the agenda of the Black experience at the center, rather than a further marginalized population on the fringes of White feminist perspectives.

Black Feminism

Black feminism is a theory of gender, race, class, and sexuality that is relevant to this research. Patricia Hill Collins' exploration of Black feminist theory highlights the intersectionality of oppressions and describes a matrix of domination that maintains these complex systems of oppressions.[35] Though Collins would likely identify the elements of her analysis I perceive as womanist to be *Black feminist,* she and I agree that at times the terms are somewhat interchangeable.[36] Like Collins suggests, the amalgamation of theoretical perspectives employed within this text are for the purposes of moving beyond the restrictions and the politics of any one theory, and to instead, apply relevant analyses to the topic of Black women's labor.[37] Therefore, though somewhat in opposition with the notion of womanism, Collins' Black feminist theory seems very much informed by a womanist perspective and clearly relevant to the topic at hand. Asserting that Black women exist within a realm of multiple oppressions; Collins contends that one cannot compartmentalize oppressions, reducing them to any one archetype. Instead, oppressions work in tandem to create the manipulation, exploitation, and abuse inherent in a stratified system. Collins further asserts that a *matrix of domination* exists within a stratified system that maintains these oppressions, as this system is actively perpetuated by the structure.

Relevant Assumptions of Critical Race Theory

Critical race theory is a perspective that asserts several assumptions about race and racism in the United States that are key to the synthesized theoretical framework applied here.[38]

Critical race theory locates the conceptualization of race in the United States as a social construction. As such, contrary to popular understandings and various scientific perspectives, race is neither rooted in phenotype nor biology. Instead critical race theory asserts that race is a fluid concept that evolves over time, as witnessed by the ever-changing conceptualization of Black and White in the United States.

Critical race theory further understands the role of racism in the United States as a structural imperative. This perspective asserts that racism holds a meaningful space within the social, political, economic, and legal structures in the United States.[39] Given its deep roots within American structures, racism in the form of White privilege becomes an invisible element that coexists within society, yet goes nearly unnoticed and is therefore infrequently challenged. This system continually reinforces a structure that standardizes whiteness and marginalizes all nonwhite groups.

Critical race theory further contends that this racism cannot be dismissed as deviant behavior as it is so often framed. Like dialectical and materialist theory, critical race theory asserts that racism will never be untangled from the fabric of the capitalist structure nor will it ever fully be discarded. As evidenced by historical moments that have seen great inroads against institutional racism, that is, the Civil Rights Acts of the 1960s, followed shortly thereafter by significant reassertions of White privilege and power in the form of assaults on Black America, that is, the growth of the prison industrial complex.

Critical race theory also asserts that racial segregation has been socially constructed for the purposes of preserving the racialized structure. Systems of first, legally enforced, then later *de facto* segregation, that persist today, are upheld by the social, political, economic, and legal power maintained by the dominating class in the United States.

Informed by dialectical and historical materialist perspectives, critical race theory contends that the ruling class only promotes the interests of Blacks when their own interests will be served even further. As evidenced throughout history, the dominating class does lend itself at times to the needs of the Black population; however, according to critical race theory, this only occurs when the results of these endeavors are too advantageous for Whites to dismiss. For instance, the struggle to end slavery has historically been reframed as northerners going to war to save southern Blacks from the institution that had bound them for hundreds of years. In actuality, threatened by the growing economic strength of the South, the North, that had little use for slavery in industrialized cities, was determined not to lose the battle for power. Therefore, the Civil War was less a struggle to emancipate slaves, but more a battle over land ownership and national and international political and economic power.[40] The Emancipation Proclamation was effectively an unintended consequence of the War Between the States.

Limitations of Historical Materialist Theory

A clear pattern of labor exploitation has developed throughout U.S. history. As such, it is evident that the capitalist structure is an impactful force in the lives of wage laborers. However, dialectical and historical materialist theory alone would miss the fact that "Women and people of color are overrepresented in the contingent workforce."[41] Chuck Collins and Felice Yeskel describe "contingent" or "nonstandard" labor as, "a number of different types of work for temp agencies, on-call workers, day laborers, part-time employees, and contract workers:"[42]

> Nonstandard workers, on average, receive lower wages than do regular full-time workers with similar personal characteristics and educational qualifications. The median wage for temp-agency workers is 75 percent of that of full-time workers.... In 2001, 31.0 percent of women worked in nonstandard employment, compared to 22.8 percent of men. Black workers comprise 10.8 percent of the total workforce, but 24.5 percent of the temp-agency workforce.[43]

Brewer, Fishman, Kuumba, and Rousseau address the historical relationship of women, particularly working-class women of color, and the state in *Women Confronting Terror: Land, Labor, and Our Bodies*. This article labels the ongoing role of the U.S. political economy in female labor–both "productive" and "reproductive"—as "state-sponsored terror."[44] Briefly chronicling this reproductive imperialism, the authors elucidate the intimate connections of patriarchy with racism, class exploitation, and heterosexism. The authors further assert that historically, Black women's relationship to the politically economy has been parasitic.

> Enslaved African women, in particular, suffered the super-exploitation of being forced agricultural and domestic labor, sexually used and abused, and being used as breeders through their reproductive labor.[45]

The authors go on to link the exploitative breeding of the slave era in the years following the embargo on the transatlantic slave trade in the nineteenth century; the coercive repression of the Negro Project of the early twentieth century; and the current oppression of neoliberal reproductive policy in the twenty-first century.[46]

Jacqueline Jones explores the relationship of Black women's labor to the national economy in the early to mid twentieth century, in *Labor of Love, Labor of Sorrow*. Jones contends that Black women, forced into very specific types of work, have historically been relegated to the margins of the national economy:

> At the very bottom of hierarchical labor force, blacks of both sexes lost their tenuous hold on employment in the agricultural, service, and industrial sectors, as economic contraction eliminated many jobs and spurred an unequal form of interracial competition for the ones that remained. Concentrated in the marginal occupations of sharecropping, private household service, and unskilled factory work, many black women's jobs had, by 1940, "gone to machines, gone to white people or gone out of style," in the words of activist-educator Nannie Burroughs.[47]

Jones goes on to assert that the state has historically controlled every element of Black women's realities, as the state serves as her employer, regulator, and her provider of social services.

Shulman's *The Betrayal of Work* explores the creation of what she refers to as a caste of low-wage workers:

> Who are the low-wage workers?...[N]early two-thirds of the low-wage workforce is white. Yet, black and Latinos are overrepresented in this group relative to their participation in the overall workforce. In fact, the proportion of minority workers in 2001 earning a low wage is substantial: 31.2 percent of blacks and 40.4 percent of Latinas in contrast to 20 percent white workers.[48]

It is no accident that women, Blacks, and Latinos are the lowest paid labor pools in the United States and even with the advancements made with the modern Civil Rights movements in the 1950s; 1960s; and 1970s, a disparity still persists for Blacks, Latinos, and women with equal education to their White male counterparts in the United States.[49]

Now we understand that dialectical and historical materialism is the most appropriate framework from which to begin this research as it offers a context by which we can explore the impacts of the needs of the political economy on social life. However, we must also acknowledge that the historical location of materialist theories solely in class inequalities causes the theory to lack some levels of analysis key in understanding the experiences of populations marginalized by the state due to racial and gender stratification. Current research has established that Black women's labor has historically been essential to the successful capitalist structure that has assisted in catapulting the United States into its position as a world superpower.[50] It is undeniable that her roles as: field laborer, reproductive laborer, and biological reproducer have contributed to every possible aspect of the U.S. political economy. What remains unclear is how this domination has continued to exist to the present day:

> The philosophy of the ruling class . . . passes through a whole tissue of complex vulgarizations to emerge as "common sense": that is, the philosophy of the masses, who accept the morality, the customs, the institutionalized behavior of the society they live in . . . to understand *how* the ruling class has managed to win the consent of the subordinate classes in this way; and then, to see how the latter will manage to overthrow the old order and bring about a new one of universal freedom.[51]

The point of substance here is that adequate analysis of the commodification of Black women's reproduction in the United States must take into consideration the prevailing economic, social, and political location of Black women. It is evident therefore that although historical materialist theory offers the foundation of economic analysis, it falls short in its exploration of race and gender. And though material feminist theory does address this omission in regard to gender, the commodification of Black women's reproduction in the United States is not a mere demographic issue resolved by the inclusion of gender. Instead it is a complex interplay of race, class, and gender oppressions mediated upon by a complex system of hegemonic institutions. The historical womanist paradigm provides a framework for analyzing these questions.

CHAPTER TWO

On Historical Materialist Method

Historical Materialist Method

A dialectical and historical materialist framework guides the methodology of this study. This historical materialist method is what allows the researcher to explore the commodification of Black women's reproduction in relation to the shifts in the needs of the political economy. The strength of this qualitative approach lies in its location of social phenomena in the material reality of the political economy. As a result, this allows the researcher to locate the commodification of Black women's reproduction in the United States within the realm of capitalist development and its fundamental link to the development of society.

This study assesses the degree to which the historical commodification of Black women's various forms of labor, specifically biological labor or reproduction, may be influenced by social, political, and economic factors (political economy). In exploring the unique position of Black women's labor, it is imperative that an analysis is formed that is not limited by racist or misogynist ideologies and considers Black women's historical relations to the economy at the center, rather than as marginal to the dominating group.

In order to explore the commodification of Black women's reproduction in the United States, this research highlights four key policy periods under three forces of production: agricultural (1845–1865), industrial (1929–1954), and global capitalism in the electronic age (1975–2009). The first policy period occurring during the agricultural era, highlights the final stages of the U.S. slave period, 1845–1865. The second period, occurring in the industrial era, examines the policies from the period of the Great Depression through post–World War II,

1929–1954. The final two policy periods occur under one overarching economic era, global capitalism in the electronic age. The first period explored in this era highlights the policies from the post–Civil Rights period through the period of the weakening of the social contract, 1975–1995. And finally, continuing the examination of the era of global capitalism in the electronic age, this book explores the policies from the period of the weakening of the social contract through the dissolution of the social contract, 1996–2009.

The Relationship of Dialectical and Historical Materialism to *Historical Materialist Method*

Both the technological conditions of producing and exchanging goods (the forces of production) and the system of ownership (the relations of production) determine the methods used by the people to secure the means of subsistence (mode of production). The chosen mode of production determines the superstructure, particularly the State, which, controlled by the economy, forms and governs social classes. The formation of these classes inevitably leads to class struggle, as it is a fundamental element in the process of capitalism. Within world history, where previously existed, "a complicated arrangement of society into various orders, a manifold gradation of social rank," we see the capitalist system replace this gradation with two major classes.[1]

> Modern bourgeois society has sprouted from the ruins of feudal society.... It has but established new classes, new conditions of oppression.... Our epoch, the epoch of the bourgeoisie, possesses, however, this distinctive feature: it has simplified the class antagonisms: Society as a whole is more and more splitting up into two great hostile camps, into two great classes directly facing each other: Bourgeoisie and Proletariat.[2]

The class relationship formed by the *bourgeoisie,* or ruling class, that owns and controls the productive forces, and the *proletariat,* or working class, demands class antagonisms. The working class exchanges their labor to the ruling class for their own survival. While, ironically, this same labor simultaneously increases the surplus product, and the capital investment of the ruling class. Thus reifying the stronghold the ruling class has over the laboring class. Furthermore, class antagonisms persist as—defined by the capitalist structure—the ruling class strives

this analysis is applied to reproduction; doesn't acknowledge how Bw individuality & collectively fought for autonomy

to glean as much surplus product from the workers as possible for the lowest possible cost; while, conversely, the workers attempt to work for the highest possible wages, under the best working conditions, for the shortest number of hours. The two classes, clearly in fundamental opposition, remain in constant struggle. The ruling class remains in control of the exploited and subordinated, workers—who are alienated from the productive process as well as from their own production.

Criticisms of Positivist Research

This qualitative method allows the researcher to examine the issue through a critical lens as opposed to the more commonly utilized positivist research methods that disallow critical interpretation and connection to the results. According to Code,

> Positivist-empiricist principles are defined around highly rarefied ideals of objectivity and value-neutrality. Objectivity is conceived as a perfectly detached, neutral, distanced, and disinterested approach to a subject matter that exists in a publicly observable space, separate from knowers/observers and making no personal claims on them. Value-neutrality elaborates the disinterested aspect of objectivity: the conviction that knowers must have no vested interest in the objects of their knowledge; that they have no reason other than the pursuit of "pure" inquiry to seek knowledge.[3]

Besides being uncritical, falsely objective, and judgmental in its supposed "value-neutrality," positivist research also suffers several other criticisms, specifically it tends to be historical and limited in its interpretability. Positivist research arguably narrowly examines statistics and utilizes inflexible categories and approaches in its analysis of social phenomena without appropriate location in the social, economic, and/or political material world. Through utilizing a historical womanist approach for this study, the researcher may assess the influence of the demands of the U.S. political economy on regulatory reproductive policies that disproportionately affect Black women in the United States during four policy stages under three economic eras and forces of production: the agricultural era from 1619 to 1865; the industrial era from 1896 to 1950; and the electronic era from 1975 to 2009.

Quantitative research maintains a positivistic approach that by its very nature focuses on an inflexible measurement of the social world through statistics. In efforts to quantitatively measure this social world, variables are assigned numeric value, and findings produced through statistical manipulation of these values. This mathematical analysis can be quite effective as it can be reproduced and proved (or disproved) regardless of the researcher. According to Goode and Hatt, "Quantification simply achieves greater precision and reliability...."[4] However, Goode and Hatt also state that,

> Modern research must reject as a false dichotomy the separation between "qualitative" and "quantitative" studies, or between the "statistical" and "non-statistical" approach.... The fundamental questions to ask about all research techniques are those dealing with precision, reliability, and relevance of the data and their analysis... "(1) how precise are their observations? (2) can other scientists repeat the observations? And (3) do the data actually satisfy the demands of the problem?"[5]

Accepting this analysis that both positivist and materialist approaches have merit, this researcher asks Goode and Hatt's questions of positivist research: how precise quantitative observations are; if the studies can be repeated; and if the data fully satisfy the demands of the research problem(s).[6]

Quantitative observations may be comparatively "precise," as they do not often rely on investigator interpretation; however, precision is a relative concept. For example, questionnaires tend to prove limiting to respondents, eliciting results that may best fit the available options, but may not contain legitimately generalizable data.

The repeatability of results, though historically accepted as a valid test, depends upon an ahistorical decontextualized approach to the research problem. As often, sociological research yields results specific to a complex configuration of variables, including race, class, gender, location, forces of production, and more, the recreation of the particular moment on history that yielded the initial results, may not prove repeatable. Does this invalidate the results? For example, could White researchers successfully repeat a quantitative experimental study of race relations, originally performed by a team of Black researchers? The positivist approach would assert that the race/ethnicity of the investigators is irrelevant, but is it?

Leading to the final question introduced by Goode and Hatt, can positivist research fully satisfy the research questions? Though the above mentioned fictional experiment could answer some questions, in what ways could the quantitative data respond to the "how" and "why" of the research questions? Why would the race/ethnicity of the researcher matter? Why are some elements of the results of the industrialized North so fundamentally different from those of the agricultural South? How do the ways race matters for some differ from others? Quantitative data cannot answer these questions, it can only tell United States that race matters do or do not exist, and depending on the formulation of the study, when, where, and in what ways.

Appropriateness of Method

While the historical materialist method is the scientific process by which we collect the data in regard to the relationships among the variables—economic, social, political, and technological. As a method, historical materialism allows this research to examine how Black women's roles within the labor force develop in relation to the demands of shifts in economic and social structures.

Historical materialist methodology is particularly appropriate for the examination of the commodification of Black women's reproduction for several reasons. Dialectical and historical materialism allows the researcher to historically locate the emergence of social phenomena in material, political, and economic contexts. Historical materialist method allows the researcher to fundamentally link the oppression and exploitation of working class labor—productive, reproductive, and biological—to the capitalist demands of U.S. political economy. Through the historical womanist method Black women's reproductive freedoms in the United States are explored in relation to the cycle of oppression and exploitation of their productive labor rooted in the ebb and flow of U.S. political economy.[7] Historical womanist theory offers critical analysis of social phenomena.

In conclusion, although quantitative research methods may prove effective and useful in identifying and predicting the relationships between certain variables in our social world, quantitative research is limiting in its results and limited in its contribution to the scientific community and therefore to the examination of social problems.

Data Collection

This study employs a historical case study approach utilizing a historical womanist theoretical foundation. The historical case study approach is an in-depth, qualitative, nonexperimental technique that examines historical events over a historical period in detail, to test a theoretical idea or hypothesis, rather than documenting trends over a length of time. According to Goode and Hatt,

> The case study...is a way of organizing social data so as to preserve the *unitary character of the social object being* studied....It is an approach that views any social unit as a whole. Almost always this means of approach includes the *development* of that unit, which may be a person, a family or other social group, a set of relationships or processes (such as family crises, adjustment to disease, friendship formation, etc.) or even an entire culture.[8]

The dialectical and historical materialist paradigm provides a framework for answering questions discussed within the context of this research and will prove useful in future analyses of social inequalities. In this study the texts for collection and analysis include journal articles, autobiographical novels, historical texts, books, and statistical data that address varying elements of the relationship between Black women's reproduction and the U.S. political economy. These sources are appropriate to this study for several reasons. The data sources include historical and contemporary information relevant to both current and future analysis. The historical and contemporary relevance of the data is a key factor in addressing the longitudinal aspects of this research. Additionally, data are collected for a variety of factors. In performing this exploratory qualitative analysis, this study completes a historical case study of the commodification of Black women's reproduction in the United States.

This study assesses the degree to which the historical commodification of Black women's various forms of labor, specifically biological labor or reproduction, may be explained by social, political, and economic factors (political economy). In exploring the unique position of Black women's labor, it is imperative that we form an analysis that is not limited by racist or misogynist ideologies and considers Black women's historical relations to the economy at the center, rather than as marginal to the dominating group.

In order to explore the commodification of Black women's reproduction in the United States, this research highlights four key policy periods under three forces of production: agricultural (1845–1865), industrial (1929–1954), and global capitalism in the electronic age

[margin handwritten note: Think about your own sources of data]

(1975–2009). In exploring these policy periods, this research focuses on several fundamental questions, that is, to what extent is there a relationship between policies that affect Black women's reproduction and the forces of production in each of the key policy periods; to what extent is social rhetoric employed as a hegemonic tool of the State; and to what extent does social rhetoric impact social and economic policies that impact Black women's reproduction.

As the investigator anticipated, answers to these research questions offer significant insight into the analysis of the commodification of Black women's reproduction in the United States. The following is an explanation of the values of each variable examined in this study. Both reproductive policies and social rhetoric are categorized as explained herein. Once measured, each variable is examined within the context of three categories of analysis: (a) nature of the U.S. economy, (b) images of Black reproduction, and (c) types of reproductive policies.

Nature of U.S. Economy

As illustrated in table 2.1, the nature of the economy for each economic stage is examined through an analysis of the forces of production of the era. In examining the tools and technologies of each era, the role of

Table 2.1 Method of analysis—Status of economic stages

Economic Stage	Mode of production, i.e., agricultural; industrialization; computerization
	How does society look in each period, i.e., economy, technology, labor, etc.?
Political Economy	What is the status of the U.S. economy? i.e., expansion, contraction, depression, etc.
Forces of Production	What are the primary tools and technologies used to produce? i.e., agricultural, industrial, computerized, etc.
	Is technology at a high or low? I.e., hand, machine, computer, etc.
Instruments of Production Labor Pool	Who are the workers? I.e., human, Black, female, etc.
Means of Production Labor Source	Where does the labor come from? I.e., Black reproduction, etc.
Relations of Production Labor Demand	Is labor in demand? Is there a surplus of available labor? Is there a stratified system of laborers and employers?

labor is assessed as well, identifying: labor needs, labor pools, and the primary labor sources of the respective eras. In assessing the nature of the U.S. economy in each era, this study is able to analyze the status of the relationship of the U.S. political economy to Black labor. This analysis includes historical descriptive data on the stages of the U.S. political economy and its relationship to Black labor. This category is significant to the analysis in that it allows the researcher to explore the relationship between the needs of the U.S. political economy and Black women's reproduction, as it links labor demand to labor source.

Images of Black Reproduction

As outlined in table 2.2, the images of Black women's reproduction are analyzed by examining the social rhetoric surrounding Black reproduction in a given economic stage. Each period examined in this study offers a collective vision of typified characteristics of Black motherhood and reproduction as well as the collective social response to the issue of Black reproduction at the time.

Social Rhetoric

The predominating images of Black women's reproduction, sexuality, and motherhood are categorized as animalistic; parasitic; pathological; or malicious, depending on the economic stage and policy period. Images that dehumanize Black reproduction and sexuality are

Table 2.2 Method of analysis—Social rhetoric

Types of Social Rhetoric Analyzed	Characteristics of Propaganda Imagery
Animalistic	Blacks are portrayed as animals, likened to monkeys in the jungles of Africa.
Parasitic	Blacks are perceived as freeloaders, funneling needed resources away from *deserving* Americans.
Pathological	Blacks are painted as fundamentally sick.
Malicious	Blacks are no longer perceived as sympathetically simple or ill, now they are seen as conniving and purposeful in their efforts to take advantage of America.

considered *animalistic*. Images that portray Black reproduction as counterproductive and/or dangerous to the American way are considered *parasitic*. Images that paint Black reproduction as symptomatic of Black dysfunction are considered *pathological*. Finally, images that depict Black reproduction as criminal are categorized as *malicious*.

Social Response

The collective social responses examined are categorized as paternalistic; separatist; reformist; and punitive (see table 2.3). *Paternalistic* societal response is categorized by periods of controlled Black reproduction. *Separatist* response categorizes periods when Blacks are segregated from the rest of the U.S. population and reproduction is shaped as dissimilar to White reproduction. *Reformist* response categorizes periods of social reform that attempt to apply technology and policy to Black reproduction. Finally, *punitive* societal response categorizes periods when Black reproduction is linked to punishable crimes.

Regulatory Reproductive Policies

These societal responses directly affect the status of reproductive policies that disproportionately affect Black women in the United States. This analysis includes historical descriptive data on the development of a societal image of Black women's reproduction. This category is significant to the research in that it allows this investigator to connect collective social consciousness to the development of reproductive policy.

Table 2.3 Method of analysis—Social responses

Types of Social Responses Analyzed	Characteristics of Social Climate
Paternalistic	Whites embrace notion that they are *responsible* for Blacks
Separatist	Laws are instituted by the state to legally separate Whites from Black society
Reformist	The state attempt to restructure Black society
Punitive	The state incarcerates Blacks in response to social problems, i.e., poverty, drug abuse, etc.

Table 2.4 Method of variable analysis

Variable Analyzed	Method of Analysis
Policy	Specific policies that disproportionately affect black women's reproduction w/in the policy period. Other significant policies may have occurred at the time, but these are specific to reproduction.
Status of Economy	Nature of the political economy, i.e., status of the economy, technology, labor, etc.
Social Rhetoric	Social rhetoric surrounding black reproduction in given policy period, i.e., animalistic, parasitic, pathological, or malicious.
Social Response	Collective social response to rhetoric campaigns, i.e., paternalistic, separatist, reformist, or punitive.
Type of Policy	Types of policies: exploitative, restrictive, controlling, or coercive.
Characteristics of Policy	Specific elements of each policy.

Types of Policies

As outlined in table 2.4, reproductive policies that disproportionately affect Black women are divided into four (4) key categories: (1) exploitative; (2) restrictive; (3) controlling; and (4) coercive. *Exploitative* reproductive policies are categorized as laws, statutes, and common practices (de jure and de facto) that encourage Black reproduction for profit. *Restrictive* reproductive policies are laws, initiatives, and common practices that discourage Black reproduction as a method of overcoming periods of economic depression and/or as a means of population control. *Controlling* reproductive policies are defined as policies and practices that vilify Black reproduction and weaken elements of the social contract as punishment for errant Black reproduction. *Coercive* reproductive policies are categorized as policies and procedures that encourage Black women to repress their own reproduction on behalf of the State as a result of coercive incentives, such as money, benefit opportunities, et cetera. This analysis includes historical data on the various reproductive policies that have affected Black women's reproduction. This category is significant in that it allows the researcher to explore the relationship of regulatory reproductive policies in the United States and Black women.

Following each of these three categories—(a) status of the relationship of the U.S. political economy and Black labor, (b) status of reproductive policy that disproportionately affect Black women in the United States, and (c) accepted social rhetoric regarding Black women's reproduction in the United States—is a summary response to the three related research questions.

Data Analysis

Exploratory research typically uses a qualitative data analysis.[9] This research analyzes information by examining data for patterns and trends. These characteristics may guide research on the national economy's impact on Black women's reproduction in the United States.

Data in this study are managed through tables and figures constructed to organize and code the findings of each of the four reproductive policy periods between 1845 and 2009. For this study's analysis, tables are constructed to organize the findings. The tables depict the data of reproductive policy analysis: 1845–2009 as follows: Black women's reproduction in the agricultural era: 1845–1865; Black women's reproduction in the industrial era: 1929–1954; Black women's reproduction in the era of global capitalism in the electronic age: 1975–1995 and 1996–2009. For this analysis, the major patterns and trends are described.

CHAPTER THREE

The Significance of Social Rhetoric

What Is Social Rhetoric?

In a nation that espouses the tenets of freedom of speech and freedom of the press, language and words and images matter. For example, when devastated by the shock and awe of the September 11, 2001 attacks (9/11), everyone told Americans to keep on living, to get out there and boost the American economy. Americans took their children trick or treating that Halloween, and went holiday gift shopping that Christmas and Hanukkah season, all the while terrified that the next major assault was coming. However in true American form, even through the overwhelming fears, Americans continued to consume. Americans soldiered on, not because we had to have another pair of shoes, but because they told us that is how we were going to win the war on terror. We understood that it was our job to set aside our fright and to keep our economy strong at all costs.

How did we know that? Because that is what we were told in every conceivable fashion—news reports, talk shows, newspaper stories, presidential addresses, even situation comedies assured us that consumption was the best way to fix the damage done by 9/11.[1] Remember how angry everyone was? Remember how acceptable it was that the president spoke on television of hunting down evil and killing it? Remember how welcome the war was in the face of all the fanatically anti-Muslim pro-American rhetoric? Remember the Patriot Act? Passed just forty five short days after 9/11, it threatened six different Constitutional amendments with the swipe of a pen, and we barely batted an eye as a nation.[2] Why did it take the sickening images of prisoners being tortured and made sport of at Abu Gharib before we started to reevaluate?[3] And even then, wasn't that a well played media blitz? Showing us women taking pictures with men in dog leashes— wow—powerful propaganda images!

Understanding both the role and impact of social rhetoric on society is fundamental to accepting the general assertions of this research. In Aristotle's critique of social rhetoric, he writes of the role of persuasion in its establishment, implying that the ability to convince one's audience is the only way to achieve social rhetoric. According to Aristotle, there are effectively three kinds of persuasion in such an exchange. The success of the first sort of persuasion is contingent upon the perceived moral integrity of the speaker. The second form of persuasion relies upon convincing the audience to share in a specific disposition dictated by the speaker. While the third form of persuasion is dependent upon evidentiary support offered within the exchange.[4] Though Aristotle is directing this philosophical analysis solely at the spoken word, his explanation of the role of persuasion within the establishment of social rhetoric is key. Whether addressing a population, a nation, or simply a small crowd, the speaker must draw its listeners in, in order to achieve the goal of spinning a narrative that his or her listeners will accept as a truth.

As we apply this classical critique of spoken persuasion to today's global context, it seems clear that the three methods of persuasion are no longer mutually exclusive, nor is persuasion solely achieved through lectures and speeches. In applying this analysis to this day and age, when we have a plethora of media resources to turn to, ranging from: Internet to television to music to talk radio, we have many means of reaching a desired population as the persuader, as well as myriad means of accessing information as the persuaded.

Continuing to apply Aristotle's critical analysis of persuasion to our discussion of the significance of social rhetoric, we must maintain a keen understanding that technological advancements have clearly impacted his original analysis. As such, we must consider Aristotle's three forms of persuasion both individually and collectively. Essentially Aristotle argues that in order to be persuaded, we must trust the speaker; trust the collective; and/or trust the proof as it is presented. Apply this analysis to the topic of Black women in the United States.

Trusting the Source

Do Americans typically trust the information source? Do we believe our media, our government? Do we assume that the radio, Internet, television, and elected officials are speaking the truth? Or rather, do we choose instead to believe communities generally dismissed as drug dealers; single mothers; prisoners; and ne'er-do-wells? The truth of the matter is that the hegemonic powers of the United States have an inherent credibility that allows the media to present Black America to the United States and the rest of the world in whatever fashion it so chooses, with the general acceptance of the majority of Americans. Contrary to the revolutionary beginnings of the nation, Americans tend to accept what we are told. And though unfortunately, the U.S. government and media are sullied with a laundry list of indiscretions, to say the least, the credibility of the America media and governance still remain somehow beyond reproach.

Trusting the Community

Further, though often critical of what we deem "nationalism" and "fanaticism" in other countries, we prescribe to a fervent patriotism in the United States that has historically entreated Americans to blend into one mindset that is considered distinctly American. Those who have dissented, though celebrated in some communities, suffer the label of pariah in the larger view. Consider celebrated activists throughout American history from abolitionists to revolutionary war heroes to women's suffragists to antiwar protesters to Civil Rights leaders. Many of our most famed and significant leaders have risen out of dissent and have had the most critical impact on our society. Often the impact has been disruptive to the status quo, leaving many of these dissenters jailed, assassinated, and/or discredited. Hindsight sometimes offers us a venerated martyr, such as Martin Luther King, Jr.; but more often than not, we have a Fred Hampton- a gifted young activist prominent in the Black Panther Party of the Civil Rights period, assassinated by FBI and Chicago police in 1969.[5] We hear little, if anything, about his work; his legacy; or his death in school or in the media. Americans, even those who have benefited from the efforts of the dissent of previous generations; even those who are non-prosperous; and even those who are nonwhite, tend to believe in America and therefore trust the collective.

Trusting the Proof

Further, Americans tend to trust the evidence. If there are more Black men in prison than any other population, then Black men must have a problem with criminality. If Black women are poor and need welfare, then they must need some guidance in choosing when and under what circumstances to have children. If the police stop a Black driver, there is an inherent assumption that s/he must have done something wrong. Americans tend not to insist on a deeper understanding of how and why these phenomena occur, we simply trust that the prevalence of Blacks in poverty, incarcerated, and underprivileged is proof that Blacks do suffer from a certain pathology as a race. We may not presume to know exactly *what* is wrong, but America does tend to accept that something is indeed *wrong* with Blacks—rather than the racially stratified system within which Blacks must maneuver. This acceptance leads us to encourage the legislation of morality, which history has proven time and again is neither possible nor humane.

Persuasion

Assuming the population has been thoroughly convinced due to ingrained trust in the source; the collective; and the proof; Americans now seem to be prime targets of manipulation. Convinced that this is a nation of free-thinkers, we often fail to perceive ourselves as the manipulable masses that today's media has created, often leaving us even more vulnerable to deception. How much does this matter?

Significance of Social Rhetoric

Patricia Hill Collins' 1990, *Black Feminist Thought* explores the impact of propaganda imagery in the United States. She asserts that various stereotypes, images, and other propaganda are employed to manipulate and exploit already marginalized populations.[6] Collins asserts that,

> These controlling images are designed to make racism, sexism, and poverty appear to be natural, normal, and an inevitable part of everyday life. Even when the political and economic conditions that originally generated controlling images disappear, such images prove remarkably tenacious because they not only keep Black women oppressed but are key in maintaining interlocking systems of race, class, and gender oppression.[7]

Manufacturing typified propaganda images of Black women assists in creating an unambiguous concept of the *other* that can legitimately be maligned and denigrated, as well as feared by White Christian society.[8]

The image created constructs a population so foreign and so loathsome that "the moral and social order" of civilized society actually feel threatened.[9] The apprehension, with which a population might approach liberating a group so horrific that instills such terror, could almost be understood, if not justified. Purposeful misrepresentation of the image of the Black woman is not solely acted out due to prejudice. Rather, controlling the images of Black women is an integral phase in disempowering her autonomy, strength, and agency as, "domination always involves attempts to objectify the subordinate group."[10] In accepting these false representations of the Black woman a larger divide forms between Black and White societies. Thus, creating two antithetical factions constantly at odds with one another, yet ironically each defining the role the other plays:

> One part is not simply different from its counterparts—they are fundamentally different entities related only through their definition as opposites. Feeling cannot be incorporated into thought or even function in conjunction with it because in either/or dichotomous thinking, feeling retards thought, values obscure facts, and judgment clouds knowledge.[11]

Rickie Solinger's 2000, *Wake up little Susie: Single Pregnancy and Race before Roe v. Wade* highlights the racialized disparities in the propagandized image of the Black and White unwed mother. While White pre-marital sex evolves from degenerate behavior into a form of social activism, that is, the notion of the "Sexual Revolution," Black sexuality becomes increasingly problematized and is considered a symptom of the so-called crisis of overpopulation, that is, the "Population Bomb."[12] Though Solinger's astute analysis perceives the conceptualization of the sexual revolution as equally, if not differently, problematized by the patriarchal establishment; I must contend that the invocation of "the bomb" in postwar America is an insurmountable image that haunts Black women to this day. These socially accepted disparate narratives situate White sexuality within the realm of liberation as White women become encouraged to assert their reproductive rights and sexual freedoms. While during the same period, Black women's sexuality and reproduction becomes the target of increasingly harsh regulation, as state reproductive policies begin to center on social responsibility and the so-called duty of the state when it comes to Black reproduction.[13] Loretta J. Ross' 1993 "African-American Women and Abortion: 1880–1970" addresses the intricacies of Black women's sexuality and reproduction in the United States between the periods following Reconstruction and immediately preceding Roe v. Wade. Located somewhere between Black American Civil Rights and women's suffrage movements, Ross asserts that Black women's struggles for reproductive freedoms and sexual liberation have been undermined on several levels. One key reason is because reproductive rights have been co-opted as a White woman's issue, not considered an issue for all women or even a general social concern of male and female members of society. A second significant reason has been the historic sexism of the Black Civil Rights Movement that has stigmatized women's issues as oppositional to and unsupportive of *The Movement*. A final important reason Black women's struggles for reproductive rights and sexual liberation have been obscured is the historical reality that women of all races in the United States are believed to lack agency as well as the ability to make their own choices.[14]

The significance of the socially accepted propaganda-enhanced narrative is no better explored than in T. Denean Sharpley-Whiting's 1999 *Black Venus: Sexualized Savages, Primal Fears, and Primitive Narratives in French*. Offering an analysis of nineteenth century French literature, Sharpley-Whiting shines a light on a historical and international perverse absorption with Black women's sexuality exemplified by a clear obsession with Black women's actual sex organs. This literary analysis reveals a historical conceptualization of degraded Black female sexuality that is based primarily in White male fantasy. This point is easily illustrated by Sharpley-Whiting as she highlights a key historically observable fact of French literature—the focus on the, "perverse nature" of sex, sexuality, and sex for sale.[15] According to Sharpley-Whiting, these literary examinations of sex slaves, courtesans, prostitutes, and fallen women are invariably presented as Black women. This reality illustrates *either* how Black women came to represent "infected sex," or possibly the very fact that they already symbolized taboo sexuality in the minds of the populace. Either choice is ironic and appalling given that historical data illustrate that only a smattering of the thousands of registered prostitutes in France were even of African descent.[16]

This exploration of French literature demonstrates the international development of the portrayal of Black woman as sexual savage. These literary depictions cast the Black woman as the epitome of taboo sexuality. A sexuality that titillates White men and proves overwhelming to the Christian consciousness and conscience. Like Sharpley-Whiting, hooks' 1981 *Ain't I A Woman: Black Women and Feminism* contends that at least some portion of Whites' tireless ongoing endeavors to regulate

Black female sexuality and reproduction through methods of: exploitation; control; repression; and coercion are generated more out of fear of their own White male sexuality, than of any issue that can legitimately be attributed to Black women themselves.

In the years following the end of slavery, as the United States moves into Reconstruction the evolution of these imaginings emerges. Previously used to justify vicious mistreatment of enslaved Black women, now the social rhetoric described by Sharpley-Whiting embeds itself into the fabric of a now free American society. Black women are epitomized as the antithesis of femininity and respectability. Barbara Christian comments on the racist misogyny displayed in post Civil War America in her "Introduction" to Dorothy Sterling's 1988 *Black Foremothers*. In her analysis Christian describes a monumental social effort to keep Black women relegated to the lowest ranks that entails discrediting her honor and reducing her to a level lower than that of prostitute. Though not explicitly referred to as "social rhetoric," by Christian, she does allude to the furthering of a negative mythology about Black women that impacts her material conditions. Described by Christian as an arsenal of cruelty against Black women, the social rhetoric of the period impacts every aspect of Black women's lives. Black women are refused common courtesies allowed other women, spoken to in the same fashion as one would address a child, and go unprotected from rape and sexual abuse, as she is believed to be so promiscuous that she cannot even be sexually assaulted. The narrative promulgated by the social rhetoric of the Reconstruction era is thorough and leaves Black women wholly mistreated.[17]

Deborah G. White's 2000, *Too Heavy a Load: Black Women in Defense of Themselves: 1894–1994*, explores the onslaught of attacks endured by Black women from the period entering Jim Crow segregation to the period entering welfare reform. Though negative social rhetoric weaves ugly narratives that assail all Blacks, Black women experience a unique brand of stereotyping. Besieged from all sides, she is regarded as contemptibly unfeminine, not only among Whites, but Blacks as well. Designed as the antithesis of the American woman by White propaganda images, she is portrayed as harmful to the Black race and accepted as such by a variety of Black male intellectuals:

> This misogyny had been in the making at least since Frazier's critique of black middle-class women and Moynihan's matriarchy thesis. African-American men, from Black Panther Eldridge Cleaver and sociologist Calvin Hernton, to psychiatrists William Grier and Price Cobbs, to ideologue Frantz Fanon, accused black

women of harming and holding back the race. Hernton, for example, explored black female history and concluded that it had produced in her a "sort of 'studism,'" which expressed itself in a "strong matriarchal drive." The black woman could be expected to be "too dominating, too demanding, too strict, too inconsiderate, and too masculine," said Hernton. . . . She is "the antithesis of American beauty," explained the two psychiatrists.[18]

The Social Construction of an Identity

As we explore the historical context of Black women's labor in the U.S. political economy, we see that the demands placed on Black women's labor vary depending on the given requirements in the specified era. Depending on the requirements of the period, the vision of Black women's reproduction is socially constructed through a system of typification. These socially constructed images project the character traits and flaws needed to support and reproduce the needs of the capitalist structure at the time. These typologies are created to supply or restrict the needed labor as dictated by the demands of the political economy during a given production era. The typologies directly relate to the ways in which Black sexuality and reproduction is exploited, restricted, controlled, and manipulated to support capitalist development and expansion during each era.[19]

These socially constructed typologies evolve over the decades from portrayals of generic members of an animalistic population lacking self control into an increasingly devious shrew bent on taking every advantage of a caring and just system that has made every effort to save her from her self. The images shift from sexual savage in the slave period, to needy surplus labor during the Depression, to pathological matriarch in the Civil Rights period, to conniving welfare queen in the current period.

The image of the sexual savage encompasses the entire slave era and endures even beyond. The sexual savage is characterized by images of an uncivilized and amoral animal. She is portrayed as a multifaceted industrious worker, who, though simple minded, follows direction well. Of course left to her own devices her instincts for sex and reproduction will consume her and overwhelm Christian society. Painted as instinctively sexual, and in turn, maternal the enslaved Black woman is in short a perfect labor source, able to provide: reproductive; productive; and biological labor in an era that relies almost entirely on Black labor.

women as surplus labor

The image of Black women as needy surplus labor emerges during the lowest economic point in U.S. history, the Great Depression. Needy surplus laborers are characterized by the image of the shiftless children and grandchildren of former slaves with no marketable skills, whose very presence drains the scarce resources available to a desperate White wage labor force in Depression era United States. Portrayed as unable to control herself, she is perceived as producing a multitude of children. This aspect of propaganda is particularly ironic, given the nation's refusal to allow women of any race; age; or marital status access to birth control. With no meaningful means of contraception and the ongoing transition from rural farm life to urban industrialism, there is an enormous increase in large poor inner city families across the nation, without regard for race. Black women's large families; however, sometimes unsupported by husbands, who are often lost to lynch mobs and the *Great Migration* in an effort to make his way in the world, are scapegoated as sources of a problem far greater than Black women could legitimately claim responsibility for.

The image of the Black woman as the pathological matriarch is prevalent in the post-Civil Rights period. This image can easily be infamously attributed to the release of the Moynihan Report. This document presents data collected by a government study with the intent of exploring the condition of the Black family in the early 1960s.[20] This poorly constructed study determines that Black families are suffering a sickness that is primarily attributed to the failings of Black women as wives and mothers. This thesis is commonly referred to as the theory of the *Black matriarchy.* Presented as aggressive, emasculating, and manipulative, the Black woman of the post-Civil Rights period is perceived as unattractive and unappealing in every sense of the term. Her lack of a socially desirous femininity as a Black woman in a nation that prizes the aesthetics of White women's appearance as the epitome of female attractiveness and her capability to survive independently in a patriarchal society make her suspect. Further, her purportedly masculine-level aggressive nature is believed to drive men out of her life. This in turn, leaves her to parent her children without fathers. The very notion of fatherless households awakens every misogynistic fear possible in this period, still fundamentally rooted in a patriarchal structure that only recognizes women, of any race, within the context of their relationship to their fathers or husbands. A Black family dependent upon the welfare system is perceived as a dangerous scenario in which Black women's children are in danger of growing uncontrollable within the confines of society. Further, Black women are perceived to be unable as well as unwilling to offer the guidance, support, and protection that is not provided when there is no father or husband in the household.

The image of the conniving welfare queen is ubiquitous in the new millennium. In this neoliberal period, Black women are now not only presented as conniving welfare queens, but wholly accepted as such, even within many Black communities. In this period, there is a common understanding of the Black female experience in the United States that is heavily warped as it is based on historical social rhetoric and conflated statistics. Perceived as persistently low-income, unskilled, poorly educated, and drug-addicted, Black women in the current period have grown to encompass all that is abhorrent in American society. And now, after so many generations of programs, services, and opportunities, America has decided that Black women simply need to be forced off of welfare, coerced into working, and dissuaded from having excessive numbers of children.

This stereotyping, advanced through media, propaganda, and other forms of social rhetoric, is employed as an apparatus of hegemonic domination performed by the state and only serves to perpetuate the interests of the ruling class.[21]

Further Readings

Alaimo, Stacy (Ed.). *Material Feminisms*. Bloomington: Indiana University Press, 2008.

Austin, Regina. "Sapphire Bound!" In *Critical Race Theory: The Key Writings that Formed the Movement*, ed. Kimberle Williams Crenshaw, Neil Gotanda, Garry Peller, and Kendall Thomas, pp. 426–440. New York: New Press, 1996.

Callanan, Valeri J. *Feeding the Fear of Crime: Crime-Related Media and Support for Three Strikes (Criminal Justice: Recent Scholarship)*. El Paso, TX: LFB Scholarly, 2004.

Churchill, Ward and Jim Vander Wall. The COINTELPRO Papers: Documents from the FBI's Secret Wars against Dissent in the United States. Boston, MA: South End Press, 1981.

Collins, Patricia Hill. "What's in a Name? Womanism, Black Feminism, and Beyond." In *The Womanist Reader*, ed. Layli Phillips, pp. 57–68. New York: Taylor & Francis, 2006 [1996].

Crenshaw, Kimberle Williams. "Mapping the Margins: Intersectionality, Identity Politics, and Violence against Women of Color." In *Critical Race Theory: The Key Writings that Formed the Movement*, ed. Kimberle Williams Crenshaw, Neil Gotanda, Garry Peller, and Kendall Thomas, pp. 357–383. New York: New Press, 1996.

Danner, Mark. *Torture and Truth: America, Abu Graib, and the War on Terror*. New York: New York Review of Books, 2004.

Davis, A.Y. 1977. "Women and Capitalism: Dialectics of Oppression and Liberation." In *The Angela Y. Davis Reader*, ed. J. James, pp. 161–192. Malden, MA: Blackwell.

Davis, Mike. *Planet of Slums*. London, England: Verso, 2007.

Gourevitch, Philip and Errol Morris. *Standard Operating Procedure*. New York: Penguin, 2008.

Helen (Charles). "The Language of Womanism: Rethinking Difference." In *The Womanist Reader*, ed. Layli Phillips, pp. 361–378. New York: Taylor & Francis, 2006.

Mankiller, Wilma, Gwendoline Mink, Marysa Smith, Barbara Smith, and Gloria Steinem. *The Reader's Companion to U.S. Women's History*. New York: Houghton Mifflin, 1998.

Mohanty, Chandra. *Feminisms without Borders: Decolonizing Theory, Practicing Solidarity*. Durham, NC: Duke University Press, 2003.

Morton, Adam D. *Unravelling Gramsci: Hegemony and passive revolution in the global political economy*. Ann Arbor, MI: Pluto Press, 2007.

Nagel, Joane. *Race, Ethnicity, and Sexuality: Intimate Intersections, Forbidden Frontiers*. New York: Oxford University Press, 2004.

Pierson, C. 1998. *Beyond the Welfare State? The New Political Economy of Welfare*, second edition. University Park: Pennsylvania State University Press.

Roberts, Dorothy E. "Punishing Drug Addicts Who Have Babies: Women of Color, Equality, and the Right to Privacy." In *Critical Race Theory: The Key Writings that Formed the Movement*, ed. Kimberle Williams Crenshaw, Neil Gotanda, Garry Peller, and Kendall Thomas, pp. 384–425. New York: New Press, 1996.

Robinson, Cedric J. *Black Marxism: The Making of the Black Radical Tradition*. Chapel Hill: University of North Carolina Press, 2000.

Rousseau, Jean-Jacques. *The Social Contract and the Discourses (Everyman's Library)*. London: David Campbell, 1992.

Rupert, Mark. "Alienation, Capitalism and the Inter-state System: Toward a Marxian Gramscian Critique." In *Gramsci, Historical Materialism and International Relations*, ed. Stephen Gill, pp. 67–92. New York: Cambridge University Press, 1993.

Simson, Rennie "The Afro-American Female: The Historical Context of the Construction of Sexual Identity." In *Powers of Desire: The Politics of Sexuality*, ed. A. Snitow, C. Stansell, and S. Thompson. New York: Monthly Review Press, 1983.

Strauss, David Levi, Charles Stein, Barbara Ehrenreich, John Gray, Meron Benvenisti, Mark Danner, and David Metlin. *Abu Graib: The Politics of Torture (The Terr Nova Series)*. Berkeley, CA: North Atlantic Books, 2004.

Torres, Sasha. *Black, White, and in Color: Television and Black Civil Rights*. Princeton, NJ: Princeton University Press, 2003.

Young, Lola. *Fear of the Dark: Race, Gender and Sexuality in the Cinema (Gender, Racism, Ethnicity Series)*. New York: Routledge Press, 1995.

PART 2

Slavery Matters!

Year	Key Historical Moments during Agricultural Slave Era (1619–1865)
1619	First Africans traded as Slaves in the United States
1622–1898	American-Indian Wars
1662	Follow the Condition of the Mother
1667	Christianity Status does not free slaves
1682	All "non-Christian" servants entering the United States are slaves
1691	Killing slaves is declared within the rights of slave-owners
1705	Illegal for enslaved Blacks to reading
1775–1783	American Revolution
1787	U.S. Constitution
1808	Embargo on Slave Importation
1846–1848	Mexican-American War
1848	Seneca Falls Convention
1857	Dred-Scott Decision reifies inequality embedded within the Constitution
1861–1865	U.S. Civil War
1863	Emancipation Proclamation
1865	Thirteenth Amendment outlawing Slavery

CHAPTER FOUR

Becoming Instruments of Production

In establishing a *New World*, the settlers of the original colonies maintain constant battles with several opponents, leaving them financially frustrated. Though initial contact is promising, they will find themselves embroiled in centuries of struggle over fertile lands the settlers wish to control. Though many other significant skirmishes certainly occur, three major conflicts characterize the struggle of the early colonies that lay the foundation for the superpower status the United States has maintained into the new millennium. First, the American-Indian Wars—a series of efforts to defeat the indigenous Indian populations— would persist for centuries.[1] On the heels of the French and Indian War, fought to protect the interests of the British Empire, the colonists enter into their next major conflict-the American Revolution.[2] Upon excessive taxation and other tyrannical policies imposed by the English monarchical rulers, the colonists begin fighting for independence from overseas sovereignty.[3] This hard-fought freedom from the British Empire is only briefly enjoyed before the turn of the nineteenth century sees the onset of the third major conflict, that with Mexico over the expansion of the United States.[4]

Throughout these battles, conflicts, and wars, the settlers-turned-occupying-conquering-slavers are determined to gain and maintain control of fertile American soil in order to develop an agricultural industry in a new land that will solidify both their financial independence as well as their political autonomy. America grew in size and economic strength through European immigration; the importation of Africans for enslaved labor; the growth of the domestic Black population; and the agricultural industry that was born of and cultivated by the institution of slavery.[5]

Why Enslave Black Africans?

As indicated by dialectical and historical materialist theory, the land-owners in the New World seek a cost-effective labor force, which is knowledgeable of agricultural production; capable of hard physical labor; and psychologically and physically controllable. Before expanding their search for this cheap exploitable labor to Africa in the early 1600s, the colonizers seek to fulfill their labor needs with White wage workers and servants.[6] This proves challenging on several levels, four of which are described here.

The first challenge that presents itself is a lack of a critical mass of employable laborers. As the New World is in transition and has only indigenous populations and European settlers, there is neither a steady stream, nor a stable population of White wage laborers.[7] The second issue is the lack of familiarity the available labor source has with farming in the region. Coming from various areas of Europe—particularly the British Isles—the colonists, often landed aristocrats, have little to no experience with the tobacco, cotton, rice, and other crops prevalent in the American territories. Thirdly, and of great significance, wage employees prove expensive. Given the goal of the enterprising endeavors of the colonizers to exploit the resources of the land to its fullest, paying wage laborers is the least profitable business plan. And a final key challenge to tapping in to the White labor source for the colonizers' agricultural needs in the New World is religious doctrine that privilege Christian Whites and women and disallow their maltreatment.[8] Farm life in the seventeenth century is harsh and unforgiving and would prove an indefensible slight against Christian peoples according to popular doctrine.

As a result of these obstacles to securing a cheap manipulable wage labor force, the planters briefly seek to enslave the indigenous populations of the region—the American Indian. This proves a failure for several reasons as well, specifically Indian's susceptibility to European germs and inability to survive in close proximity to Whites. Also, the Indian knowledge of the land allows more opportunities to escape enslavement. Ultimately, neither White wage labor; indentured servants; nor Indians prove as profitable or as acquiescent as the Black African population:

> For a number of reasons, Native Americans were seldom held as slaves in the colonies. For one thing, it was too easy for them to run away. They were also susceptible to European diseases and, when they lived around whites, their mortality rate was high.

Besides, enslaving whole tribes was beyond the capability of most groups of colonists, so enslaving individual tribe members could lead to reprisals. And so, for slave labor, that left Africans and African Americans-black people.[9]

Black Africans are proven knowledgeable farmers, experienced hard laborers, with readily identifiable appearances, and due to the sadistically complex nature of the transatlantic slave trade, would prove to be fairly docile captives.[10] *Not exactly docile*

Only after these described efforts to tap into White and Indian labor sources fail, do the White colonizers turn their search for a mass of manipulable labor outward and begin to exploit a cheap and profitable labor source from Africa—and the Black woman. Of course both male and female Africans are forced into slavery; however:

> ...it was a widespread belief among white plantation owners that black women were often better workers than their male counterparts.... Given their African heritage, it was easy for enslaved black women to adapt to farm labor in the colonies. Not only was the displaced African man unaccustomed to various types of farm labor, he often saw many tasks as "feminine" and resented having to perform them.[11]

Further, due to differing labor needs from the Caribbean and both Latin and South America, unlike other ports in the Americas, the Colonies imported a fairly even number of African men and women to be enslaved. This led to a significant number of American-born Blacks and eventually a premium on the worth of enslaved Black women of childbearing age. As a result—although the colonies imported the smallest number of Africans for enslavement in the Americas, they grew to have the largest population of Blacks in the New World.[12] The *breeding* of enslaved Blacks, though employed throughout the slave era, would prove particularly profitable in the half century between the embargo on slave importation that is finally imposed and enforced in 1808 and 1865—the date of Emancipation.

Slavery and the Capitalist Structure

In analyzing the development of capitalism in the United States, the role of slavery, though reprehensible, should be clear. Slavery, though profoundly inhumane, proved to be a fundamentally profitable endeavor.

Slavery in the agricultural era propels a region of settlers into the role that the United States maintains nearly four hundred years later. The Black woman is a vital element in the historical relationship between the slave mode of production and the developing capitalist economy, as, together with her male counterparts, she becomes a significant labor force of the U.S. economy.

In keeping with capitalist ideology, the landed planters, who would become slave owners, seek the most cost effective labor force they can access. Though several of the myriad factors that lead to the decision to enslave Black Africans have already been discussed in this volume, three key justifications for the exploitation of Black women's various forms of labor during slavery are outlined here. These three key justifications are the Black African woman's familiarity with farm labor; the preexistence of a patriarchal structure in Africa; and the lack of Christianity on the Continent.

As previously mentioned, one major justification employed is the practical fact of Black African women's farming and domestic capabilities. Coming from agricultural societies, with a previously established gendered division of labor, African women are familiar with effective reproductive and manual labor:

> As much of the work to be done in the American colonies is in the area of hoe-agriculture, it undoubtedly occurred to slavers that the African female, accustomed to performing arduous work in the fields while also performing a wide variety of tasks in the domestic household, would be very useful on the American plantation.[13]

A second justification is the pre-existence of male patriarchy within the African communities. The planters see populations of women already accustomed to both being controlled by men and hard physical labor:

> White male observers of African culture in the 18th and 19th centuries were astounded and impressed by the African male's subjugation of the African female. They were not accustomed to a patriarchal social order that demanded not only that women accept an inferior status, but that they participate actively in the community labor force.[14]

And finally, after identifying the Black African woman as a manual laborer, acquiescent to male control and skilled in both farm and domestic labor, a third justification employed is the Black African woman's lack of Christian "morality," that would allow the White planter to take full ownership of her, spirit and body:

> Christian mythology depicted woman as the source of sin and evil; racist-sexist mythology simply designated black women the epitome of female evil and sinfulness. White men could justify the de-humanization and sexual exploitation of black women by arguing that they possessed inherent evil demonic qualities.[15]

In accepting the Black African woman as a hedonistic heathen, the White slaver could separate her from her humanity and justify claims of absolute ownership of her as though she were mere property, rather than a fully sentient being:

> The white slaver could exercise freely absolute power, for he could brutalize and exploit her without fear of harmful retaliation...rape was a common method of torture slavers used to subdue recalcitrant black women. The threat of rape or other physical brutalization inspired terror in the psyches of displaced African females.[16]

In every attack, assault, abuse, and rape, the White slavers reify their false assertions that the Black African women are not human beings, but slaves. They are imagined as savages without God and humanity, with insatiable sexual appetites, who need the structure of slavery for survival as much as the state relies on slavery to survive.

This false consciousness created by the ruling class in support of ruling class domination over the poorest members of society—in this case an enslaved people—is typical in a capitalist structure. The state will protect the interest of the ruling class, as the state has historically been the organic extension of the ruling class that serves as an apparatus to control the other classes, often through violence. This control is seldom simply a matter of economic power; instead it encompasses far reaching controls of culture, norms, and values, and ensures ongoing domination by the ruling elite. This domination is felt no deeper than by Black women. Instead of taking her place within the capitalist structure, as a worker—whose labor is exploited and whose humanity is alienated true enough, but with the ability to survive by *choosing* to trade her labor power for survival—Black women's labor is instead taken from them. As a result of this exploitation, Black women (and men) enter this country as the actual instruments of production, rather than as possessors of a commodity—with autonomy over their own labor, which they are able to sell.[17]

This is clearly evidenced by the state's treatment of U.S. slavery as the mid to late 1600s see a barrage of inhumane legislation further embroiling Blacks in the institution of slavery. By 1667, though initially cited as a fundamental justification for enslavement of Black Africans, conversion to Christianity could have no impact on one's slave status. However, by 1682, all servants entering the country who were not Christian would be considered slaves. If religion has no bearing on slave status in 1667, then why would it matter fifteen years later in the case of new arrivals? This contradiction highlights the development of a double standard instituted to support the dominating class at all costs, *non-Christian,* is an obvious euphemism for Black. Meaning only Blacks could be forced into slavery. By 1691, it is not considered a felony to take the life of an enslaved person. And in fact, as long as you are the *owner* of said *slave,* it is not even considered a crime. This depth of authority administered by the state is inflexible in regards to the oppressed classes and can only be dismantled by a fundamental restructuring of the system.[18]

Reproduction for Maximum Production

The history of the oppression and exploitation of Black women's biological labor, or reproduction, in the United States begins with the forced breeding of enslaved women in the 1600s.[19] Obliged to submit to livestock-type breeding goals of plantation owners, enslaved women are coerced through a variety of methods—including: violence, bribery, threats, and more, to reproduce and reproduce often.[20]

Black women are exploited for various types of labor, including productive labor, in the form of field labor; reproductive labor, in the form of domestic work; and biological labor, that is, breeding. Given the versatility of her contributions to the system, one could argue that the Black woman herself is the key to the development of the capitalist economy in the United States. And though all forms of Black women's labor are critical to the slave economy, no one proves more essential than her biological labor. With an eye on profit, the slavers import comparatively few people directly from Africa for enslavement. Rather, they primarily exploit the nearby markets in the Caribbean nations who supply them with seasoned workers and encourage domestic Blacks to breed, in order to increase their numbers. As such, U.S. slavery quickly develops into a system that breeds human beings for profit as humans breed livestock for food.[21]

If the Black U.S. slave experience is exploitative and alienating, then the position of the Black female slave is uniquely dehumanizing in that the success of the very structure that oppresses her immensely relies on her abilities to sustain it through production and reproduction. The added ignominy of sexual abuses, regulated reproduction, and forced reproductive labor further exacerbate Black women's labor exploitation during and after slavery.

Enslaved Black Women as Breeders

The ruling class continues to dominate Black labor—both male and female; however, the means of control have arguably been different for the two populations. According to bell hooks, "In a retrospective examination of the black female slave experience, sexism looms as large as racism as an oppressive force in the lives of black women."[22] The fundamental domination over Black women that occurs could only exist within the patriarchal structure that is the very foundation of the United States:

> Institutionalized sexism—that is, patriarchy—formed the base of the American social structure along with racial imperialism. Sexism was an integral part of the social and political order white colonizers brought with them from their European homelands, and it was to have a grave impact on the fate of enslaved black women.[23]

Hooks' *Ain't I a Woman: Black Women and Feminism,* offers a historical feminist analysis of the social, cultural, economic, and political location of Black women in the United States. In so doing, hooks describes the first sexual and reproductive roles of the Black woman in the United States, that of the reproducer of the slave laborer. According to hooks, the latter portion of the slave era sees a significant push toward the breeding of slaves.[24]

Hooks asserts that planters are besieged by "virulent attacks on slave importation" and turn to breeding slaves to encourage profit.[25] As such, beginning with legislation in 1662, children born of slave women are legally mandated to follow *the condition of the mother.* This exceptional mandate means that all children born to enslaved women would be slaves, no matter the mother or child's religion, nation, or race.[26] Further, according to hooks, since nineteenth century settlers already "defined the primary function of all women to be that of breeding workers," their exploitation of vilified enslaved Black women "was a widespread and common practice."[27]

Hooks further elucidates the breeding process as it often played out in its various forms, describing a system of offering incentives to enslaved Black women to encourage reproduction during the slave era: "Some slave owners devised a system of rewards to induce women to breed."[28] These incentives were comprised of elements for survival, not small luxuries.

Enslaved Black women might be provided with extra food for herself and her family as *compensation* for producing a child. Consider that enslaved peoples survive at a subsistence level, consigned to the most meager of diets. Trapped in a circumstance that precludes healthy foods and meats, they are of good fortune if they receive the leftover meat from parts of animals that Whites would not even consider eating, such as the lining of the pig's stomach; its feet; and its intestines. Under the tortuous conditions of malnourishment and abuse, *extra food*, in the form of a small pig, could be the difference between life and death.

Some slave-owners might offer the enslaved Black woman clothing as payment, enticement, or gift when she produces a healthy child; while others might even at times offer small sums of money. Some slave owners even go so far as to promise freedom upon the delivery of any number of children. Of course, no laws protect the enslaved women to ensure that the owner follows through with his promises. And further, this *freedom* would not encompass the family of the enslaved Black woman, and would therefore be a bittersweet victory, if ever there was such a thing.[29]

According to hooks, these petty offerings manifested themselves as both reproductive exploitation and rape, forcing Black female slaves into the role of reluctant (but powerless) prostitute. Hooks expresses this final role—of prostitute—as the saddest irony, given that "prostitutes are women and men who engage in sexual behavior for money or pay of some kind, it is…inaccurately used when applied to enslaved Black women [being used as] sexual latrines."[30]

Slave Resistance

Though enslaved Blacks—both male and female—find themselves at the mercy of a brutal and inhumane system, with opportunities to communicate effectively, organize, develop a coherent plan, and execute a full blown revolt few and far between, many revolutionary acts rise up in defiance of the disgraceful institution of enslavement. As with so many other exploited, abused, and marginalized populations throughout world history, enslaved Blacks find ways to resist.

Many enslaved Blacks escape from plantations. Some of those who escape make countless journeys back and forth between the North and the South helping others in their escape. Some go on to publish articles and books that speak against the institution of slavery and even become activist leaders. Beyond these significant numbers of men and women, countless Black women who cannot escape the shackles of slavery, take another route and revolt in a profoundly impactful and personal way.[31]

Some enslaved Black women refuse to have children born into slavery. At times, the refusal of these women to breed is obscured by other pregnancies on the plantation; however, it eventually becomes common practice for slave owners to keep specific enslaved Black women for the primary purpose of reproducing more slaves.[32] And though this makes this covert resistance more dangerous, there are a great number of instances reported over the generations of slavery that illustrate the myriad ways that slave women refuse to accept this forced role of breeder:

> A planter had kept between four and six slave women "of proper age to breed" for twenty-five years and that "only two children had been born on the place at full term." It was later discovered that the slaves had concocted a medicine with which they were able to terminate their unwanted pregnancies. He also found evidence of a master who claimed that an older female slave had discovered a remedy for pregnancies and had been "instrumental in all...the abortions on his place."[33]

Enslaved Black women, aware of their shared status, conspire together to strategize a method to deny the slaver their children's lives.[34] Though homeopathic remedies play a significant role in enslaved Black women's resistance to the role of breeder, lack of medical care and scientific knowledge often leave them with few options in regards to reproduction. However, an even more devastating and drastic option that requires little medical know-how, always remains-infanticide:

> Possibly the most psychologically devastating means that the slave mother had of undermining the slave system was infanticide.

The frequency with which this occurred is not at all clear.... However, it is important to note that the relatively small number of documented cases is not as significant as the fact that it occurred at all.[35]

Though there is some debate about the frequency of such resistance, as stated above, the very fact that such action would have ever been taken is a testament to the vicious and cruel nature of a life of enslavement. Though it is clearly tragic to remember the women who literally took their newborn's lives into their own hands, it is important to note that this is not only a sacrifice on the part of the mother, to save her child from the pain of enslavement, it is also an assault on the owners and the very system that enslaves her and would enslave her child given the opportunity:

> The daily resistance of enslaved women was, as White stated, 'seldom politically oriented, consciously collective, or violently revolutionary,' but it was effective. It often changed their own lives and those of their children. At the same time, it affected the slaveholders in a practical, often economically related way. And out of the spirit of resistance came a stronger and stronger impulse toward the kind of action that would change the country itself.[36]

Loretta J. Ross also writes of resisting forced breeding in the slave era in her 1993 "African-American Women and Abortion: 1880–1970." In this piece, Ross cites essays written by nineteenth century physicians, asserting that forced to breed, Black women came up with effective methods of inducing homeopathic abortion. These probable methods varied, from "medicine, violent exercise, or by external and internal manipulations," but all succeeded in the destruction of "the foetus at an early age of gestation."[37]

References to the conspiracy among Black slave women to wrench reproductive control from slave owners is also addressed in Brodie's 1994 *Contraception and Abortion in Nineteenth-Century America*. Though Brodie admits her analysis is sorely lacking depth as it relates to the issues of contraception, abortion, reproductive rights and biological regulations of slave women; she does acknowledge both the complexity of the topic as well as the need for further research on the various means and motivations of Black slave women's covert contraception and abortions.[38]

Regardless of the debates over the extent to which enslaved Black women employed abortion and infanticide to resist forced breeding, it seems clear that the fewest number of cases remain testament to the inhumanity of the system and the indomitable and courageous spirit exhibited by enslaved Black women. The enslaved Black woman activist simply refuses to perpetuate this system, at whatever costs. Even from her depressed location, the enslaved Black woman can see that this system is dependent on her in order to continue successfully. She sees her power from the most impotent of locations, and when all other options are exhausted, she takes the only meaningful action possible. She internalizes the pain of her choice to resist and carries on with the life of a slave.

She will likely be violently punished for this resistance. Undoubtedly, given her circumstances, short of death, or an unforeseen biological determinant, she will likely be impregnated again. With no regard for her will, her safety, or the psychological impact of having lost a child, she will be forced to go on. Her resistance however, cannot ever be considered futile, because the child she lost will never become a slave. She has saved her child from a fate worse than death and cost the slaver the only thing that matters to him—profit. The loss of that child will cost the slave owner, if only a few dollars or a few months, the loss will be felt. Thus her resistance is effective and though the slave system may not have been overthrown, it has been disrupted.

CHAPTER FIVE

Is This the White Man's Burden—Or Ours?

Barring the resistance described in the previous chapter, gaining the absolute physical and psychological power over Black Africans necessary to maintain such an inhumane system, the slave trade proves incredibly lucrative and catapults the United States into a strong position of agricultural production for the world economy. Slave ownership is the most profitable investment in the nation next to land ownership in 1860, with 60 percent of the nation's wealth invested in the agricultural south (see table 5.1). In the period between 1845 and 1865 the United States is in a state of expansion. And though farming receives a significant boost from developing technologies—particularly the cotton gin—the fundamental force of production of the agricultural era remains human labor.

With cheap abundant labor in high demand and the slave economy profoundly dependent upon Black slave labor for profit, every effort is made to justify the institution of slavery and rationalize rampant (Black) slave reproduction. These rationales come in the form of state-sponsored legal sanctions, mentioned in the previous chapter, as well as collectively embraced images of Black women's sexuality and reproduction.[1] Painting Blacks as ignorant animalistic heathens, White America comes to accept the notion that Blacks are somehow less than human. The slave era sees the establishment of an ever-present theme of negative propaganda surrounding Blacks in the United States and Africa. Not only meant to widen the gulf that separates Blacks and Whites, this ongoing propaganda campaign is further justifies the enslavement of Blacks, as it is rooted in the belief that Whites bear a responsibility to tame and supervise savage peoples for the sake of the greater society, the so-called White man's burden.[2]

Table 5.1   Status of political economy in agricultural era

Mode of Production	Slavery
Political Economy 1619–1865	• Increasingly expanding throughout agricultural era • 60% of nation's wealth invested in agricultural South by 1860
Forces of Production	• Technology at a low in seventeenth century • Cotton Gin increases production exponentially in eighteenth century • Hand Labor remains primary technology for harvesting crop through 1865
Instruments of Production Labor Pool	Primarily Human Labor • White indentured servants through eighteenth century • White wage laborers minimally used throughout • Native American wage labor minimally used throughout • Native American slave labor primarily practiced in late seventeenth through early eighteenth century, but remains in various forms through late nineteenth century • Black Slaves from 1619 to 1865
Means of Production Labor Source	After 1808, Black reproduction becomes the sole source of replenishing labor pool
Relations of Production Labor Demand	Cheap abundant labor is in high demand Indentured servant vs. Employer Wage laborer vs. Capitalist Slave vs. Master

During the agricultural era the notion of the "White man's burden" is introduced at the core of a multilayered series of *responsibilities* that fall upon the White race. This "burden" is described as the bringing of Christianity to a supposedly heathen people. Ignorant of Christian doctrine, Africans are painted as childlike, unknowledgeable, and hedonistic. With the acceptance of this image, one might *almost* consider slavery a sort of twisted kindness toward a "savage" group in need of parental structure and guidance.[3]

Image of Sexual Savage

Though social rhetoric is circulated about the Black race in general, there is much negative propaganda specific to female slave sexuality and reproduction. Presented as lewd; sexually deviant; and animalistic,

Table 5.2 Themes of social rhetoric in the agricultural era

Theme of Social Rhetoric 1845–1865	Representation of Sexual Savage
Heathen	Portrayed as being *Godless*
Savage	Depicted as uncivilized
Puerile	Described as childlike
Hedonistic	Represented as having a lascivious nature
White Man's Burden	Responsibility of Whites to manage and control Blacks
Animalistic	Imagined as being instinctively maternal

Black reproduction is perceived as an animal instinct of an inhuman population (see table 5.2). Depicted as lacking the moral compass that leads civilized peoples to modesty, temperance, and humility, Black African women are often illustrated as naked savages wallowing in an overt and foul sexuality that threatens to corrupt their supposedly moral Christian captors.

Propaganda images illustrating the hypersexual "savage slave" myth includes artwork; political cartoons; even dramatic characters in books and stage plays. Paintings of the slave period can be found often depicting naked bodies of Black Africans arriving on American shores, seemingly writhing in the still images, as though unable to control their insatiable desires. Subliminal hints abound implying that Black men and women are not only animals, but even demonic. Rarely did the media representations of the seventeenth, eighteenth, and nineteenth centuries include images of mortified confused strangers in a strange land. Often sick and abused in countless ways, women arriving without clothing, never did so by their own choosing. Having been raped, humiliated, and tortured, these women are now forced to stand on an auction block where she will be sold. Yet, she is perceived as the animal?

As a result of this persistent social rhetoric, Black women, purportedly lacking the morality of White women, suffer intolerable indignities at the hands of their White *Christian* oppressors. As owned property, sexual abuse is perceived as a right of the *moral* slave owner, rather than an illegal and immoral crime:

> Generally, when sexual liaisons did occur between the female slave and the slave owner, the compelling image of the bad-black-girl, or Jezebel, was used to explain this relationship. That is, slave owners who privately coerced their female slaves, or surreptitiously offered them harsh alternatives if they were unwilling to

submit to their owner's sexual whims, attributed these liaisons to
the hypersexuality of the female slave who was purported to be
the aggressor or seducer. Therefore, the bad–black–girl image as
a symbol of African American women has been used to depict
the African American woman as an eager, available and willing
sexual partner for her slave owner and for other males, with relative degrees of power and wealth, in American society.[4]

Further, enslaved Black men are at a loss to protect the Black women
of their communities, as they suffer some similar elements of sexual
exploitation, as they themselves are commodified as instruments of
production—for both manual and biological labor.

Womanhood in Society

Also, impactful rhetoric on Black women in U.S. society is the fabled
notion of the *Cult of True Womanhood*. Common social rhetoric from
the mid to late 1800s, the Cult idea reasserts the power of the patriarchal structure over White women as they are called upon to eschew
employment outside the home and take their place as wives and mothers,
reproducing the labor pool and caring for the male laborers. According
to Giddings,

> For White men, the cult [of true womanhood] was convenient.
> In an increasingly industrialized economy, more of them were
> forced to leave the farms for occupations that middle–class women
> had enjoyed. During the early rise of the factory system, the main
> source of labor was proud-if needy-Puritan girls who saw their
> work as a stopgap until they married. Although the work was
> strenuous and the wages low, such employment still carried a cer-
> tain status.[5]

With these radical economic changes, these women find themselves
forced back into the home. As housewives and mothers, no longer wage
earners, any sense of autonomy previously enjoyed by White middle
class women is lost:

> With the coming of the cult idea, however, work outside the
> home lost its prestige, and women...were no longer expected to

be *in* the labor force but to stay home and *reproduce* the labor force. So when the cult of the lady took hold, they were replaced by poorer immigrant women, a cheaper, more permanent, and more exploitable source of workers.[6]

The cult of true womanhood presents itself as a reification of the vision of the American woman as White and middle class, and cements the Black woman's role as an interloper:

> For women, the vehicle for these aspirations was what became known as the "cult of the lady" or the "cult of true womanhood." Now a woman had to be true to the cult's cardinal tenets of domesticity, submissiveness, piety, and purity in order to be good enough for society's inner circles. Failing to adhere to any of these tenets-which the overwhelming number of Black women could hardly live up to-made one less than a moral "true" woman.[7]

Being a woman takes on new meaning in the age of true womanhood. Enveloped in class and status, this position falls far out of reach for both slave and free Black women. Now faced with insurmountable rhetoric that firmly situates Black women in the role of incomprehensible *other*, Black women have no means of overcoming the social conception that she is less than a "lady." According to Giddings,

> Free Black women in the North also had to struggle with the consequences of being perceived as a "different kind of humanity." Abolition hadn't erased the taint of their alleged immorality, and converging social and economic forces in the 1830's added a new challenge. With the emergence of a self-conscious middle class, Black women had to overcome notions about the relationship of class—as well as color—to morality.[8]

And though the notion that women should behave as ladies and be treated as such is, today, clearly acknowledged as misogynistic tyranny and an overt exertion of patriarchal domination; working; living; and surviving in the nineteenth century, is far more dangerous and less manageable for any women perceived as anything less than a lady. This common rhetoric ensures that Black women are even further wounded by society's refusal to accept her as a woman, rather than as a manual and reproductive workhorse for physical and sexual exploitation.

Paternalistic Response

The social response to these omnipresent campaigns is paternalistic (see table 5.3). Americans embrace the notion that enslaved Blacks need to be tamed and supervised and that Blacks require patriarchal Whites to take care of both enslaved Black mothers and offspring, through the organized system of slave ownership, for the very survival of Blacks.

Throughout the period the State imposes more and more stringent legislation that controls every breath of the enslaved Black human being. And though the response to the social rhetoric that implies that Blacks need White supremacy and control for their own well-being is paternalistic, the manner in which this paternalism is conveyed upon enslaved Blacks varies from one White slave owner to the next.

Some feel it is their duty to spread the word of God to the heathen non-Christian population. As the religious doctrine is spread, many enslaved Blacks convert to Christianity. So many in fact that the State feels threatened and implements a number of policies to circumvent the acceptance of Blacks as Christian peoples. Claiming that Blacks are too ignorant to comprehend the word of God, many assert that Blacks could only mimic their White owners' devotion to Christianity and could not actually feel it themselves.

Conversely, it is argued that Blacks could be misrepresenting themselves as true believers. Instead they could potentially be cunning enough to feign conversion in order to take advantage of the kindness of Whites who offer them the word of God, as part of a larger scheme to escape slavery. If this is the case, then all Blacks attempting to convert should be considered suspect, and perhaps even denied acceptance into the Christian faith.

This tactic is of course dangerous as it implies that Blacks are thinking intelligent human beings, rather than the ignorant animals they are portrayed as. Regardless of the logic behind the sentiment, policies are set in place by the latter part of the seventeenth century to dismiss these

Table 5.3 Snapshot of social response to rhetoric campaigns in the agricultural era

Social Climate 1845–1865	Characteristics of Social Climate
Paternalistic Social Response	Society believes all Blacks, both free and slave, need to be tamed and supervised (*White Man's Burden*)
	Society believes enslaved Blacks require patriarchal White owners of both mother & offspring to survive

converted peoples and keep them relegated to slave status. Further, by 1705, though it had historically been taboo, it becomes illegal to teach an enslaved Black person to read. This particular policy challenges efforts to bring Christianity to Blacks, as it becomes illegal for Blacks to read the Bible.

The paternalistic response of the era extends much further than the few supposedly sympathetic Whites who choose to confer Christianity onto their slaves. This paternalism embeds itself in the very culture of the day. Whites perceive themselves to be located in several key locations essential to Black survival, including that of: parent; protector; and owner. Emboldened by the perception that they are righteous in their endeavors, Whites in the slave period, develop a false consciousness that supports the evil enterprise in every way.

As mythical parent, the general sentiment of the era is akin to the adage: *spare the rod and spoil the child*. As such, it grows customary to abuse enslaved Blacks—*for their own good*. The conceptualization that enslaved Blacks are mindless children and Godless heathens instills within Whites a sense of moral superiority that facilitates the widespread justification of physical, psychological, and emotional abuse of enslaved Blacks. This allows Whites to beat and torture enslaved Blacks without reservation.

As professed protectors of their Black slaves, Whites perceive themselves as deserving of enslaved Blacks' respect, loyalty, and hard work. The White slavers actually see themselves as saving the Blacks from either the White images of the *jungle* in Africa or from harsher slavers who would treat them more cruelly, or even from themselves. Fully embracing the false notion that Black people are lesser beings, there is a genuine belief among Whites (around the world) that left to their own devices; lazy, shiftless, and ignorant Blacks would suffer far worse than they ever could in the grips of slavery.

Finally, Whites believe themselves to be the owners of enslaved Blacks. Contrary to all religious doctrine, Whites hold tight to the notion that they control Blacks mind, body, and spirit. This is perhaps the most dangerous element of the paternalistic view that arises in the slave era. Whites place themselves in the role of gods, determining every aspect of Black reality. This misguided belief leads Whites to unthinkable levels of abuse. Rape becomes a common and expected practice within slave life. So common in fact that policy has to be implemented to address the visibly White children being born to enslaved Black women.[9] Whites even begin choosing when Blacks live and die, even when they reproduce.

CHAPTER SIX

Age Old Pimpin': Exploitative Reproductive Policies

As highlighted in table 6.1, due to economic expansion, low technology, and high demand for cheap manipulable labor, Black reproduction is encouraged for the sake of profit in the agricultural south. This encouragement comes in the form of several policies and protocols that directly affect Black reproduction in the slave era. As illustrated in table 6.1, the reproductive policies of the agricultural era are exploitative as offspring of enslaved Black women are legally owned by White slavers and enslaved Black women are forced to breed through coercive and forced policies such as cash incentives for reproducing and threats of violent retribution for refusal of reproduction for profit.[1]

Establishing the Value of the Female Slave

As a struggling new agricultural society, the colonies tap into the labor capabilities of Black African women early on. Already accustomed to patriarchal farming communities in Africa, enslaved Black women in the United States are assigned to: cooking; cleaning; child rearing; fieldwork; and more. In fact, enslaved Black women of childbearing age are such multifaceted workers—useful for biological, reproductive, and manual labor—that they are actually *worth* more money on the slave market.

Receipts for enslaved people often include the cash amount of the sale alongside a space to notate miscellaneous information about the purchased person. These notations might describe any number of issues

Table 6.1 Examples of relevant policies in the agricultural era

Influential Policies of the Slave Era	*Characteristics of Influential Policies of the Slave Era*
Forced Breeding ⎫ ⎬ Practices Coerced Breeding ⎭	Forced impregnation of enslaved Blacks through rape and "mating." • Cash and extra food and privilege incentives to reproduce Black slave labor force.
Slave Codes	Codes were instituted throughout the slave era and varied from state to state but were often similar • Slaves are not allowed to be armed—1650 • Black babies "follow the condition of the mother"—1662 • Baptism does not change slave status—1667 • Non-Christian servants entering the country are considered slaves—1705 • Illegal for slaves to read—1705 • Killing a slave is legal—1705
Value of Black Reproduction	• Enslaved Black women of childbearing age purchased and sold for more money than non-childbearing enslaved women.

deemed important and relevant to the sale, such as: the slave's fertility; demeanor; and/or general constitution. Women of childbearing age are often described as fertile or the number of children she has given birth to is listed with a promise or guarantee that she is able to produce more children. While infertile women, though of a lesser cash value, are just as aggressively marketed as domestic laborers. Referred to as *Auntie* or *Mammy*, they are often sold with the guarantee that, though infertile, she will contribute to the reproduction of slave labor in other ways. As a reproductive laborer, she will perform any number of tasks, including: cooking; cleaning; sewing; tending to community children, both enslaved and the "master's" children; often alongside the promise that she can perform significant field labor as well.

Managing Black Populations

Accepting the cruelty of the institution of slavery does not come easily to all of the new Americans:

Defining slavery was not an easy task in a democracy, or rather, a group of democracies. And it is not easy for patriotic Americans to accept the fact that it was going on at the very time that colonists were chafing under the oppression of British rule and talking in lofty terms about freedom and the rights of man. Essentially, slavery, as a legal category, defined certain people as part people and part property. In the half-century or so following 1641, hundreds of laws would be passed clarifying the position of these "part-people" socially and economically. But the most significant laws were those that defined exactly who could be classified as a slave and who could not legally be slaves.[2]

Slave Codes

As the culture of farming, trade, and slavery takes shape in the colonies, so does the legal structure; and countless laws regarding slavery and Black women's reproduction pass throughout individual states across the nation in response to every aspect of the slave system. The slavers institute various and sundry policies related to production, sales, and myriad other aspects of the slaving business, often as the issues present themselves. The effort to control the enslaved population through legislation culminates in the development of _slave codes_. These codes are comprised of a host of restrictive policies and laws that maintain the system of power between White slavers and enslaved Blacks. Codes cover a broad range of issues, such as: establishing the fine for stealing or killing someone else's slave; the punishment for harboring fugitive slaves; and the consequences for running away from slavery. Some codes, like the 1705 statute, prevent Black children from learning to read; while others declare that White women who dare to marry a slave will themselves become slave to her husband's _master_; while still others proclaim that Blacks are not allowed to be armed as free men are; while others preclude Blacks from accessing the legal system or of accusing a White slave owner of a crime; or even resisting any orders given them.[3] "These 'slave codes' were based on force and violence—in short, white terrorism," acted out domestically, White against Black.[4] The list of codes goes on and on, each one varying slightly from one state to the next. The peculiar institution of slavery is fraught with minutiae detailing how the system is organized.

Efforts to dominate the Black Africans begin at the moment of capture. Rape, humiliation, and other forms of torturous brutality are the weapons of choice. Oftentimes, African women, having survived the horrors of the Middle Passage, arrive at the slave auction already pregnant, having been raped and tortured throughout the rigorous voyage across the ocean. Sexual abuse is so prevalent that even often silent White women would be moved to comment on its role in the structure

of the slave system—no matter how unforgiving the characterization
of the victims:

> The sexual exploitation of enslaved women by white men was
> so common that South Carolinian Mary Boykin Chestnut would
> write in the middle 1800s, "Like the patriarchs of old, our men
> live all in one house with their wives and their concubines; and
> the mulattoes one sees in every family partly resemble the white
> children."[5]

African women who survived the Middle Passage unimpregnated are
forced to create a new home amongst the slave quarters in a strange new
land. Though a wholly unnatural environment, families begin to form.[6]
In the early years of slavery these families are often interracial, as Black
Africans work and live in close proximity to White indentured servants
and Native Americans, two other systematically exploited labor populations of the period. Faced with the implications of having fostered a new
indigenous American population, southern planters are compelled to
address the legal status of these new biracial "Americans:"

> Children were born who were black *and* white. Or black and
> Native American. This was a completely natural result of the liv-
> ing condition at the time, as enslaved Africans and indentured
> white servants often worked side by side. They relaxed together,
> rebelled against their situation together, became friends, and cre-
> ated families.[7]

Having established early on that Whites are barred from enslavement,
the slave owners now need to mandate the legal status of the offspring
of the enslaved, who are no longer exclusively Black:

> This mixed population was problematic to the lawmakers. Could
> they be enslaved? Did their white blood protect them or did their
> black blood condemn them...? In the early 1600s-beginning
> with the 1662 Virginia law-the American colonies without excep-
> tion passed laws stating that "all children born in this country
> shall be held bond or free only according to the condition of the
> mother."[8]

With the passing of these laws, arguably for one of the first times in
world history, a mother's status, not the father's, would determine the

child's future. From 1662 through 1865, individual state policies dictate that any child born to an enslaved woman would him/her self become a slave owned by the same "master" that owns the mother of the child. In a system that incorporates rape and ongoing sexual abuse into its very foundation, this policy protects the White slave owners from having to free their own offspring. Instead, a child born to an enslaved Black woman, even if the father is White, would always be considered Black and always be born a slave. Black women are at the absolute mercy of a sadistic slave system that protects the White slave owners' capital interests above the humanity of the enslaved Blacks:

> [Children] born to slave women would be slaves and, of course, the property of the woman's owner. . . . [The law] altered the status of black women in the most profound way, by redefining their position as women. From then on, black motherhood is, at least for slaves, a legal curse. . . . Henceforth, black women would be valued not only for their work, but for their ability to produce more workers.[9]

In the thirty years, from 1700 to 1730, the number of Africans and African Americans living in the colonies rises from 26,000 to 70,000.[10] Between 1740 and 1780 a reported 210,000 more Africans are imported into the colonies. Forced Black labor is an extremely profitable endeavor that helps accelerate an agricultural boom in the United States that predicates the United States' position as a major superpower in later eras. With the rising number of Blacks in America, the status of children born to slave women is no longer the only issue involving slavery the White slave owners need to be explicitly defined.

Other Impactful Policies

Having been assailed with policy that dissolves their right to parent their own children, and being forced to reproduce the very system that enslaves them, by providing the labor pool for the next generation; motherhood becomes—on some levels—a "curse" for enslaved Black women.[11] Black women's reproduction is systematically forced and harshly regulated by U.S. policy. Under threat of torturous, yet legal, repercussions, such as, being sold away from her family; being beaten with a whip; and/or being subjected to violent, painful, and degrading sexual abuse; enslaved Black girls are expected to begin reproducing as early as age twelve. Legally sanctioned sexual exploitation of children for profit is an unthinkable concept in the United States in the new millennium, yet a customary expectation of slave production in the seventeenth, eighteenth, and nineteenth centuries.

Evidenced by the 1860 U.S. Census, the final period of slavery, 1845 to 1865, sees the southern owning class fiercely clinging to their established slavocracy. According to the 1860 Census, there is a consistent increase in the number of slaves between 1840 and 1860, averaging 25 percent per year. This steady increase seems inconsistent with the policy of the day, given that slave importation ends in 1808 due to a federally enforced embargo. Evidently this federal restriction on slave importation, though ending the nearly two hundred years period of abduction and trade of Africans for involuntary enslavement; simultaneously exacerbates the reproductive exploitation of Black slaves in the United States. This has a particularly profound impact on enslaved Black women.

In order to maintain the trend of increasing slave numbers in the generations following the embargo, enslaved Black women, already condemned by the invasive and cruel laws that obligate their children to slavery, are now forced to acquiesce to unofficial policies that promote black slave reproduction. Enslaved Black women are raped, mated like animals, and/or coerced with violence and through incentives, such as small amounts of cash, extra food, and other basic necessities in order to increase the labor pool, thereby increasing agricultural production, and in turn maximizing profit.[12]

Other Significant Edicts

None of the previously discussed policies, laws, and edicts proves more damaging to Blacks than the very document that liberates the colonists—the Constitution. The Constitution itself is the culmination of one hundred fifty years of constructing a system of chattel slavery in the New World.[13] This damaging document is clever and illusive in its institutionalization of racism in the United States:

> Not even the term 'slavery' was allowed to mar the sublime concepts articulated in the Constitution, which euphemistically refers to 'persons held to service of labor' as those exceptional human beings who did not merit the rights and guarantees otherwise extended to all.[14]

Table 6.2 Reproductive policy analysis: 1845–1865

Slave period Exploitative Reproductive Policies	Nature of Economy 1845–1865	Social Response 1845–1865	Type of Policy	Characteristics of Exploitative Reproductive Policies of the Slave Period
Forced Breeding Forcing Enslaved Black Women to Produce Children	• Expansion • Low technology • Hi labor demand • Black reproduction is primary labor source	Paternalistic • Channel savage behavior	Exploitative protocol to maximize profit-applied throughout slave era, particularly salient 1808–1865	• Black women are raped by White owners to increase reproduction • Black women are mated w/male slaves like animals to increase reproduction • Black women are forced to submit to Black male slaves by White owners to increase reproduction • Black women are violently punished for not reproducing
Buying Black Babies Cash, Food, & Clothing Incentives for Reproduction	• Expansion • Low technology • Hi labor demand • Black reproduction is primary labor source	Paternalistic • Channel savage behavior	Exploitative protocol to maximize profit-applied throughout slave era, particularly salient 1808–1865	• Black women are forced to trade their reproduction for minimal incentives, otherwise typically denied them
Owning Black Babies Co-Opted Ownership of Black Babies	• Expansion • Low technology • Hi labor demand • Black reproduction is primary labor source	Paternalistic • Tame wild animalistic Blacks	Exploitative law to maximize profit-custom throughout slave era, government sanctioned 1662–1865	• Slave offspring "follow the condition of the mother" • Whites legislate absolute autonomy over Black women's offspring • Slave owners often "own" their own biological biracial offspring after rape of Black slave women
Establishing Cash Value Reproductive Capabilities Determine Black Woman's Value	• Expansion • Low technology • Hi labor demand • Black reproduction is primary labor source	Paternalistic • Glean some value from savages	Exploitative protocol to maximize profit-custom throughout slave era, particularly salient 1808–1865	• Black woman is only worth as much as she can produce

In its conspicuous silence on the explicit topic of slavery, the Constitution implicitly consents to the "peculiar institution."

Two other profoundly damaging blows dealt to Blacks by the Constitution are the "three-fifths rule" and "states' rights."[15] The three-fifths rule determines that one Black person only constitutes three-fifths of a human being. As such, Blacks, both free and enslaved, hold no political strength. In fact, the enslavement and customarily cruel mistreatment of Blacks carries with it no moral or legal retribution. While states' rights give each individual state the power to determine local laws that govern voting qualifications, slavery issues, and Civil Rights. The Constitution thoroughly eliminates any possibility of federal support or protection for Blacks in the current and future eras. This maltreatment would remain a constant in the United States for nearly the next two hundred years. Even continuing to dog Blacks after the Emancipation Proclamation; Blacks would not achieve any meaningful inclusion or protection from the U.S. government until the passing of the Civil Rights Acts of 1957, 1960, and 1964. These policies finally offer federal intervention into legalized state discrimination and the systematic disenfranchisement of Blacks through cruelty, intimidation, and social, political, and economic exclusion.[16]

Summary

In sum, as illustrated in table 6.2, historical data show that the needs of the national economy during the policy period between 1845 and 1865 are clearly linked to the passage of exploitative policies as they relate to enslaved Black women in the United States. In this period the U.S. economy is in a state of expansion with low technology and high labor demand. Black reproduction is depended upon as the primary source of labor. In order to justify the commodification of this labor source, various forms of media present Black women as savages needing their sexual energies channeled. A pseudo-paternalistic social response develops *justifying* the enslavement of Black women. As a result of this paternalistic social climate and the reliance of the White owners on the institution of slavery as a system of controlling a cheap manipulable labor force, exploitative types of policies and protocols are developed that dehumanize the Black mother and maximize the profits of the White owners.

Further Readings

Botti, Timothy J. *Envy of the World: A History of the US Economy and Big Business.* New York: Algora, 2006.

Gillham, Nicholas W. "Sir Francis Galton and the Birth of Eugenics." In *Annual Review of Genetics* 35: pp. 83–101, 2001.

Gordon Linda. *Woman's Body, Woman's Right: A Social History of Birth Control in America*, revised and updated edition. New York: Penguin Books, 1990.

Green, Ronald Walter, *Malthusian Worlds: U.S. Leadership and the Governing of the Population Crisis (Polemics).* Boulder, CO: Westview Press, 1999.

Himes, Norman Edwin. "Note on the Early History of Contraception in America." In *New England Journal of Medicine* 205: pp. 438–440, 1931.

Jones, Jacqueline. *A Social History of the Laboring Classes: From Colonial Times to the Present (Problems in American History).* Malden, MA: Blackwell, 1999.

Jordan, Winthrop D. *White over Black: American Attitudes toward the Negro, 1550–1812.* Chapel Hill, NC: University of North Carolina Press, 1968.

Katz E. "The History of Birth Control in the United States." In *Trends in History* 4: pp. 81–101, 1988.

Ledbetter Rosanna, *A History of the Malthusian League, 1877–1927.* Columbus: Ohio State University Press, 1976.

Leung M. "Making the Radical Respectable. Little Rock Clubwomen and the Cause of Birth Control during the 1930s." In *Arkansas Historical Quarterly* 57: pp. 17–33, 1988.

MacFarlane, D.R. and K.J. Meier. *The Politics of Fertility Control. Family Planning and Abortion Policies in the American States.* New York, 2001.

Perrin, L.M. "Resisting Reproduction. Reconsidering Slave Contraception in the Old South." In *Journal of American Studies* 35: pp. 255–75, 2001.

Reis, Elizabeth (Ed.). *American Sexual Histories.* Malden, MA: Blackwell, 2001.

Smith, Merril. *Sex and Sexuality in Early America.* New York: New York University Press. 1998.

Solinger, Rickie. "Racializing the Nation: From the Declaration of Independence to the Emancipation Proclamation, 1776–1865." In *The Reproductive Rights Reader: Law, Medicine, and the Construction of Motherhood,* ed. Nancy Ehrenreich, pp. 261–274, New York: New York University Press, 2008.

Tucker S. 1988. "The Black Domestic in the South: Her Legacy as Mother and Mother Surrogate." In *Southern Women,* ed. C.M. Dillman, pp. 93–102. New York: Hemisphere.

Williams, P. Autumn 1988. "On Being the Object of Property." In *Signs* 14: pp. 5–24.

PART 3

Emancipated . . . Not Liberated

Year	Key Historical Moments during Industrial Era (1866–1950)
1866–1877	Reconstruction
1870	Fifteenth Amendment-No race restrictions on Suffrage
1877	Tilden-Hayes Compromise
1907	Fist Court-Mandated Sterilization
1910–1940	The Great Migration
1914–1918	World War I
1920	Nineteenth Amendment—Woman's Suffrage
1921	American Birth Control League
1927	*Buck v. Bell*
1929	Stock Market Crash
1929–1939	The Great Depression
1933–1936	New Deal Policies
1939–1945	World War II
1939–1942	Negro Project
1942	Planned Parenthood Federation

CHAPTER SEVEN

Labor in the Industrial Age

Having contextualized the historical sexual exploitation of enslaved Black women in the agricultural era, we now turn our attentions forward, toward a second watershed moment in Black women's reproductive history—reproductive policies of the industrial era, specifically between 1929 and 1954. As the slave era enters its last generations, industrialization begins to take hold of the nation and to show itself in innumerable ways. According to Giddens these changes were

> Symbolized by the humming New England textile mills, northern industrialization was reaching new heights in this period. The consequent broader flow of capital created a new middle class striving for upper-class status.[1]

The end of slavery sees nearly four million slaves freed and thousands of former owners who have lost land and capital.[2] Without the labor; land; and capital resources available in the previous era, many of the former slave owners find themselves no longer able to maximize agricultural profits. As a result, the nation sees its wage labor force increase exponentially and for the first time in U.S. history Black reproduction becomes symptomatic of the financial crises of society, rather than its successes. Following their emancipation from slavery, Black women's manual and reproductive labor continues to be exploited; however, the economic landscape changes such over the decades following the Civil War—due to the national move toward industrialization—that the general need for Black labor diminishes significantly. Whereas the United States previously relied on Blacks as instruments of production and reproduction for maximization of agricultural profit; now, Black

production has become a threat to White production and Black reproduction has become a social problem.

Though in using the term, *instrument of production,* Marx is references
any slave system not, not specifically Blacks in the United States, having been the *instruments of production* for 246 years, Black workers had
historically been both literally and figuratively chained to the shifts
in the U.S. forces of production; even further alienating Blacks from
American society. Marx asserts that,

> . . . laborers are free in two senses. . . . The typical laborers of capi-
> talism are neither a part of the means of production, as are slaves
> and bondmen; nor do they possess means of production of their
> own. . . . Laborers under capitalism have been 'freed' or *separated*
> from their means of production.[3]

If Marx's definition of laborers in the working class is correct, then
Black women are even further alienated from U.S. society as their former position as slaves predisposes them to exist on the margins of an
already classed culture. With Emancipation and this transition from
agricultural to industrial forces of production, many formerly enslaved
Black women find themselves still trapped in the fields, continuing to
provide manual labor for their former masters and other White land-
owners. A significant portion of these Black women laborers are married mothers forced to work outside the home in a system which expects
honorable women to stay home and care for their husbands and children.
Just five years after Emancipation, statistics show that 40 percent of
married southern Black women work outside the home; while more
than 98 percent of married southern White women do not.[4] Excluded
from factory opportunities, that at least carry a certain prestige, those
who do not join the sharecropper ranks are often relegated to domestic
service, effectively continuing the reproductive labor that many Black
women performed while previously enslaved.

Sixty years later, by the onset of the Great Depression, 90 percent of
Black women's labor remains either agricultural or domestic. Due to
the shifts toward industrialization, though many Black women and men
continue to work in farming, Black women are no longer primarily
employed in agriculture. Instead she is largely employed as a domestic
employee, typically performing as: laundress; maid; seamstress; nanny;
and cook in White women's homes. Due to the nature of such private
employment, Black women are offered no organizational protection,
and are left wholly unprotected by the reform policies of the New Deal

era.[5] Hit hard by the status of the economy, Black women suffer the highest unemployment rate across the nation. Black women are denied basic labor rights of fair compensation and employee benefits. Further, Black women only earn 38 percent of White women's wages—who themselves do not earn a fair wage. It is evident that within this historical context of former slave laborers, Black women exist within a particular social location in the United States, rooted in socially accepted discrimination and institutionalized misogyny and racism. This location, arguably, makes Black women more vulnerable to the attacks of the political economy than the other classes.

As shown in table 7.1, it is apparent that, with the dissolution of slavery, Black women's productive and reproductive labor, though continuously exploited, ceases to play as significantly positive a role in the U.S. economy as in the previous era. As a result, Black women's labor—both reproductive and productive—becomes problematized,

Table 7.1 Status of political economy in industrial era

Mode of Production	*Industrialization*
Political Economy 1896–1950	• Nation is in a state of increasing expansion through 1929 stock market crash
	• Nation experiences significant period of Contraction-The Great Depression from 1929 through end of World War II
	• Nation experiences booming expansion from 1945 beyond 1950
	• Industrial production for world Economy
Forces of Production	• Technology at a high
	• Factories are significant source of capitalist profit
	• Mechanical labor is employed in factories and on farms
Instruments of Production Labor Pool	• Human Labor is primarily Black sharecroppers, Black domestic and service workers.
	• Blacks are excluded from union and factory work
	• Blacks, White Americans, and primarily European immigrants vie for wage employment
Means of Production Labor Source	• Blacks, Whites, and immigrants
	• Black reproduction is no longer necessity for profit and is problematized for the first time
Relations of Production Labor Demand	• Labor demand is low as there is a surplus of now free Blacks, immigrants, and Whites vying for limited employment
	• Industrial age serf vs. Landlord in the form of sharecropping
	• Wage laborer vs. Capitalist

rather than sought after, as it had been in the past. With the dissolution of slavery Black women find that—previously encouraged to reproduce for profit—the nation now deems Black reproduction as a social problem that clogs the workforce and overwhelms the White population.[6] No longer marketable and without capital in a capitalist system, the Black woman is unlike others of the subordinated working class in the capitalist United States, having been exploited, both sexually and physically as slaves and forced to provide "free" productive; reproductive; and biological labor.

The Great Depression

With the stock market crash of 1929, the United States falls deeply into an economic depression that persists throughout the 1930s. Technological development is at a standstill. Unemployment rates are at the highest the United States has ever seen. Labor demands are at their absolute lowest. Further, the U.S. experiences the lowest birthrate the nation has seen before or since this period of severe contraction. In the years following the Great Depression, the United States emerges successfully from World War II into an era of economic prosperity and into the role of global superpower. By 1945, technology is at an absolute high and industry loses its dependence on human labor and instead relies on automation. And though not widely commercially produced until the 1960s, various incarnations of the computer and other computer-assisted technology are developing rapidly beginning in 1937. These technological advancements are launching the United States head-on into the next age of computerization. In the meantime, White Americans and (mostly European) immigrants continue to vie for wage labor. This competition leads to anti-immigration and anti-Black propaganda. This social rhetoric leads to policies that encourage discord between the marginalized groups and systematically excludes Blacks from unions. The social rhetoric of the period will eventually lead to the racial segregation or ghettoization of both Blacks and immigrants, such as Italians, Poles, Irish, and Ukrainian. Though White middle-class reproduction is encouraged in the prosperous post–World War II era (postwar era), Black reproduction is condemned as a drain on American resources.

CHAPTER EIGHT

Becoming a Social Problem

The ongoing mechanization of the agricultural industry coupled with the significant shifts in the relations of production drive many former agricultural laborers to the already industrialized North in turn of the century America. Though typically referenced as a *Black* migration period, the four decades before the U.S. entry into World War II see tremendous migration of both Whites and Blacks, who are unable to thrive in the new South. As a result of this migration of Blacks and Whites, as well as primarily European immigrants, by the onset of the Great Depression of the 1930s, the United States finds itself with an overabundance of labor and little to no labor demand. As a result of these changes in the national economy, there is an end to the previously high demand for Black labor. At this point, Black women's reproduction of the primary labor pool is no longer tantamount to economic success and in fact becomes a national concern.

These economic concerns impact significantly on the development of restrictive reproductive policies between 1929 and 1954. Having already begun the debate on the nature and intelligence of Blacks in previous eras, the twentieth century begins with a renewed "scientific" examination of the *Negro* problem. Originally published in 1859, Charles Darwin's seminal work, *The Origin of Species,* becomes a key element within the ongoing debate. The impact of this issue is evidenced by the political platforms that drive the 1868 presidential campaign—White supremacy and the degradation of the human species by Blacks. According to historian Eric Foner, Francis P. Blair, Jr., the vice-presidential candidate for the 1868 election,

> ...embarked on a speaking campaign.... In blatantly racist language...[Blair spoke of] "a semi-barbarous race of blacks who are

worshippers of fetishes and polygamists."...Having read Darwin's *Origin of Species*, Blair now asserted that racial intermixing would reverse evolution, produce a less advanced species incapable of reproducing itself, and destroy the accumulated improvement of the centuries.[1]

Having long been considered a burden to the White race; Blacks had most recently been blamed for the so-called disenfranchisement of White men. As many White slave owners and their families had been unable to recover from the Civil War; Reconstruction; and the nation's moves toward industrialization, they found themselves alienated from the political structure; unable to secure economic stability; nor to obtain gainful employment. Much of this was blamed on Blacks as they had already historically been deemed a threat to the *morality* of White men and women; a threat to their livelihood was not inconceivable. Now, on top of everything else, according to the predominant scientific theories of the day, Blacks are also a danger to the future of the species. As a result, during the early part of the twentieth century, inside a period that is already rife with struggle for the Black population, Black reproduction is reviled in both intellectual and popular communities as a deleterious parasitic drain.

With the onset of industrialization, the state reasserts its position of patriarchal authority over Black women's biological; manual; and reproductive labor; radically redefining her previous contributions to the system. Similarly to the manner in which Black reproduction is framed as a social concern through vehement social rhetoric; White reproduction is crafted as a social responsibility of the middle class. The historical notions of "true womanhood" and the new emerging middle classes both buy into and feed into eugenics ideologies.

Rise of Eugenics

In the years following the forced labor of the slave period, the United States undergoes significant political and economic changes. As the nation approaches its lowest point, economically—The Great Depression—Black women are not only discouraged from reproducing, but legislation rooted in eugenics ideology is designed to enforce these policies.

Eugenics is a pseudo-scientific theoretical perspective originated in the late nineteenth century by Sir Francis Galton.[2] A British polymath by all accounts and cousin of Charles Darwin, Galton is taken with the concepts discussed in Darwin's 1859 work *The Origin of Species*. Picking up where his cousin leaves off, Galton begins devising a theory that includes the analysis of "survival of the fittest," "nature vs. nurture," and both "positive" and "negative" reproduction. By 1883 Galton presents the theory of eugenics.[3] Derived from the Greek for "well born" or "good breeding;" Galtonian eugenics proposes the improvement of the human species by controlling reproduction through: (1) stemming the reproduction of the undesirable members of the species; and (2) encouraging the reproduction of the "fittest" most desirable members of the species. A racist condemnation of nonwhite populations is inherent in eugenics philosophies. Galton, along with countless other scientists; educators; activists; and politicians continue to develop the *theory* well into the early twentieth century. Eugenics can be found at the core of the most insidious state sponsored crimes against humanity that have ever been enforced in the United States and around the world. Including the era of segregation in the United States; compulsory sterilization programs that run rampant throughout the United States; Australia; Europe; Asia; and some Latin American countries; and the rise of the final solution in Nazi Germany.[4] Some would assert that scientific analysis rooted in eugenics ideologies persist even today.

Kline's 2001 *Building a Better Race* argues the rise of eugenics philosophies is the result of a nation afraid of its own changing morality. According to Kline, the further away the United States moved from its Victorian "passionlessness," the closer its White upper classes were drawn to eugenics ideologies.[5] In the late nineteenth century the growing concern for "mental and moral deficiency," was focused on the lower classes, immigrants, and Blacks.[6] However, after a period of attempting to segregate members of these populations—primarily women perceived as *promiscuous* and *morons*—proved unsuccessful in thwarting changes to traditional sexual mores; by the turn of the century, sterilization became the answer to the plight of the human race.[7] In the age of the "new morality" and the roaring 20s, eugenics is embraced as a way to save the collective American soul.[8] A nation, fundamentally rooted in both White and male supremacy, according to Kline, understandably gravitates toward a philosophy that would not only legitimize, but justify, racial and gender inequity as, "an appealing solution to the problem of moral disorder."[9]

Luker's 1996 *Dubious Conceptions: The Politics of Teenage Pregnancy* asserts that America's fears for future generations has existed for generations before the emergence of policies regulating mainstream reproduction. However, according to Luker, the United States did not see the advent of legislation that would police reproduction until the nineteenth century,

> ...only in the nineteenth century did the United States institute formal, legal policies ensuring that some people would never

contribute to those coming generations. Limiting the right to
marry, incarcerating "wayward girls," and passing laws to sterilize
the poor, the criminal, or the "unfit" from reproducing.[10]

Luker further asserts that to focus solely on the push towards negative
eugenics tells only a piece of the history. In order to fully examine the
United States' relationship to eugenics ideology, one must also examine
the push for the upper classes to reproduce:

> Influenced by Darwinian thought and its domestic variants,
> Americans realized that policies to keep the unfit from reproduc-
> ing needed to be matched with policies encouraging childbearing
> among the fit.[11]

This fear of the *fit* failing to reproduce at rates commensurate with
those of the foreign-born, poor, and black populations led to federal
policies restricting contraception:

> The differences in fertility between immigrants and the native-
> born, between blacks and whites, and between the well-off and
> the poor were so striking that in 1903 Theodore Roosevelt coined
> a term "race suicide" to describe this long-standing and worri-
> some phenomenon.... Clearly, the government had to ensure that
> the 'fit' bore their fair share of children, and it did so by limiting
> access to contraceptives and abortions.[12]

Consistent with the eugenics rhetoric of the day, intrinsic with the cultural push for Black women to stop reproducing is the push for White
middle-class women to have more children. According to Davis,

> During the first decades of the twentieth century the rising
> popularity of the eugenics movement was hardly a fortuitous
> development. Eugenic ideas were perfectly suited to the ideologi-
> cal needs of young monopoly capitalists. Imperialist incursions in
> Latin America and in the Pacific needed to be justified, as did the
> intensified exploitation of Black workers in the South and immi-
> grant workers in the North and West. The pseudo-scientific racial
> theories associated with the eugenics campaign furnished dramatic
> apologies for the conduct of the young monopolies. As a result, this
> movement won the unhesitating support of such leading capitalists
> as the Carnegies, the Harrimans and the Kelloggs.[13]

The Image of Needy Surplus Labor

The image of Blacks is already firmly rooted in historical social rhetoric that presents Blacks as lazy; ignorant; and unable to take care of themselves. During a period in American history when nearly everyone is hyper extended, this leaves a palpable sentiment of resentment. During such desperate times, such as the Great Depression; World War II; or dramatic industrial transitions. It is far less improbable to propagate social rhetoric that portrays millions of Blacks as a surplus labor force; contributing only to the population density in urban America; adding extra mouths to feed in soup kitchens; and draining the nation of its available resources; when Americans are already vulnerable and economically unstable. Particularly given that a population has already been exiled from mainstream society, as in the case of Blacks who can only live in designated areas; work particular types of jobs; and socialize in certain race-specific venues. They already occupy a space outside of American society. Having historically been indoctrinated with the image of hedonistic Black slaves, who, supposedly lacking humanity, *need* White ownership and guidance; Whites are quick to embrace images of a freeloading useless rabble in the industrial era. Thus the notion that they could be culpable for the social; economic; and political crises of the era is not at all farfetched for much of White America.

Though the Great Depression is a period of economic struggle throughout the nation, and Blacks seldom benefit from New Deal reform policies; Blacks are seen as a threat to the social safety net created to protect White Americans during this tumultuous period. Blacks are presented as sexually corrupt, morally bankrupt parasites in dire need of already dismal resources. Black women bear the brunt of this perception as their previously sought after ability to reproduce the labor force, is now reimagined as burdensome and problematic.

As the development of the Black woman as surplus labor is a key moment in the historical development of capitalism in the United States this industrial period is a fundamental moment in the development of the relationship between Black women's reproduction and the national economy. As stated previously by Marx, the ruling class must continuously revolutionize its instruments of production in order to profit.[14] The economic transition from agricultural forces of production to industrial must be analyzed as Zeitlin argues.

For a proper understanding of the concept of "productive forces," we must remember that Marx makes a fundamental distinction

between capitalist and precapitalist modes of production. Modern
capitalist industry, Marx writes, "...never looks upon and treats
the existing form of a process as final." The technical basis of that
industry is therefore revolutionary, while earlier modes of production were *conservative*.[15]

When examining the processes of revolutionizing the instruments of
production one should consider technological advancements as well as
the labor force. As, according to hooks, before the advent of the technologies that lead to the invention of the cotton picking machine,

> ...harvesting of crops depended heavily on the labor of black
> females. Although both black women and men labored to pick ripe
> cotton, it was believed that the more delicately tapered fingers of the
> black female made it easier for her to gather cotton from the pod.[16]

These new technologies are key in separating Black women from their
previous position as *instruments of production* and forcing them into
the role of surplus labor. Though Black women remain agricultural
laborers with the onset of the new tenant farming, often referred to as
sharecropping, and continues to perform domestic work; having previously been the very backbone of the economic structure, the Black
woman in the United States now finds her labor obsolete, and herself
irrelevant. Black reproduction at this point becomes perceived as a burden on society and Black women depicted as needy surplus labor. At
which time, as described in table 8.1, Black reproduction is vilified
and alleged as parasitic. Once firmly established, this public image that
reinforces a nationwide derision is used as a political platform from
which contraceptive movements firmly attached to anti-Black rhetoric
are launched.

Table 8.1 Themes of social rhetoric in the industrial era

Theme of Social Rhetoric 1929–1954	Representation of Needy Surplus Labor
Freeloading	Image of free Blacks overrunning United States
Irresponsible	Illustrated as unable or unwilling to take care of themselves or their offspring, leading to degeneracy
Immoral	Seen as destroying moral fiber of nation
Indigent	Perceived as overwhelming nation's workforce, leaving no space for White workers
Parasites	Believed to consume the few resources available to White Americans

Postwar Reproduction

As the nation pulls itself from the depths of the Great Depression and positions itself as an international superpower in the postwar era, Americans are absolutely intoxicated by both *positive* and *negative* eugenics.[17] Buying into eugenical rhetoric that perpetuates images of superiority, competitions are held to prove who has the "fitter family" and the "better baby."[18] Textbooks include eugenics as a valid science. Advertisers for soap and cleaning supplies even get on board, as cleanliness is considered one of the tenets of the eugenically superior. According to Stephanie Coontz,

> ...the 1950s sitcoms were aimed at young couples....The message was clear: Buy these ranch houses, Hotpoint appliances, and child-raising ideas...and you too can escape from the conflicts of race [and] class....There was tremendous hostility to people who could be defined as "others": Jews, African Americans, Puerto Ricans, the poor, gays or lesbians, and "the red menace."[19]

As sterilization laws and policies aimed at Blacks are supported by all of the nation's major institutions: education; church; media; government; et cetera; the image of the "American Dream" is inculcated into society and intertwined with the notion that White reproduction is good for society and Black reproduction is wrong.

Baby Boom vs. Population Bomb

Baby Boom

A term coined by the media, the b*aby boom,* is commonly accepted as the period of extensive reproduction from 1946 to1964.[20] Not specific to the United States, a boom is a natural phenomenon that typically occurs after a major war. However the notion of the American baby boom has been co-opted as the very image of hometown America. Having survived the struggles of the Great Depression and the horrors of World War II, the postwar era is considered the height of American suburbanization. A period of rampant reproduction, the baby boom is commonly revered as the most prosperous and nostalgic stage in U.S. history. Even today the nation honors this brief period in American history with a commemorative postage stamp series designed to encapsulate the joy of propagation and the simple pleasures of the American family. Characterized by images of a cherubic faced healthy White child and excited and anxious new fathers seeing their new children for the first time through a pane of glass in the hospital nursery, the baby boom is nostalgia at its very best.[21]

The 1950s, in particular, has been venerated as a period when White middle class American families; like their television counterparts— *Ozzie & Harriet, Donna Reed,* and *Leave It To Beaver*—have achieved the *American Dream.* Mom and Dad relish their unaffected gender roles—he, the sole breadwinner and head of household and she, the homemaker and mother. Though this purportedly ideal reality is short-lived, and specific to a select population of Americans, the myth of the all-American nuclear family has transcended reality and become locked in our collective memory as America's glory days.[22]

In truth, the suburbanization of the 1950s is an attempt at the reorganization of the American institution of family. According to Coontz, "1950s family forms and values . . . [is an] *experimentation* with the possibilities of a new kind of family, not as the expression of some longstanding tradition."[23] In previous generations families had often been extended, as newlyweds lived with parents; in-laws; siblings; and grandparents. The 1950s sees the kinship community that in the past had helped with finances, childrearing, and offered emotional and psychological support, abandoned. In the 1950s, with the creation of the *nuclear family,* for the first time young couples are on their own, with the responsibilities of a mortgage, expensive cars, and the cultural insistence that they become an active consumer.[24]

And though, for a few years, many of the men and women in these suburbanized families find comfort in their positions and even thrive in their roles, the harsh realities of life are inevitably revealed. In fact, Coontz reports that the same White middle class families that are so revered in contemporary memories as having lived the American dream; are actually fraught with social; culture; and economic crises of their own. War veterans returning to families that no longer accept his authority, wives often having "two or more children in diapers," leaving them clearly overwhelmed and tethered to a role that many women and men in the 1950s take on as early as eighteen.[25] According to Coontz, the postwar family is comprised of,

> . . . couples who had married in haste, women who had tasted new freedom during World War II and given up their jobs with regret, veterans whose children resented their attempts to reassert paternal authority, and individuals disturbed by the changing racial and ethnic mix of postwar America.[26]

Such glaring incongruities between the actual circumstances of American history and Americans' collective musings, is a key insight into the American psyche. These contradictions illustrate the American people's willingness to accept false realities, when instilled by media and other major U.S. institutions. It further demonstrates Americans' willingness to deny evident truths that are clearly exemplified in the lived history of the United Sates. As America's historical context prior to the postwar era is replete with slavery; exploitation; poverty; and abuse. During the supposedly prosperous 1950s the nation begins to witness the outcomes of these centuries of abuse. The experiment of the postwar era is shattered by strife; chaos; turmoil; and revolution in the form of a variety of activist struggles, including: Black Civil Rights movements; women's rights movements; gay rights movements; antiwar movements; and a significant number of ethnic and youth movements. Leaving one to reconsider the commemorative postage stamp series mentioned earlier, disseminated by the U.S. post office to venerate the so-called baby boom. In its efforts to stir up nostalgic visions of the White American Dream, it only serves to reinforce the institutionalized racist patriarchal misogyny of yesteryear.

Population Bomb

This cooperative denial that dismisses the varied disaffected members of society is further illustrated by the cavalier disregard for the contradictions of being Black in America. While in a reality parallel, and in appalling contrast, to White middle class America's cheerfully revered *baby boom;* rooted in Malthusian, Darwinist, and Galtonian philosophies, Black reproduction is termed a metaphorical *population bomb.*[27] Blacks exist in a hostile reality where they fight tooth and nail for the slightest civil freedoms: choosing his/her own seat on a public bus; the option of eating in any restaurant; or even to attend a good public school. As Whites live the so-called *American Dream,* Blacks are mired in a centuries-long struggle for the recognition of their very humanity.

Separatist Response

The response to the imagery of the period, as highlighted in table 8.2, is devastating to all Blacks, male and female. Bearing the brunt of blame for the status of the political economy, Blacks again find themselves at the center of whirlwind debates demanding what to do about the "Negro problem." The first half of the twentieth century sees the rise of industry and shifts in migration patterns. Blacks, drawn to northern

Table 8.2   Snapshot of social response to rhetoric campaigns in the industrial era

Social Climate 1924–1954	Characteristics of Social Climate
Separatist Social Response	Society believes all Blacks, both free and slave, are draining American resources
	Society believes all Blacks, both free and slave, should live lives separate from White America

cities, such as Chicago and Detroit; are vehemently attacked in a deluge of so-called race riots in the early part of the century.[28] White America enforces rules that Blacks must remain separate from Whites at all costs. Controlled by angry lynch mobs of Whites, Blacks are kidnapped, assaulted, and killed—in short lynched—in record numbers. Under the threat of death, Blacks are relegated to small sections of major cities, such as the Black Belt on Chicago's south side or Harlem in New York City.

Perhaps it not so surprising that near the end of the first decade of the new millennium, facing, arguably, the most significant economic crisis in U.S. history since the Great Depression; the media offers a familiar refrain—blame the poor and "minority."[29] Perhaps this is not the *exact* language being employed. It is true that the constant chatter about the collapse of the housing market being a direct result of poor *urban* residents going into foreclosure could hypothetically be a reference to anyone who has fallen upon hard times. However it is evident that media references to terms such as *urban; inner city;* and *welfare*, have all come to be coded language for the more controversial *Black*. In the words of much of the American media and many elected officials, including George W. Bush, many of these urban and inner city borrowers *should not* have received a home loan in the first place. Inserting urban in lieu of Black does not lessen the implication of culpability.

Thus the belief that Blacks are ultimately responsible for social problems. Be the issue: urban crime; lack of education; or unemployment, at the core Blacks are scapegoated as the antithesis of American prosperity. Supporting their continued victimization within an unforgiving structure rooted in systematic racial; gender; class; and labor oppression and exploitation. This image results in generations of state sponsored racial segregation.

CHAPTER NINE

Morons, Mental Defectives, Prostitutes, and Dope Fiends: Restrictive Reproductive Policies

Becoming African Americans

After the Civil War, the thirteenth amendment is passed abolishing slavery. Unfortunately the mere abolition of slavery does not offer instant inclusion for the Africans who had become Americans over the many generations of forced servitude. Instead, Blacks suffer a terrible backlash to federal efforts to incorporate them into the U.S. structure, such as Reconstruction policies and the Civil Rights Act of 1866. As the nation continues to plod clumsily forward out of the depths of slavery and the anguish of civil war, desperately grasping at de jure segregation and terrorism along the way, there is a brief period of rigorous and significant federal mandates to correct the misdeeds of the previous generations.

Throughout this period known as Reconstruction (1866–1877), the U.S. government attempts to demand inclusion of Blacks through political and military force. Similarly to the laws governing slavery in the preceding era, freedom requires a number of amendments, laws, and policies that regulate equality, inclusion, and access for Black Americans. For a length of time, at least during Reconstruction, Blacks finally enjoy some political freedom and inclusion. However, with the Hayes-Tilden compromise of 1877, it becomes apparent that Blacks have been used as pawns in a political struggle, rather than integrated into the national political structure.[1]

Even still, Reconstruction is a meaningful historical moment for Blacks. At one point, over 800,000 Blacks are registered to vote due to Black suffrage movements attached to Reconstruction.[2] Further, for the first time in American history Blacks—now Americans—hold elected posts within the U.S. government.[3] It is a new era; and for the first time in their history in America, there is hope for African Americans. Reconstruction is a period, not only of restoration, but also of bestowing citizenship on a previously denied people. Reconstruction sees more Black political involvement in the U.S. democratic process across the nation than in any years since.[4]

Unfortunately the successes of the period are short-lived. Even with the passing of the fifteenth amendment, which specifies Blacks' right to vote, de facto and de jure violence and intimidation tactics occur both at the ballot and in the streets by terrorist organizations, as well as by city, state, and government officials.[5] According to Giddings,

> Racial hostility was especially focused on Afro-Americans who had made substantial economic gains in the postwar period-gains now being checked by the South's counterrevolution, the eclipse of the Freedmen's Bureau, and later the depression of 1893.[6]

Southern states respond almost immediately to the successful federal efforts with their own state-sanctioned vigilante anti-incorporation efforts, by implementing "Black Codes" and launching an organized series of terrorist attacks. Southern Blacks, having just escaped the degradation and dangers of slavery are now inundated with these new policies of disenfranchisement and violence. Prohibited from the freedoms to: bear arms; organize; own property; vote; or fully integrate into American society; Blacks, particularly in the South, also live under the constant threat of terror.[7]

American Terrorism

Terrorist organizations, such as the Ku Klux Klan, are launched and avidly take up the cause to enforce these Black codes across the South in order to keep Blacks from gaining any further social; political; or economic ground. The Ku Klux Klan is a White supremacist terrorist organization, known colloquially throughout the nation as the KKK. It is launched "in 1866 as a Tennessee social club, the Ku Klux Klan spreads into nearly every southern state, launching a 'reign of terror.'[8] The lawlessness; mayhem; and mass murder perpetrated by the organization is unprecedented. The former Louisiana governor, George

Michael Hahn declares that, "murder and intimidation are the order of the day in this state."[9] They target and assassinate politicians; Blacks; and anyone who would stand in their way. Attacking as angry mobs; they are known to have killed hundreds of people in a single strike. Their mob rule becomes so feared that White supporters of Black inclusion must rescind their backing and accept that the previous inroads would soon be reversed.[10] The Ku Klux Klan's campaigns of violence prove incredibly effective in their war against Black progress in the late nineteenth century. Even after successfully disenfranchising Blacks from political power after the Civil War, they would continue to evolve as a violent terrorist organization over the generations. The Ku Klux Klan has seen many incarnations over the decades, presenting themselves as: concerned citizens; vigilantes; and even politicians. They continue to thrive across the nation today.

Though reportedly condemned by the northern part of the nation, the Black codes of the nineteenth century are federally supported by legally sanctioned anti-integration laws that follow. Specifically, the 1896 Supreme Court ruling of *Plessy v. Ferguson* which determines that "separate but equal" accommodations for Blacks and Whites are constitutional.[11] This ruling ushers in the Jim Crow segregation era that persists for the next half a century. Terrorist actions, further fueled by "Jim Crow" segregation laws, enforce the harsh and unreasonable policies and laws assailing, now free, Blacks. These policies range from: voting regulations, such as: literacy tests; poll taxes; and the grandfather clause; substandard educational institutions; disparate healthcare; and unequal access to community resources, including: retail stores; restaurants; and public parks.[12]

Though still drowning in discrimination, many Black men fight in World War II. Upon returning home, having travelled to Europe and northern cities in the United States, many could no longer reconcile the reprehensible systemic racism of the south.[13] Failed by the U.S. government, many southern Blacks choose to leave the poverty and hopelessness of their rural communities. In the mass exodus of this Great Migration, many Blacks are forced to leave their families and head north, either until they establish themselves in the north or because many Black women who had not travelled remain wary of the unknown and remain mired in familial ties—such as senior kin care. Those who do choose to migrate, head north in search of enfranchisement, civil freedoms, work, and above all—hope. According to Giddings,

All these things added to the pressures on Black family life that were exacerbated by Black migration to the cities, both southern and northern. Between 1890 and 1910, as many as 200,000 Blacks left the soil that had borne so much of their blood and tears. Blacks were beleaguered. The Black family was under siege.[14]

Restricting Black Reproduction

In search of a freedom of opportunity not afforded them in the rural south, Blacks now find themselves in competition for work in ways they had not experienced in the past.[15] This new reality is not lost on White America. By 1907, as a result of powerful lobbying on behalf of eugenics philosophies, sterilizations could be court-mandated to control criminality, amorality *incompetence, imbecility, and degeneracy.*[16] These policies are most often invoked in poorer rural regions and urban inner cities.

American Eugenics

Illustrated by the image of a large tree sprouting roots and limbs in all directions, eugenics is presented as an organic and biological reality that impacts every aspect of our humanity. Supported by the intertwining roots of knowledge labeled with various disciplines, such as: the humanities; social sciences; the law; medicine; mathematics; and physical sciences. The allegorical reference to the *tree of life* as it were, stands tall surrounded by a caption that reads, "Eugenics is the self direction of human evolution."[17] The very idea of eugenics is presented as the pathway to knowledge, self-improvement, and the future of humanity. Though wholly inhumane in its blatant and overt message of forcible and coercive sterilization of the so-called unfit—which typically means Blacks; Latina(o)s; Native Americans; the poor; and/or the mentally ill, eugenics is presented as an intelligent, logical, even harmonious way to better civilization.[18] A burgeoning notion at the end of the nineteenth century, eugenics ideologies are so embraced in American society midway through the first half of the century, that according to Angela Y. Davis,

> By 1932 the Eugenics Society could boast that at least twenty-six states had passed compulsory sterilization laws and that thousands of 'unfit' persons had already been surgically prevented from reproducing.[19]

By 1935, thirty-three states have eugenics-based sterilization statutes on their books across the nation.[20] Though the invocation of these laws for the purposes of forced sterilization falls out of favor and therefore declines in use in the late 1970s and early 1980s, many of these laws remain on the books in individual states, and are even periodically updated. Further, local policies continue to be implemented across the nation to disproportionately force and coerce poorer; Black; Latina; and Native American women into sterilization.[21]

Margaret Sanger

A women's rights activist and a trained nurse, Margaret Sanger, prescribes to Galton's theories of eugenics and applies its ideologies to the ongoing battle for contraceptive rights in the United States. Margaret Sanger is an activist who protests on behalf of women's rights her entire career. In 1921 Sanger attends a court hearing wearing a gag over her mouth protesting a judge's refusal to allow her to speak in court. In violation of federal law, Sanger publishes pamphlets and articles illuminating female reproductive issues, such as menstruation; pregnancy; avoiding pregnancy; and female sexuality. In 1921 Sanger founds the American Birth Control League, which eventually becomes the Planned Parenthood Federation in 1942. Sanger is so committed to negative eugenics that listed among the eight goals of the organization, is

STERILIZATION of the insane and feebleminded and the encouragement of this operation upon those afflicted with inherited or transmissible diseases, with the understanding that sterilization does not deprive the individual of his or her sex expression, but merely renders him incapable of producing children.[22]

There are explicit contradictions in the legacy of Margaret Sanger's active involvement in the fight for reproductive rights of women. Though contrasted with her overtly racist ideologies, Sanger has made many significant gains on behalf of women's reproductive rights in the United States. However, there has been much debate as to her role in oppressing Black women's reproductive rights and the overall goals of her efforts. Though her work is credited with much of the reproductive freedoms of all American women today, according to Angela Davis, Margaret Sanger is quite blatantly an avid negative eugenicist.[23] According to Davis, in a radio interview Sanger reports that,

Morons, mental defectives, epileptics, illiterates, paupers, unemployables, criminals, prostitutes and dope fiends; ought to be surgically sterilized, [Sanger] argued in a radio talk...if they wished, she said, they should be able to choose a lifelong segregated existence in labor camps.[24]

Sanger's legacy persists today in the ongoing work of Planned Parenthood. This organization that has stood for nearly one hundred years; continues to maintain the role as leading provider of gynecological, contraceptive, and general medical healthcare services to poorer women and women of color throughout the nation to this day. Unfortunately, its connections to Sanger and its original goals make the organization suspect. Tainted by this history, the debate continues today as to whether or not the organization's dedication to providing abortion; contraceptive; and sterilization services is due to a commitment to reproductive rights or to negative eugenics. That said the organization's current mission clearly denotes an explicit commitment to bioethics; education; and patient's rights to privacy, in stark contrast to Sanger's initial vision.

Victims of Eugenics

Just as Sanger's struggles for women's reproductive rights have not impacted on a singular population; it must be noted that the eugenics movement is not specific to Blacks only. The push by Sanger and many of her contemporaries for negative eugenics has severely impacted many populations other than Black women. Though this research highlights the historical relationships of Black women's reproduction to the state, it is by no means meant to purposefully ignore other populations impacted by these abuses. I would be remiss if I did not acknowledge the effects that sterilization abuse ha had on populations other than Black women. A great number of physically and sexually abused children; Native American women and men; Asian women and men; immigrants; mentally ill and otherwise infirmed or impoverished people—both men and women—are victims of eugenics ideology.[25] In fact, the first court mandated sterilization procedure, in 1907, is performed on a White male inmate in Indiana.

Arguably, the population most heavily impacted by sterilization abuses of the state may be Latina women. As Roosevelt's government had determined that the economic problems in Puerto Rico should be attributed to overpopulation, many overt and covert efforts were employed to reduce the number of children produced.[26] As such, since then, any opportunity to perform permanent surgical sterilizations has been exploited. At times these sterilizations are performed openly through government programs instituted to reduce the population. At other times, more covert methods are employed.

In the 1970s pharmaceutical companies exploring various contraceptive devices and technologies routinely perform clinical trials on animals and inner city Black and Latina populations in the United States and in the U.S. territory of Puerto Rico.[27] As such, as the U.S. medical community seeks methods of perfecting the permanent surgical sterilization procedure, they perform the surgery on thousands of women in Puerto Rico. Initially a process by which the fallopian tubes are simply cut; doctors eventually learn that nature tends to find a way and that given time, the tubes may reconnect and resume functionality. Through performing the surgery on countless Puerto Rican women, they eventually discover that the ends should not only be cut, but also cauterized, in order to achieve a truly permanent procedure. More than 35 percent of Puerto Rican women of childbearing age had been sterilized by the 1970s.[28] Today, it is said that up to half of the women of childbearing age in Puerto Rico have received this surgery, which has become so inevitable and commonplace that many refer to it as simply, *the operation*.

That said, there is a tangential movement born of eugenics philosophies known as the Negro Project, which *is* specific to Blacks.[29] Arguably, as illustrated in Table 9.1, these forced sterilization policies and

Table 9.1 Examples of relevant policies in the industrial era

Influential Policies of the Industrial Era	Characteristics of Influential Policies of the Industrial Era
Eugenics	State supported eugenics Movement to discourage Black reproduction and encourage White reproduction
The Negro Project	Negro Project to encourage Black contraception and sterilization
Jim Crow	Jim Crow laws enforcing "separate but equal" from 1896 to 1954
Compulsory Sterilization	State imposed forced sterilization programs leading to over 70,000 court-mandated sterilizations from 1907 to mid-1980s. Many state laws remain on the books today.
The New Deal	The New Deal Reform Policies, first instituted in 1933, exist in various forms through the turn of the century. Begin moving towards dissolution in the 1990s.

programs, such as the Negro Project are part and parcel of a concerted effort to rid White America of the burden of Black reproduction. The reproductive policies of the industrial era are restrictive, as the nation legally forces Black women into sterilization procedures through eugenical sterilization laws and initiatives such as the Negro Project.

The Negro Project

By the 1930s Black women are commonly considered feeble-minded, promiscuous, and generally degenerate. There is both a social and political push to regulate Black populations that is *legitimized* by the eugenics movement. According to Giddings,[30]

> The birth control movement which, though legalizing contraception in this country, and launched with the idea of eradicating poverty, degenerated into a campaign to 'keep the unfit from reproducing themselves with all its Social Darwinist implications.'[31]

Well before the inception of the Negro Project, compulsory and coercive sterilization programs had already begun targeting Blacks. What's more they would continue to target Black women well after the program's end. The Eugenics Commission of North Carolina, which had diligently administered eugenics sterilization policies since 1933, admits that of the 7,686 sterilizations that had been performed in the state by the early 1960s, "about 5,000 of the sterilized persons had been Black."[32] They assert their purpose for sterilizing Black girls as young as ten years old is, "to prevent the reproduction of 'mentally deficient persons.'"[33] North Carolina continues to perform sterilizations at the same alarming rate, of 65 percent Black compared to 35 percent White, for the next twenty years.[34]

In the late 1930s Margaret Sanger commissions a government funded project that centers on Black reproduction—the *Negro Project*. Though presented as a program to offer marginalized Black communities access to reproductive information and healthcare, through the manipulation of Black doctors and clergy, the project actually serves as a vehicle to persuade Blacks to curb reproduction and volunteer for surgical sterilization. In fact, Sanger writes in a letter to a co-conspirator on the Negro Project that they must be particularly careful that the Black community does not learn that the primary goal of the program is the extermination of Blacks. To that end, she suggests the use of religious leaders to mollify the Black masses and undermine any Black rebels.[35] Though the nation remains adamantly against contraception throughout the first half of the twentieth century, Sanger, alongside other significant advocates, such as Mary Lasker and heir to the Procter and Gamble fortune, Clarence Gamble, manage to garner powerful supporters of the *birth control movement*, as it promises to resolve one of the nation's most pressing issues–*population control*.[36]

Sanger leads the Negro Project from 1939 to 1942. Though the program does not end for another decade, Sanger leaves the project in the capable hands of the largely Black volunteer staff she has trained. At which time she opens a clinic in Harlem, where Black women in New York City are sterilized through similar initiatives employed in the south. Little information is available on the depths of the Negro Project. What is known is that they are incredibly successful at their endeavors. Sanger is able to enlist the support of several major Black leaders, such as Mary McCleod Bethune, activist and educator; Rev. Adam Clayton Powell Sr., pastor of a famed Harlem church; and Charles S. Johnson, president of Fiske University.[37] The public face of Sanger's initiatives varies depending on her audience. For White communities she clearly advocates the extermination of Blacks and perceives them as a detriment to the human race. While in front of Black audiences she presents herself as a progressive who offers only support of Blacks and women's causes.[38] Much debate on this matter continues to this day.

In the public discourse, much of the discussion of Margaret Sanger and the Negro Project is reduced to a simplistic level. Too often the Negro Project is invoked today as a part of some effort to discourage Black women from using birth control or from having abortions. Though within the context of the tragic history that locates forced sterilization programs within an ongoing struggle against genocide, there is a certain logic to these concerns. And within that context, the fear of the abortion industry is, if not unadvisable, somewhat understandable. However, it is unfortunate that this history has been co-opted by extremists whose goals include curbing Black women's reproductive rights. And even worse, this horrid blight in American history has not been taught in schools and openly acknowledged in the media. Instead it has been reduced to a publicity stunt for misogynistic conservative politics that would deny a woman's right to choose in order to prove a political point.

Table 9.2 Reproductive policy analysis: 1929–1954

Industrial Era Restrictive Reproductive Policies	Nature of Economy 1929–1954	Social Response 1929–1954	Type of Policy	Characteristics of Industrial Era Restrictive Reproductive Policies
Court Mandated Sterilizations	• Contraction • Expansion • High Technology • Surplus labor supply • Broad unskilled labor force	Separatist • Curtail danger of Black overpopulation and future intermingling	Restrictive • To keep Blacks from multiplying • Save government funds for future children	• Criminalization of undesirable heredity, i.e., race, illness, sanity • Criminalization of undesirable characteristics, i.e., poverty, perceived intelligence, chastity • Criminalization of undesirable status, i.e., orphan status, prisoner
The Negro Project	• Contraction • Expansion • High Technology • Surplus labor supply • Broad unskilled labor force	Separatist • Curtail danger of Black overpopulation and future intermingling	Restrictive • To keep Blacks from multiplying • Save government funds for future children	• Manipulate Black doctors and clergy to convince Blacks to volunteer for sterilization

Summary

In sum, the data, as seen in table 9.2, show that in the policy period between 1929 and 1954, the nation experiences periods of both contraction and expansion as well as an explosion of technology leading to the obsolescence of Black women's labor—both productive and reproductive. Once Black reproduction is no longer directly linked to the forces of production, as it had been during slavery, Black reproduction—previously encouraged for profit—becomes problematized in the social consciousness. The new demands of the industrial forces of production in the United States render Black women's labor superfluous and push Black women's production and reproduction to the periphery of society. Policies in this period are restrictive in an effort to maintain distance from Blacks who are freely migrating across the country and to stem concerns of Black overpopulation. In restrictive reproductive freedom of Black women in the period, Black reproduction is criminalized and vilified.

Further Readings

Bennett, Lerone. *Black Power U.S.A.: The Human Side of Reconstruction, 1867–1877.* Chicago, IL: Johnson, 1967.

DuBois, W.E.B. *Black Reconstruction in the United States, 1860–1880.* New York: Simon & Schuster, 1995.

Franklin, John Hope and Alfred Moss, Jr. *From Slavery to Freedom: A History of African Americans,* seventh edition. New York: Knopf, 1994.

Gordon, Linda. *Pitied but Not Entitled: Single Mothers and the History of Welfare.* New York: Free Press, 1994.

Jones, Jacqueline. *The Dispossessed: America's Underclass from the Civil War to the Present.* New York: Basic Books, 1992.

Leavitt Judith W. (Ed.). *Women and Health in America. Historical Readings,* second edition. Madison: University of Wisconsin Press, 1999.

Lehmann, Nicholas. *The Promised Land: The Great Black Migration and How It Changed America.* New York: Vintage Books, 1992.

Miele, Frank. *Intelligence, Race, and Genetics: Conversation with Arthur R. Jensen.* Cambridge, MA: Westview, 2002.

Schoen, Johanna. *Choice & Coercion: Birth Control, Sterilization, and Abortion in Public Health and Welfare.* Chapel Hill: University of North Carolina Press.

Tarry, Ellen. *The Third Door: The Autobiography of an American Negro Woman.* New York: D. McKay, 1955.

PART 4

A Brand New Day

Year	Key Historical Moments during Era of Global Capitalism in the Electronic Age (1975–2009)
1954	Brown V Board of Education
1957	Civil Rights Act—Voting Rights Act
1960	Civil Rights Act—Federal inspection of Voter Registration Polls
1964	Civil Rights Act—Outlawed Segregation
1968	Civil Rights Act—Fair Housing Act
1959–1975	Vietnam War
1960	Legalization of Birth Control Pill
1962–1975	Antiwar Movement (Vietnam)
1965	Moynihan Report
1964–1975	Modern Civil Rights Period
1964	War on Poverty
1971	War on Drugs
1973	Roe V Wade
1990	Human Genome Project
1990–2002	Norplant
1992	Depo-Provera
1996	Welfare Reform

CHAPTER TEN

Global Capitalism in the Electronic Age

With hundreds of thousands of Blacks having already migrated north between 1890 and 1910; the postwar era sees upward of 5 million Blacks join their ranks by 1970.[1] Already previously abhorred as a drain on American resources, urban cities now feel overrun with Blacks, who in this new market are considered a glut on the labor force. Black reproduction, now unnecessary with the new skilled labor and access to international labor pools, is portrayed as a pathological danger. As the industrial forces of production strive to new heights due to the exploitation of significant new technologies, specifically the computer chip leading to automation, industry is revolutionized in the United States and around the world.

Black labor becomes even less profitable in the latter years of the twentieth century, due to technological advancements that exclude the unskilled worker and allow access to a global labor force.[2] The policy period between 1975 and 1995 sees the nation experience cycles of expansion, contraction, and recession. The policy period between 1996 and 2006 sees expansion persist for the wealthiest and contraction for the poorest. While 2007 through 2009 sees the collapse of the housing market and a significant recession still debated as a possible depression; which has the potential to impact labor and capital alike.

The expansion of exploitable technologies continues to expand at an extraordinary rate throughout both policy periods allowing access to a global labor force, as illustrated in table 10.1. Black labor, dismissed as unskilled and unprofitable, continues to be devalued throughout the twentieth century and into the twenty-first. The automation of industry that occurs in this period even further alienates the unskilled laborer from *productive* American society. The technological advancement

Table 10.1   Status of political economy in era of global capitalism in the electronic age (1975–2009)

Mode of Production	Global Capitalism in the Electronic Age
Political Economy	• Expansion • Recession • Expansion for wealthier/Contraction for poorer majority
Forces of Production	• Automation for global consumption • Computerization for global consumption
Instruments of Production Labor Pool	• Technology at an all time high with the introduction of the computer chip • Mechanization of work-machines replacing skilled labor • Computerization • Specialization of Skills • "skilled" employment replaces previously "unskilled" wage labor
Means of Production Labor Source	• There is a surplus of available labor globally • Working class Blacks, Latinos, & Caribbean immigrants vie for "unskilled" employment that remains • Emergence of global corporations, outsourcing, & "sweatshops"
Relations of Production Labor Demand	• Cheap abundant labor is in high demand • Wage laborer vs. Capitalist

of industry in the electronic age, not only brings unemployment for Blacks, it also carries with it significant reproductive technologies that aid in the repression of Black women's reproduction. In the years following civil rights gains for all Blacks, Black women are beleaguered with regulatory reproductive policies that undermine the Black family and continue the historic assault on Black motherhood.

Brief Status of 1970s Economy

The 1970s is a period of some despair for the nation. The country's leader impeached; a previous president assassinated; kids protesting in the streets; the nation had been violently snatched from the Rockwellian vision of the postwar period before it. And though the Vietnam War is finally ended in April 1975, the nation emerges changed. Among many tumultuous years of the period, 1975 can easily be designated as a watershed moment in the history of the U.S. economy as well as in the consciousness of America. For those who fought in the war and returned home to skyrocketing unemployment; antiwar sentiments; and for many, lingering illness and drug addiction; the end of the war is only the beginning. While others who had fought against the war find that now that the draft had ended, they no longer have a defined path to follow. The first baby boomers are turning thirty years old and of those who had identified with the counterculture of the previous period, many become lost in substance abuse and dysphoria. Further, Americans experience inconceivable inflation that sees a profound elevation in the cost of living, including unaffordable home prices; energy crises; and other major cost increases.

Brief Status of 1980s Economy

Neoliberal policies begun in the 1970s, starting with the degradation of the efficacy of the New Deal reform policies through deregulation of: the savings and loan industry; communications; and energy; give rise to Reagan's deregulation policies of the 1980s, which send an unmistakable ripple through the U.S. economy.[3] As such, the 1980s sees tremendous spikes in unemployment and poverty. With this, there is an explosion of homelessness and drug abuse, the likes of which Americans had not seen in the past.

No longer hippies choosing to *turn on, tune in, and drop out.* Instead these diverse populations of people are often beset with a number of social; physical; psychological; and economic issues. Frequently: mentally ill; physically challenged; and/or poor people; the many in homeless communities often self-soothe by abusing a number of substances, including alcohol; heroine; and cocaine.

The use of drugs by the poorer communities is only rivaled by that of the indulgent hard-partying *yuppie* that emerges in the same era. A bastardized amalgamation of the previous two generations, the twenty- and thirty-somethings of the 1980s resist the counterculture leftist philosophies of the 1960s and early 1970s; yet rebuke the quiet suburbanization of the 1950s. Instead, the 1980s sees the ascension of young urban capitalist greed and excess that still remains legendary in the new millennium.

Brief Status of 1990s Economy

The neoliberal policies of Reagan era economics, supported by the legendary greed of the 1980s is challenged when the nation experiences a significant recession in the early 1990s. Bolstered by the savings and loan crisis as well as numerous failing banks, the U.S. government is forced to fund hundreds of billions of dollars through FDIC insurance. The United States, though deeply in debt emerges the victor of the decades-long *cold war* with the collapse of the Soviet Union. In the mid 1990s amid a flurry of technological expansion that includes cell phones; home computers; and the Internet, an information explosion occurs. Catapulting the world into an innovative global age, these revolutionary technologies drastically impact our methods of telecommunications and industry; and redefine our cultures; thus reducing a previously compartmentalized world into what some consider one accessible community. It is important, however to note that along with the growing accessibility for some, this *globalization* also sees industrial, economic, political, social, cultural, and ecological impacts, the world over.[4] And though often framed as an evolutionary aspect of civilized humanity, actually the globalization occurring in the neoliberal era is often a process that reinforces global inequity and reifies structural economic divides. Now more than ever the disparity between the wealthy minority and the poorer majority is painfully evident in the United States.

Brief Status of Millennium Economy

By the year 2000 the initial thrill of the unchartered terrain of the Internet had clearly waned and the so-called *dot-com bubble* burst. In the wake of this economic crisis, the nation experiences the first attack on American soil since Pearl Harbor, the September 11, 2001 attacks on the World Trade Center and the Pentagon. The impact of this attack is felt throughout the economy. Coupled with the devastation of a U.S. attack and the deaths and injuries of thousands upon thousands of people, primarily civilian, the U.S. economy grinds to a near halt. Billions of dollars are lost in the state of New York and by the airline industry. The stock market is closed for a week following the attacks and suffers record losses. The nation is at a virtual standstill. Less than one month later, the U.S. military invades Afghanistan in its search for the perpetrators of the American attacks. Nearly a decade later there has been much controversy over the so-called war on terror, as many consider it "unwinnable" and misleading.[5]

Four years after the September 11 attacks, while still firmly embroiled in the war, the nation is faced with another crisis, Hurricane Katrina.[6] August 2005 a gargantuan tropical storm attacks the Gulf Coast.

Though many cities across several states in the United States and the Caribbean are impacted, none prove as heartbreakingly tragic as the effects on greater New Orleans, Louisiana. Thousands of people die; hundreds of thousands are displaced, some permanently; and there are over one hundred billion dollars in damages.

Meanwhile the United States sees an unprecedented rise in home prices, reifying the divide between working and middle classes. Home prices begin moving out of reach of average working class families supplying the impetus for the growth of a subprime lending market. Within this inflated market, a fraction of loans begin to cater to so-called subprime borrowers, who often have little or poor credit and scant resources to secure a deposit for a home. Often the loans themselves are *subprime,* as they are frequently attached to variable interest rates and involve balloon payments that working class borrowers typically cannot afford. As evidenced by the increase in foreclosures and subsequent collapse of the housing market in the second half of the millennium.

Global Economy and the Black Labor Pool

By the dawn of the new millennium companies had already begun production in international territories. A now truly global economy, the United States has come to embrace the cycles of war, recession, technological advancement, expansion, recession, war, et cetera. This cycle leads to unemployment fluctuations, downsizing, layoffs, and changing labor markets. No longer wedded to the available domestic labor pool, the less than desirable populations in the United States—Blacks, immigrants, et cetera—are no longer (even periodically) sought after. Even the small proportion of the working poor still exploited for service and care work are in danger of losing their status, as computerized labor is increasingly replacing human production.

CHAPTER ELEVEN

Pathologizing the Black Woman

As feared in the previous periods, an explosion of civil disobedience and unrest does indeed ignite throughout the nation in the 1950s; 1960s; and 1970s. However, it is no *population* bomb as once feared. It is instead a direct result of the longstanding ongoing exploitation and abuse endured by marginalized Americans. The overt divergence of experience between marginalized peoples and middle-class White America leads to a series of uprisings of the oppressed populations of the nation, including: Blacks; women; gays and lesbians; antiwar protesters; Latina(o) populations; and more. As a result, the nation sees a shift from the homogenized nuclear family of the 1950s into a stage of sexual liberation and political dissent in the 1960s and 1970s.

Ironically, as effective as the Civil Rights and women's liberation movements are for Blacks and women respectively, they are equally as *ineffective* for Black women.

Indeed, the late 1960s and early 1970s were a period of learning for many groups, including black women who felt betrayed or somehow underrepresented by the black and women's movements of the civil rights era.[1]

Marginalized from both Black politics and women's rights, Black women find themselves lost in the shuffle in the efforts to gain civil liberties, and vilified in the efforts to blame someone for the ongoing unrest. In an unfortunate backlash to the successes of these movements, Black women, persistently trapped in a misogynistic and racist structure, find themselves held morally responsible for the perceived immorality of a nation.

By 1965, the year the notorious Moynihan Report is released, Blacks have made tremendous strides as Americans.[2] They are still, however, intellectually, scientifically, and morally considered failures. Over the next ten years, between 1965 and 1975, White American women will make meaningful progress. White women gain the freedom of reproductive choice. Both married and single women are able to experience the liberation of the birth control pill. White middle class women will be able to reject motherhood and marriage as their only options. And for the first time since World War II White middle class women will be able to earn a living outside the home in force. But unlike their experiences in the previous era, they can now unabashedly embrace paths that lead to education and careers. During this same period, Black women are labeled as the root cause of a sickness destroying Black America.

At the same time, White women are discovering their own freedoms; Blacks continue to be embroiled in the ongoing fight for civil liberties that had heretofore not been won. As Black women and men express their discontentedness through grassroots organizing and purposeful protests, various forms of propaganda emerge to portray the Black woman as the ultimate culprit behind the catastrophic state of Black America. As illustrated in table 11.1 depicted by government reports; social science research; radio; television; news; and film, as a failure as both a woman and as a mother, Black women become the scapegoat for historically institutionalized racism endemic to American society. According to White,

"Depreciated by her own kind, judged grotesque by her society, and valued only as a sexually convenient laboring animal," the black girl, they reasoned had the cards stacked against her.... The failure of a black female to develop a healthy narcissism in girlhood caused her, later in life, to neglect her figure, allow herself to become obese, concern herself more with the utility of clothing and less with style, and resign herself to the "asexual maternal role in which work and hovering concern for the family" occupied her entirely. According to the argument the black woman's concern with family was emasculating. This put black women in league with white men in their attempt to destroy black men.[3]

Rendered as emasculating of Black men, overbearing to her family, and sexually and emotionally abandoned due to a supposed general unattractiveness, the Black woman is held responsible for the

Table 11.1 Themes of social rhetoric in the era of global capitalism in the electronic age (1975–1995)

Theme of Social Rhetoric 1975–1995	Representation of Pathological Matriarch
Black "Pathology" Myth	Myth of sickness among Blacks that causes failure in society
Aggressive/Angry	Perpetuate notion of antagonistic Black women and hostile Black men
Emasculating	Image of belligerent Black women that renders Black men and therefore Black society as impotent
"Welfare Queen"	Portrayed as indigent and irresponsible, forcing taxpaying Americans to support Black families
Drug Addicted	Depicted as addicted to Crack cocaine, and at the root of a drug epidemic that is destroying the nation
Part of "population bomb"	Seen as having children indiscriminately

dysfunctionality of the Black family and the so-called *pathology* of Black America.

From Reproductive Freedom to Fertility Control

Just as there had been a purposeful manipulation of the image of Black women in the previous periods; there is a purposeful degradation of Blackness and Black womanhood that occurs in the 1970s. This social rhetoric campaign serves to further the political agendas of a system fundamentally rooted in racism; misogyny; and class antagonisms. According to hooks,

> . . . most people tend to see devaluation of black womanhood as occurring only in the context of slavery. In actuality, sexual exploitation of black women continued long after slavery ended and was institutionalized by other oppressive practices. Devaluation of black womanhood after slavery ended was a conscious, deliberate effort on the part of whites to sabotage mounting black female self-confidence and self-respect.[4]

In the wake of the conceptualization of the Black population bomb and the revolutionary movements of the previous era, Black reproduction takes on a new meaning. Within this context of impending disaster,

Black reproduction ceases to be a mere ideological issue, it becomes perceived as an actual threat and treated as such.

Reagan's 1997 *When Abortion Was a Crime* asserts that the birth control movement and the population control movement, though two separate and distinct agendas, with one rooted in feminist liberation and the other in state-sponsored control, are inexorably linked. This occurs as a result of philosophical changes in major women's rights platforms, characterized by organizations such as *Planned Parenthood*,

> The emphasis on planning that the birth control movement adopted in the 1940s would haunt the movement to decriminalize abortion. The movement's new name, "Planned Parenthood," implied that *planned* children were better and *unplanned* children undesirable.[5]

This approach advocates the planning of wanted pregnancies and labels unplanned pregnancies; that is unwanted children, as socially irresponsible. This shift does not come without consequence,

> Exercising [family planning], however, was a middle-class privilege and virtue. Many, particularly in the working class, did not "plan" their families and did not necessarily regard an unplanned pregnancy…as unwanted. The emphasis on family planning had the unfortunate [implication]…that "accidental" childbearing was reprehensible.[6]

As a result of the fight for women's reproductive freedoms being enveloped by a push toward contraception as a way to combat so-called overpopulation, the birth control movement becomes a threat to Black women's reproduction.[7] The national reproduction agenda is felt most saliently in "low-income and 'nonwhite neighborhoods,'" prompting "urban black nationalists" to deem birth control as 'black genocide.'"[8]

Bernard Asbell's 1995 *The Pill: A Biography of the Drug that Changed the World* focuses on the journey of access to oral contraception. Asbell explores the pill in the context of a journey toward reproductive freedom–which it often is for White middle class women. In the recounting of this history Asbell briefly touches on the reaction of the Black media to the Negro Project.[9] In December 1967, the Pittsburgh branch of the NAACP charged Margaret Sanger's Planned Parenthood with attempting to keep "the Black birthrate as low as possible."[10] The statement released called Planned Parenthood's commitment to contraceptive services in non-White communities tantamount to "genocide for the Negro people."[11] Though Dr. Charles E. Greenlee, the NAACP representative who had originally made the statement, later concedes that "genocide" might have been too strong a term, he and the NAACP still assert that Planned Parenthood is a detriment to Blacks:

> He [Greenlee] said that Planned Parenthood coerced disadvantaged black people to employ birth control by sending workers door-to-door until women feel they are forced to go to a clinic. I don't oppose contraceptives *per se*, but I'm against this "Pill-pushing" in black neighborhoods where many people are made to feel that they'd better obey official suggestions' to visit a birth control clinic or risk losing their monthly welfare checks.[12]

Dr. Greenlee is not alone in his assessment of the politics of contraception and its relationship to Black communities.[13] Both the mainstream middle class Black reformist organizations as well as the grassroots working class Black radical organizations agreed, that the Negro Project and Planned Parenthood are indeed suspect. As a result, though Dr. Greenlee effectively recants his charge of 'genocide,' the Black media picked up on the term and continues to use it widely in connection with Planned Parenthood, the eugenics movement, and the Negro Project.

Loretta J. Ross' 1993 "African-American Women and Abortion: 1880–1970" states that "birth control advocacy quickly becomes a tool of racists who argued in favor of eugenics, or other population control policies, based on fears of African-Americans and others thought to be 'undesirable' to the politically powerful."[14] Ross depicts her own personal history of fighting social stereotyping of Black women's sexuality. She describes, "doctors' diagnoses of African-American women [that] were distorted with theories of diseases brought back by soldiers returning from Vietnam."[15] Ross' personal analysis then shifts to reflections on her own experiences as a Black woman seeking contraceptive and reproductive care during the electronic age, stating, "My pelvic infection from the IUD is treated as a mysterious venereal disease. I wondered who really controlled my body."[16] Ross' analysis reveals the affects of regulating private reproductive decisions and begs us to acknowledge the personal impact on Black women of the period.

According to the 2005 documentary film, *The Pill*, that illustrates the origin and life of the birth control pill, Black women are in general agreement with Black organizations and Black media regarding the political undertones of the Negro project. However, according to the documentary, when faced with the choice of taking a political stance against genocidal mistreatment or having the freedom that comes with the pill—as do the majority of women around the United States—they choose contraception.[17]

Birthing the Image of the Pathological
Matriarch (1975–1995)

Painted in the image of a poor single mother with several children and no male partner, the Black woman in this period is imagined as a moral and financial drain on her own community as well as the nation. Her perceived promiscuity is only matched by her allegedly aggressive nature and therefore, she is only able to seduce men long enough to get pregnant, but fails to have the ability to keep him involved in her and her children's lives. Her children are portrayed as unkempt and poorly cared for; learning more from the harsh and unforgiving city streets than from his/her Black mother and absent father. This imagined home life is believed to be the start of a cycle, referenced as a culture of poverty by some and an underclass by others.[18] These allegedly inadequately parented children grow into adult Black men and women who struggle to become constructive members of society. These generations of Blacks are believed to be the most in need of reform.

Crack

Broadly labeling Black women as drug addicts in an era overwhelmed with addiction brings to mind the onset of the U.S. AIDS epidemic. Though the disease couldn't possibly have set its sights on any one population, the nation becomes convinced that it is a "gay plague." Hopefully you are equally appalled by such a foul and ignorant reaction to an illness that, let's face it, can impact any of us at any time. And no matter: our nation; our gender; our race; our class; our religion; or our sexual orientation; the sickness would have the same detrimental effect on any of our lives.

Similarly, in the same period, characterized by excess and partying on the one hand and severe economic depression on the other, it seems the nation meets in the middle and becomes addicted to drugs. It first reveals itself in Black communities, but over the generations has come to show itself as an equal opportunity addiction. Cheap, accessible, and powerfully addictive, no one could have known the impact this drug would have on society. Theft; overdose; prostitution; mental illness; vagrancy; and worst of all *crack babies*. Though these are all monumental social problems, one wonders why these same things cannot be said for Crystal meth in the 1990s or Oxycontin in the millennium; or for that matter *powder* cocaine. The same is not said because the social rhetoric around crack cocaine has created a stigma around the user and the offspring of the user that has never before been applied to another population.

Reformist Response

The primary focus of this work is certainly on Black sexuality and reproduction. However it must be noted that significant changes in the prison industrial complex begin to emerge in this policy period. This same period that experiences a meaningful shift in the nation's response to Black women and Black reproduction and motherhood, also begins to envision Blackness differently. As the prison industrial complex evolves from a reformist endeavor into a punitive approach to crime, so does the social climate regarding Blacks; Black women; and Black reproduction. No longer the innocent simpletons, they had been perceived as during the slave era; nor even the rural farm laborer of the first half of the century. Blacks have now permeated every aspect of American industrial society, standing up and demanding to be noticed, no doubt vexing much of White America.

Blacks are now perceived as spreading their so-called pathology and fears erupt about the relationships with the White children with whom

Table 11.2 Snapshot of social response to rhetoric campaigns in era of global capitalism in the electronic age (1975–1995)

Social Climate 1975–1995	Characteristics of Social Climate
Reformist Social Response	Believes nation need to returns to "family values" Nation feels responsible for "epidemics" that are "destroying" America
	Believes nation must reevaluate the social safety net that has allowed blacks

they now attend school. Perceived as taking over the cities and infiltrating the youth culture, Americans look toward reforming the Black population. Unlike the Reconstruction period of the previous century, the goals of this reform period are rooted in controlling Blacks, rather than integrating them into White society. Whites perceive Blacks as overrunning city streets and changing the face of the nation, and therefore take their reformist stance seriously.

As it grows increasingly apparent that Blacks no longer fear expressing their discontent, be it on television; through music; in their writings; or in person, the state becomes increasingly focused on controlling their behavior. Tools employed to control *pathological* Blacks in the period include: increased incarceration; the growth of a child welfare industry; assaults on welfare programming; and increasing sterilization efforts.[19]

CHAPTER TWELVE

She's Out of Control: Controlling Reproductive Policies

Population Control Policies

One meaningful result of the dissent that follows the postwar era is the introduction of oral contraceptives in the 1960s and 1970s. In exploring the road to the pill, it is impossible to ignore the hypocrisy of the national emphasis on securing reproductive freedoms for White women while establishing *fertility control* for "other" populations.

According to Angela Davis' 1983 *Women, Race, & Class*, Depo-Provera—a test drug in 1973—is in use in U.S. hospitals. Though a test drug it is dispensed to third world; poor; illiterate; and Black women and girls as young as twelve years old in efforts to curb undesirable reproduction. Through animal testing on monkeys and dogs it is discovered that the drug is carcinogenic. Wanting to continue to inhibit the reproduction of these undesirable populations; health administrators resort to far more drastic measures. They begin invoking the states longstanding eugenics policies as justification for sterilizing women and girls, often with neither their permission nor their knowledge. In one instance, the Montgomery Community Action Committee orders the sterilization of two sisters, one twelve and one fourteen, after coercing their illiterate mother into signing a consent form with the mark of an "X."[1]

In the aftermath of the publicity exposing the Relf sisters' case, similar episodes were brought to light. In Montgomery alone, eleven girls, also in their teens, had been similarly sterilized.

HEW-funded birth control clinics in other states, as it turned out, had also subjected young girls to sterilization abuse.[2]

According to Davis, "Moreover, individual women came forth with equally outrageous stories [including threats] to discontinue...welfare payments [without] surgical sterilization...[and being told that the permanent surgical sterilization procedure] would be temporary."[3]

Eventually, the mandatory sterilization laws are repealed in the mid-1970s, having survived for over seventy years; however not before over 70,000 court-mandated surgical sterilizations are performed.[4] Rickie Solinger's 2000 *Wake Up Little Susie: Single Pregnancy and Race before* Roe v. Wade examines women's reproductive policy from both an economic and historical perspective. Solinger focuses on the post-war period from 1945 to 1965; highlighting the growth of dissimilar views of White and Black reproduction as the nation moves into the Civil Rights era. According to Solinger, even in the years following the end of compulsory sterilizations, the practice continues to dog Black women:

> Even without state laws or a national, public mandate for sterilization of black women who had illegitimate babies, the practice of this form of population control remained a part of the de facto race-specific population policy of some states.[5]

As illustrated in table 12.1, Black women become perceived as a genuine threat that needs to be controlled. These efforts to control Black populations become more and more dangerous for Black women as reproductive policies and practices become more adamantly anti-Black reproduction, as outlined in table 12.2. No longer relegated to special programs or court cases, the sterilization of Black women becomes a common occurrence at inner city hospitals. The eugenics movement remains a strong force within the United States—aimed primarily at Black women—through the mid-1970s:

> Fannie Lou Hamer [Black female activist] created a big stir when she was quoted in the *Washington Post* to the effect that "six out of every ten women were taken to Sunflower City Hospital to be sterilized for no reason at all. Often the women were not told that they had been sterilized until they were released from the hospital."...She was never effectively refuted.[6]

Concerns for Black women's reproductive health and freedoms become so intense in Black communities that various forms of community level

Table 12.1 Themes of social rhetoric in the era of global capitalism in electronic age from 1996–2009

Theme of Social Rhetoric 1996–2009	Representation of Conniving Welfare Queen
Single-mother "Epidemic"	See Black women as part of an epidemic of irresponsible indiscriminate mothering of children without fathers
Teen Mother "Epidemic"	See Black teens, particularly girls, as part of an epidemic of teen pregnancies
Black Mothers are Irresponsible and Childlike	Depicted as lazy, abusive, and neglectful mothers
Black Motherhood is a Tool of Manipulation	Perceived as using pregnancy and childbirth as a scheme to manipulate the State into financing their lifestyle
Black Motherhood Leads to Overwhelmed Prison System	Imagined as the root cause of the overwhelmed prison system, as Black women are portrayed as poor mothers who are unable or unwilling to maintain a two parent household, thus leaving Black sons to run wild.

Table 12.2 Examples of relevant policies in the era of global capitalism in the electronic age from 1975–1995

Influential Policies of the Global Era in the Electronic Age	Characteristics of Influential Policies of the Global Era in the Electronic Age
Post-Civil Rights	Backlash to Civil Rights gains made by Blacks
Depo-Provera Medical trials	Medical Trials of long-acting contraception on inner city girls; dogs; and monkeys
Short Term Chemical Sterilization	Introduction of long-acting injection and implantation contraception
Weakening of Social Contract	Welfare reform debate sees New Deal Reform policies in danger
State Sponsored contraception	State medical centers pay to insert long-acting contraceptive devices-removal is not an option
War on Poverty	Initiated national discussion of how to fix the "problem" of the inner city-term is first coined by Lyndon B. Johnson in 1964
War on Drugs	Criminalization of drug addiction for Black mothers/having drug affected babies-term is first coined by Richard M. Nixon in 1971

organizing rises up around the issue. Black Consciousness and Black Power organizations; historically dismissive of women's issues even begin to warn Black women of the dangers of forced and coercive sterilization. A pamphlet is produced and widely circulated in 1968 with three articles debating the situation of black female reproductive freedoms in the United States.[7] The language of the pamphlet is clearly one of alarm. There is a growing concern that black women are being used in the fight for reproductive freedoms, but will be the victims of its successes.

Eventually the monumental technological advances in the field of reproductive technology, along with the legalization of contraception in 1960; and the wide availability of the pill beginning in 1972; and the decriminalization of abortion in 1973, replace this antiquated system of forced sterilization.[8] Long-acting contraception begins being distributed through state-funded facilities in urban centers, even before FDA approval, including: intrauterine devices (both the traditional and copper IUD); depot medroxyprogesterone acetate (Depo-Provera); progestin levonorgestrel implants (Norplant); and more recently Ortho-Evra (The Patch).[9] New reproductive technologies also refine the previously "reversible" surgical sterilization, ensuring the permanency of the sterilization procedure.[10]

Early Methods of "Welfare Reform"

As discussed throughout this study, along with the advances in reproductive rights in the 1970s comes a torrent of previously ignored sterilization abuses against Black women. Black women receiving welfare benefits are subjected to horrific abuses at the hands of the system designed to aid them in their times of need. The government agencies have such power over the women's private lives that they actually dictate that women receiving benefits are legally mandated not to engage in extramarital relationships with men. If they do, it is presumed that he could assume responsibility for the woman and her child(ren), and she will be discontinued from public assistance. If a woman is discovered in a relationship with a man, then any efforts she makes to consume services are tantamount to fraud in the eyes of the law. To that end, beginning in the 1950s and lasting well into the 1980s, policies implemented forcing welfare recipients, almost always Black female recipients, to endure "midnight raids."[11] These raids force her "to allow agents into her home at any time, day or night, to check for a man, or she would jeopardize her welfare allotment.[12] These statutes exist across the nation, in locations as varied as New York and Arizona. In fact, Phoenix, Arizona, carries along reporters on their midnight raids, dubbed "a 'pre-dawn safari' to emphasize the African connection."[13]

Included in economy-minded state and local welfare policies were provisions for sterilization and for midnight raids on the homes of unwed ADC mothers. Both provisions, of course, allowed for the violation of the personal safety and physical integrity of the black woman's body.[14]

Child Welfare Industry

Along with an explosion of rhetoric that degrades Black women's sexuality and reproductive rights, the period from 1975 to 1995 sees the implementation of an assault on Black motherhood as well. Black women perceived as being in dire need of reform, see the contemporary child welfare industry begin to take root. Black mothers are inundated with claims of abuse and neglect. No longer allowed to resolve personal issues through private family intervention, Black women are ten times more apt than White women to be turned in to authorities for consuming drugs or alcohol during pregnancy. This even though there is no discernable difference in the prevalence of substance abuse by pregnant Black women than there is for White women.[15] This period sees Black women's parenting become a punishable offense within the social justice system.[16] Before World War II less than a quarter of all child welfare facilities admit Black children. More often than not a parentless Black child is deemed a delinquency problem and thrown in prison, rather than taken in by the state. Until a 1973 lawsuit demands change, the child welfare system remains deeply segregated, typically leaving Black families to resolve parenting concerns from within the confines of extended relatives. Between 1980 and 1999 the number of children within the child welfare system absolutely explodes placing over half of a million youth in custody. And though Black children make up less than one quarter of the national youth population, they constitute a whopping 43 percent of children in care.[17] In 1999, this is 238,560 Black children who have been removed from their parents' custody and have been involuntarily placed in the home of a subsidized guardian—someone who is paid to take care of them. This industry continues to expand throughout this period and into the next, with the racial and class demographics growing increasingly more and more visible. Further, the implication that Blacks, particularly black women, cannot or will not take care of their own children, will haunt Blacks into the next millennium.

CHAPTER THIRTEEN

Vilifying Black Motherhood

The theory of the *Black matriarchy* discussed earlier leads into later conceptualizations of a Black "underclass" that would persist into the next millennium.[1] William Julius Wilson, for instance, reaches back to the Moynihan Report to argue a similar pathology, arguing that a *ghetto* mentality quickly develops into a ghetto culture for this Black *underclass*.[2] Wilson's analysis is socially damning. And were he not so adamantly opposed to what he refers to as liberal researchers' and theorists' perspectives on race/racism, one could very well perceive his exploration of a so-called underclass as a contemporary revisioning of Marx's classic *lumpen proletariat*. Though he aggressively denies it, Wilson's theory of the underclass could be perceived as a reinterpretation of Marx's historic class analysis. This could have been readily achieved by transfusing Marx's class analysis with Frantz Fanon's variation, which interweaves Marx's theory with the ravaging impacts of colonization along with contemporary critical race theory.

However, rather than presenting this analysis within this enduring historical context, it is presented as further "proof" that poor Blacks are a detriment to the American way. The so-called underclass culture described by Wilson includes: teen parenting, drug abuse, crime, poor work ethic, et cetera. Capitalizing on these images, the United States government, now backed by traditional sciences, social sciences, and public opinion, devotes itself to a *war on crime* and a *war on drugs*. The focus on the notion of the *welfare queen*, and the reinvigorated rhetoric inciting *fear of an explosion of Black reproduction*, with oft invoked media references to an *epidemic of crack babies*, is a direct attack on the perennial Black *matriarch*. As a result, over the last forty years since: the legalization of abortion; Civil Rights; and technological advancements in birth control devices, Black women have continued to be at the epicenter of a debate on immorality and irresponsibility.

Throughout the period, Black and White women continue to exist within two different Americas. Reproductive technology for White women means, "designer babies," being able to have children later in life; more opportunities to become a mother; and to have as many children as science allows.[3] While reproductive technology for Black women in the United States is reduced to efforts to reduce perceived fiscal and social burden. Thus leading Black reproductive technology to explore methods to slow population growth through perfecting birth control and sterilization procedures, so as to offset the financial and social pressures caused by the welfare system.

Dorothy Roberts' 1997 *Killing the Black Body: Race, Reproduction, and the Meaning of Liberty* offers a historical, economic, and political analysis of the history of regulating Black women's reproduction in the United States. Roberts also explores the welfare reform debate that occurs over the decade before welfare reform becomes a reality. Within this analysis Roberts draws an ongoing historical connection between Black women's reproduction and the U.S. political economy. Roberts states that the late twentieth century sees "an explosion of propaganda and policies that degrade Black women's reproductive decisions."[4] Roberts further asserts that this "wave of reproductive regulation" is fundamentally rooted in the historical pattern of subjugation and control of Black women's bodies and choices for the purposes of economic gain.[5]

Creating the Image of the Conniving Welfare Queen (1996–2009)

As the nation watches poorer classes of Black America descend deeper and deeper into poverty, drugs, and ghettoization, Black women are treated as the scapegoat at every turn. Perceived as manipulative and pathological in the early years of Civil Rights, she later becomes a malicious blight on society. Seen as a drain on resources, she is imagined to be so amoral and heartless that she would go so far as to have an illegitimate child for the sake of garnering a larger welfare check. This fear of abuses by the Black woman has been cited *ad nauseam* as a justification for welfare "reforms":

... women's rights to reproductive freedom which to [the National Welfare Rights Organization] meant their right to have children. The stereotype of the welfare mother whose libido and fertility were out of control had potentially severe consequences for poor black women during these years when the Pill and other devices revolutionized birth control. In the nineteenth century, when white men controlled black fecundity, they manipulated the enslaved women's childbearing to maximize their profits. Now, there were many who thought it would better profit the nation if they could limit the number of children poor black women had.[6]

No longer the ignorant savages of yesterday; Black women are envisioned as savvy and manipulative products of generations of failing Black women. This is a significant shift in the perception of Black womanhood that is felt at every level of the Black community. With the condemnation of Black women's abilities to parent Black children; her perceived ineffectuality in interpersonal relationships with Black men; and her supposedly antagonistic nature; the belief that both Black men and Black women would require even more regulation of both their public and private behaviors becomes a plausible conclusion. With the numbers of Black men being incarcerated growing exponentially, many fingers point in judgment of the so-called failings of Black mothers and wives, rather than at a system rife with institutionalized racism. Where previous generations of white America had unsuccessfully attempted to restrict and control Black reproduction, the current policy period seeks to compel the Black woman to control Black reproduction herself through coercive policies.

Punitive Response

In reviewing this policy period the negative social rhetoric surrounding Blacks serves as the incentive needed to urge American society forward from the drive to reform Blacks to the need to punish them. It is no accident that the vigorous

Table 13.1 Snapshot of social response to rhetoric campaigns in the era of global capitalism in the electronic age (1996–2009)

Social Climate 1996–2009	Characteristics of Social Climate
Punitive Social Response	Believe Black mothers need to be trained to be members of society
	Equates Black motherhood with welfare and various epidemics
	Believes Black mothers must be forced off of welfare and made to work as contributing members of society
	Criminalizes Black motherhood

growth of the prison industrial complex begins in the period immediately following the final years of the Civil Rights movement, nor that its growth coincides with a media blitz assaulting Black women and the Black family. During this same period we see the explosion of a booming prison industry that develops into the overpopulated prison industrial complex that continues to increase its rolls at alarming rates even today.

In a state of expansion for over thirty years, by midyear 2006 the United States can claim that one in nine Black men between the ages of twenty and thirty-four are currently behind bars in some fashion, whether in local jails or federal prisons. As compared to only one in 106 White men over the age of eighteen incarcerated in the same period. This same punitive agenda leads to one in one hundred Black women between the ages of thirty-five and thirty-nine being held behind bars as of midyear 2006, compared to only one in 355 White women also aged thirty-five to thirty-nine who are incarcerated at midyear 2006.[7]

These statistics point to what Angela Davis contextualizes as a socially constructed *racialized fear of crime*.[8] She quite astutely asserts that, just as the fears of communism had previously consumed the first half of the twentieth century; a socially constructed *war on crime* has been meticulously invented in its place. These fears have been driven by decades of social rhetoric designed to instill fear, panic, and dread of Blackness in White America. This rhetoric is so deeply ingrained, that though the disparities are evident and the inhumanity clear the prison populations continue to grow. While new technologies are constantly being revolutionized: to fortify the prisons; add so-called security measures to the streets; and to maintain control of ex-offenders; the nation continues to passively allow the prison industry to make billions of dollars in profit.[9] Beyond the tragedy of the growth of the prison industrial complex, these efforts at punishing Blacks further include the development of controlling reproductive and parenting policies and practices that continue to degrade Black women's reproductive rights to this day.

Operationalize criminalization

CHAPTER FOURTEEN

Gettin' Your Tubes Tied: Coercive Reproductive Policies

Policies of the electronic age are first controlling and then coercive in the state's efforts to manipulate Black reproduction. Table 14.1 illustrates the efforts to control Black reproduction as both a labor force and as a reproductive force come in the form of the welfare reform debate. After years of perfecting reproductive technology through testing contraceptives and procedures in poor; Black; and Latina(o) communities, the state implements programming to subsidize long-acting birth control devices. Often, these devices place these women in dire medical situations, as the state provides subsidized implantation; yet charges exorbitant fees for the removal of the device. As a result, a significant percentage of inner city and third world women are left at the mercy of health care providers in state sponsored facilities. This sort of deceptive programming signals the state's transition from covert methods of controlling Black and other marginalized populations' reproduction, to efforts to actively coerce Black women into voluntarily sterilizing themselves, either through permanent surgery or through long-acting barrier and chemical sterilization procedures, such as the copper IUD, Norplant, and Depo-Provera.

Grassroots Organizing for Reproductive Freedoms

Unsupported by White women's liberation movements in the struggles against these violations, Black women are forced to form organizations of their own to help safeguard against sterilization of black women.[1] Though Black and White women's organizations make efforts to ban

Table 14.1 Examples of relevant policies in the era of global capitalism in the electronic age (1996–2009)

Influential Policies of the Global Era in the Electronic Age	Characteristics of Influential Policies of the Global Era in the Electronic Age
Welfare Reform	Period after initiation of welfare reform ushers in the period after the dissolution of the Social Contract
State Sponsored Short Chemical Sterilization	Cash incentives for long-acting & permanent contraception
"No Child Left Behind"	State sanctions policies to "save" inner city America— euphemism for Black youth
State Sponsored Permanent Surgical Sterilization	Sterilization of Black mothers under 21 standard protocol
War on Poverty	Criminalizes poverty as an exploitative effort to extort money from the government
War on Drugs	Continues to criminalize drug addiction for Black mothers/having drug affected babies

together politically in the 1970s—their agendas are so disparate that Black women remain leery of White women's historic reproductive rights struggles:

> The failure of the abortion rights campaign to conduct a historical self evaluation led to a dangerously superficial appraisal of Black people's suspicious attitudes toward birth control in general. Granted, when some Black people unhesitatingly equated birth control with genocide, it did appear to be an exaggerated—even paranoiac—reaction. Yet white abortion rights activists missed a profound message, for underlying these cries of genocide were important clues about the history of the birth control movement. This movement, for example, had been known to advocate involuntary sterilization–a racist form of mass "birth control."[2]

Welfare Reform in the Neoliberal Era

With the media so closely associating Black women with the frightful drug and poverty "epidemics" sweeping the nation, the disdain for Black reproduction reaches astounding new heights in the late 1980s, as illustrated in table 14.2.[3] The climate is ripe for a new approach to welfare reform. This new assessment of an old issue moves beyond identifying Black women as the problem and blaming Black women for their

Table 14.2 Reproductive policy analysis: 1975–1995

Controlling Reproductive Policies in Age of Global Capitalism in the Electronic Era	Nature of Economy 1975–1995	Social Response 1975–1995	Type of Policy	Characteristics of Controlling Reproductive Policies in Age of Global Capitalism in the Electronic era
Welfare Reform Debate	• Expansion • Contraction • Recession • Hi technology • Low labor demand • Global labor force	Reformist • Heal Black pathology	Controlling policies • Force Black women to pay own way • Save government funds	• Begins to weaken the strength of social contract • Stigmatizes people who receive Public Assistance • "Midnight Raids" • Criminalizes dating for single Black mothers
Medical Trials of Long-acting Contraception in State-funded Facilities	• Expansion • Contraction • Recession • Hi technology • Low labor demand • Global labor force	Reformist • Heal Black pathology	Controlling protocols • Force Black women to use contraception • Save government funds for future children	• Test long-acting contraception in state facilities in urban centers that primarily service poor Blacks. • Administer contraception that has yet to gain FDA approval • Practice drugs on poor Blacks
State-sponsored Long-term Contraception	• Expansion • Contraction • Recession • Hi technology • Low labor demand • Global labor force	Reformist • Heal Black pathology	Controlling protocols • Force Black women to use contraception • Save government funds for future children	• Family cap • Families leaving welfare • Healthy marriage initiatives • Responsible Fatherhood initiatives • Working for welfare eligibility • Parenting training
Growth of Child Welfare Industry	• Expansion • Contraction • Recession • Hi technology • Low labor demand • Global labor force	Reformist • Heal Black pathology	Controlling protocols • Force Black women to use contraception • Save government funds for future children	• Explosion of Blacks in care • Blacks 10 times more likely to be reported • Criminalization of drug addicted parents. • Forced parenting Training

reproduction. Instead, the state; reminiscent of the *White man's burden* of a century before; claims a *responsibility to train* Black women how to become contributing members of society. This means she must be *taught* to take financial responsibility for her own children and *earn* her right to a public safety net, by working in the wage labor system. This is of course ironic, as Black women have historically been significant assets to the U.S. labor system, as both slave and wage laborers.

As a threat to illustrate how serious the state's ultimatum truly is, welfare recipients are suddenly dropped from the rolls of a number of states across the nation at dramatic rates beginning in the early 1990s.[4] The small percentage allowed to regain access to some form of benefit assistance are now required to participate in degrading programs such as *earnfare; workfirst; and Wisconsin Works.* Under such programs the recipient is required to provide free labor to an employer as a means to *pay back* the cost of the monthly food stamp allotment. Upon fulfilling the *debt,* the employee or welfare recipient or involuntary indentured servant, depending on one's perspective, is free to earn more money, providing it falls within the miniscule parameters of allowable income; often less than $50 for up to thirty-five hours of work.

Beyond the attack on the "work-ethic" of welfare recipients, the state also focuses on its "moral" concerns. The state finds common lifestyle choices and social circumstances, such as: extra-marital cohabitation; pre-marital sex; single motherhood; and teen pregnancy, as intolerable abuses of the welfare system. As, such the U.S. government, with a falsely righteous indignation, strips away the social contract meant to support American families, leaving in its place radical policies that protect the ongoing interests of neoliberal America. Now instead of forced sterilization, the state offers cash incentives to the same populations previously documented as *undesirable,* paying them to take long-acting birth control *voluntarily.* Black women with drug addictions are coerced into permanent surgical and short term chemical sterilization as well as long-acting birth control procedures through threats of imprisonment and the loss of their children. Now, fully exploited and left no discernable sense of dignity or privacy, welfare recipients numbers begin to decline dramatically.[5]

Current Status of Black Female Surgical Sterilization (1996–2009)

Beyond the devastating effects of welfare reform on Black women's lives and reproductive options, sterilization continues to disproportionately affect Black women's reproduction, as illustrated in table 14.3. More than one hundred years since the first eugenics-based sterilizations in the United States, Black women continue to be the most inclined to use permanent female surgical sterilization as their means of birth control, as is commonly advised by their community healthcare providers. By 2002, 17 percent, or 10.3 million, of women aged fifteen to forty-four (who use contraception), receive permanent female surgical sterilizations.[6]

According to a 2004 report from the National Center for Health Statistics, up to 4 percent of women receiving female surgical sterilizations are only between the ages of twenty to twenty-four years old. Though ostensibly a relatively small number, 4 percent of the second leading form of contraception is over 400,000 sterilizations performed on women as young as 20 years old every year. Further, the 22 percent or over 2.2 million women receiving the highest number of sterilizations annually are Black; followed closely by Hispanic women, with 20 percent or over 2 million permanent surgical sterilizations per year. Though Blacks and Hispanics of all races and genders combined only constitute one quarter of the U.S. population, together they account for nearly half of all female surgical sterilizations.[7]

For years little data had been collected that could address the extent to which these sterilizations have been voluntary, coerced, and/or forced. However, per the National Center for Health Statistics, as of 2002, White non-Hispanic women, who have received a family planning service in the past 12 months, experience the lowest rates of sterilization counseling and procedures from their health care providers. This compared to Black women being counseled more than 1⅓ percent more often than White women, and to Hispanic women, who experience sterilization counseling at nearly twice the rate of White women.

Reminiscent of the early years of eugenic sterilization programs, the overwhelming majority of women receiving surgical sterilizations have little education. As over half of twenty-two- to twenty-four-year-old women using female surgical sterilization, are not even high school graduates. A vast number of women having surgical sterilizations are living at or below the poverty line. And though the data do not currently offer the combined statistics of age, parity, educational attainment, and race it is a valid assumption, based on the data that do exist that the majority of women receiving female surgical sterilizations in the United States are poorer Black women under the age of 24, with little education.

Arguably, ongoing efforts to vilify and criminalize Black reproduction have proven somewhat successful as Black women themselves

Table 14.3 Reproductive policy analysis: 1996–2009 ✄

Coercive Reproductive Policies in Age of Global Capitalism in the Electronic Era	Nature of Economy 1996–2009	Social Response 1996–2009	Type of Policy	Characteristics of Coercive Reproductive Policies in Age of Global Capitalism in the Electronic Era
Sterilization of Mothers Under 21 with Multiple Children	• Expansion for wealthier • Contraction for poorer • Hi technology • Low labor demand • Global labor force	Conniving Black mothers require Punitive response • Punish Black girls/women for being sexually active • Punish Black girls for having multiple children	Coercive Protocol • To keep Black girls from having more children • Save government funds for future children	• Standard to approach girls at statistically most vulnerable period–directly after childbirth • No longer "reversible" • Procedure subsidized by the State • Waive parental consent for girls under 18
Cash Incentives for Long-acting/permanent Contraception	• Expansion for wealthier • Contraction for poorer • Hi technology • Low labor demand • Global labor force	Conniving Black mothers/girls require covert/proactively punitive response • Punish Black girls "crimes" not yet committed • Punish Black girls for being sexually active	Coercive Policy • To avoid new children in need of government funding • Save government funds for future children	• Standard within state-sponsored institutions, i.e., foster care; board of health facilities; Medicaid services • Attached to welfare benefits • Over 40% of female surgical sterilizations are on Black women.
Welfare Reform	• Expansion for wealthier • Contraction for poorer • Hi technology • Low labor demand • Global labor force	Conniving Black mothers require punitive response • Punish Black women for needing Public Assistance	Coercive Act • To force poor off of Public Assistance • Save government funds	• Family cap • Families leaving welfare • Healthy marriage initiatives • Responsible Fatherhood initiatives • Working for welfare eligibility • Parenting training
Expansion of Child Welfare Industry	• Expansion for wealthier • Contraction for poorer • Hi technology • Low labor demand • Global labor force	Conniving Black mothers/girls require covert/proactively punitive response • Punish Black girls "crimes" not yet committed • Punish Black girls for being sexually active	Coercive Policy • To avoid new children in need of government funding • Save government funds for future children	• Increasing Numbers of Black youth • Criminalization of drug addicted parents. • Reduced efforts to return children home • Increased efforts to place for adoption and guardianship • Privatization

are consenting to permanent surgical sterilizations at alarming rates. Whether this trend is a result of coercive policies—that threaten welfare eligibility, criminalize poor and drug-addicted mothers, or pay cash incentives—or if this is simply Black women's reproductive choice is questionable given the historical and current climate of institutional attacks on Black reproduction. Either way, sterilization remains the number one method of contraception among Black women using contraceptive methods, with them receiving over one-fourth of surgical sterilizations annually—up 10 percent since 1982.[8]

In trying to decipher the reason for such a large percentage of Black and Hispanic women receiving surgical sterilizations; one might turn to the state-sponsored healthcare providers which continue to employ century-old policies and procedures that discourage nonwhite reproduction and encourage poor and "minority" sterilization. For instance an organization called, *Salud Chicago*, offers a Web site with *information* about Hispanic women receiving a tubal ligation procedure.[9] The site claims that though the procedure is *considered* permanent, 50–80 percent of the time it can be successfully reversed. The site fails to state that only 1–2 percent of women who have been sterilized are medically cleared to attempt a reversal.[10] The site assures Hispanic women that life changes that may impact their decision, such as remarriage or divorce, should not be of concern as they can likely have the procedure reversed. Only a passing reference is made to the necessity of hiring, a costly and often difficult to find, tubal ligation reversal specialist.

Other similarly coercive and misleading abuses occur as well. In many urban centers it is local policy to offer young women less than twenty one years of age free tubal ligation services, if they have had multiple children. Several studies have determined that women are more inclined to regret having the procedure performed when they: are under thirty years of age; have the procedure performed immediately after childbirth; and when they are unmarried or in a relationship with significant conflict.[11] Teenage mothers tend not to be married, nor in stable relationships. Many state funded facilities consider it common practice to offer sterilization procedures to these young women literally moments after giving birth as a matter of economy and because they may have some concern about the young girls exhibiting the responsibility to return at a later date. Age is one of the most significant predictors of regret that has ever been researched.

Given all of these facts, it seems clear that the well-being of these women of color is not paramount to this programming, if considered at all. And though none of these policies claim specific focus on Black or Latina women and girls, given their location and coded language assigned them, they are clearly manifested as such. Again, reifying this study's assumption that reproductive freedom is not the same for all women in the United States.

Child Welfare Industry

Eerily reminiscent of the prison industrial complex, the child welfare industry disproportionately impacts Black youth and families. Like the prison industry, the child welfare industry lays the blame of its rise, on the Black family itself; with special consideration of the *crisis* of single Black mothers. Having been considered the root of the pathology of Blacks and the Black family for forty-five years, the child welfare industry has taken up the cause to finally end the perceived crisis.

I am keenly aware of this industry as I spent five years working with troubled youth in the child welfare system during the policy period between 1996 and 2009. First I worked with runaways in California. Then I worked with kids on probation and parole in Chicago. Some had been in jail from the time they had been small children. Then I became an emergency case manager for a prominent Chicago area child welfare agency. The agency offered every service imaginable, they trained foster parents, they counseled children, they trained social workers—they did it all. As an *emergency* worker, I was responsible for working with youth whose home has been suddenly disrupted. Sometimes it is due to having only just been taken away from their birth parents. Other times it is because the foster parent they are assigned fails a home inspection. And other times, actually, as heartbreaking as it is, the majority of the time, the placement no longer wants the child.

I cannot count the number of times I rushed to work because the office secretary had called and told me a foster parent had dumped a child off at the front door of the agency when the doors opened. When I'd arrive, the child would always be sitting, all of his or her worldly belongings next to them in a trash bag, just waiting. Waiting for someone to take them to wherever they would sleep that night. I spent my final year in the industry working as the case manager for a group home for girls who themselves were current wards of the state, and had children of their own in their care. The goal of the facility is to teach the young girls how to parent, how to love, and how to take care of themselves on their own. The girls all attended school and worked and cared for their children with minimal assistance from the staff.

With a caseload that peaked at fifty-two, and changed every ninety days, I worked with hundreds of families. Over five years, in two states, three major cities, and countless suburbs, I only encountered three White families in the system—and these were the most extreme cases that anyone in any of the facilities had ever witnessed. One fifteen-year-old White client threw her one year old son off of a third floor back porch one Saturday afternoon because she had gone off of her schizophrenia medication. Another White client would fall into hysterics rather than be forced to have a supervised visit with his mother, a diagnosed paranoid schizophrenic, who often went off of her meds, leaving the child in constant fear. This was contrary to my Black clients, who often preferred their families with all their flaws to any foster facility. I seldom experienced a Black family that had a history of beating the children and I never once had a case against a Black family that did not involve drugs and poverty.

In the years following welfare reform the private agencies that had previously been used by the state to pick up a certain amount of overflow, were now to be employed as the full service provider. With this push toward privatization the agency would begin to play both sides of the fence, offering services to: the clients; that is, the children; the foster parents; *and* the biological parents.

It was in this period that I learned the hard way that child welfare is a business, not a service. I was working diligently to get a child returned home, which according to the court is always the first plan of resolution. Both parents had attended every class; completed all their assigned services; secured housing; done it all. They clearly loved each other and their child and we all thought that we were progressing well. Until one day my supervisor tells me I should start proceeding toward securing a subsidized guardianship for the child in their current placement. I was shocked and appalled. She had never mentioned this before. She knew all too well how hard the family had been working and had no logical reason to change the plans. I was later informed that due to budget cuts and some high profile media snafus that implied poor performance, the agency was in need of a financial boost. This boost would be earned by obtaining the cash bonus it would receive when a long term guardian was established for the child. This bonus would not be offered if the child was returned home. The agency sought as many bonuses as possible during that 1998 fiscal year.

An entire industry has grown from the expansion of the business of foster care in the 1980s and 1990s. And it is the children in the welfare system—overwhelmingly Black—who have a price on their foreheads.

Emergency care youth are worth almost $300 per month by the year 2000; while treatment care youth (kids with physical and profound psychological or emotional issues) are worth $355. The list of charges and fees and stipends and bonuses goes on and on. Expanding well beyond its youth in care numbers, the child welfare industry has staked its claim as a business at every level. From: subsidized guardians; to private agencies contracted by the state; to state oversight; to the court systems; to substance abuse programs; to parenting class services; to special education services and alternative schools; to adoptive parents—there is money to be made on all sides.

Since 2006

Since 1997 an organization known as *Project CRACK* has paid 2,546 *clients* up to $500 each to be either surgically or chemically sterilized.[12] According to their website, the mission of the program "is to reduce the number of substance exposed births to zero."[13] In achieving this goal they report considering all of the options. Per their own marketing site, they even claim to have considered incarceration of potential parents who are drug addicted and/or alcoholics. However, their website further contends that in the end, the goal of the organization is most "cost effective" and expeditiously achieved through sterilizing *undesirable parents*.[14]

Though not explicitly stated, with 99 percent of the program participants being female, this program has clearly targeted women.[15] And though roughly *only* one third of their paid clients have been Black, their adamant claims that they are not targeting African Americans would at least appear valid, were the organization not so pointedly named *Project CRACK*.[16] Choosing to focus their sterilization efforts on crack cocaine consumption, which has clearly been deemed a Black problem; smacks of racism. Regardless of claims, through ad campaigns; media exposure; and their website that the organization "targets a behavior, not a racial demographic," nearly three-fifths of their sterilized clients have been nonwhite—and at least half of them have been Black.[17] African Americans make up only approximately 12 percent of the U.S. population, while Whites constitute a whopping 75 percent. Further, among the approximately 6.3 million women of child bearing age annually who require substance abuse treatment, only 7.8 percent were African American between 2004 and 2006, while 10.7 percent of women who were in need of substance abuse treatment between 2004 and 2006 were White.[18] Given the national data and *Project CRACK'S* own statistics, it seems evident that they are disproportionately *servicing* Black communities and that it is no accident they have never called themselves *Project Crystal Meth* or *Project Oxycontin*.[19]

Though they offer several temporary chemical contraceptive options, *Project CRACK* is proudly responsible for permanently surgically sterilizing nearly one thousand men and women since 1997, and they continue to expand today. In fact at the time of this writing, the organization had established its *services* in 45 cities within 39 states across the country, plus the District of Columbia, as well as an RV travelling cross country, to promote their program. According to a local newspaper in Harrisburg, PA,

> A 30-foot RV covered with pictures of young women drinking and doing drugs pulled into Harrisburg on Friday with a very clear mission—give female drug addicts and alcoholics $300 if they will get long-term birth control or undergo sterilization…The RV itself if [*sic*] mainly a promotional vehicle. There is a picture of a young girl drinking, another injecting drugs and there is the image of an infant connected to medical tubes. On the back of the RV, a sign reads, 'She has her daddy's eyes, and her mommy's addiction.'[20]

This mobile campaign seems to have proven very effective, as *Project CRACK* added 446 paid clients to their records between 2007 and 2008 alone.

September 24, 2008—Louisiana state representative, John LaBruzzo (R), member of the Committee on Health and Welfare, announces his interest in pursuing research on a cash incentive program that will offer $1,000 to poor women who elect to undergo permanent surgical sterilization. This same program would offer tax incentives to wealthier families who opt to *have* babies.[21] Reminiscent of April 30, 1991, when the Shreveport Times reports that, then representative of LaBruzzo's current District 81, David Duke, had put forth a bill offering poorer women an annual cash incentive to accept short term chemical sterilization, in the form of Norplant implantation.[22] Unlike Duke, LaBruzzo claims his interests in creating such a program are not at all race related. Instead, he asserts that such a program is the only way to save us from a future where our children are the minority forced to work, in order to support the lazy masses, who suffer from a clear sense of entitlement and refuse to take care of themselves.[23]

As it turns out—fortunately— by the time of this writing LaBruzzo had decided against pursuing this particular sterilization program in Louisiana. When asked why, he reports that upon further investigation, he had learned the state of Louisiana already offers free sterilization services to women receiving welfare benefits and feels that his program would essentially duplicate the already available service. As such, he does not feel that the program would be supported, financially or otherwise. He further indicated that he has suffered some personal moral and religious reservations. However, after discussing the matter with his spiritual advisor, he still maintains that sterilization is a moral, practical, and legitimate method of resolving the issue he refers to as "generational welfare."

Having abandoned the original sterilization idea, LaBruzzo contends that something still needs to be done sooner rather than later as "these people," presumably Blacks, "start teaching children at a very young age to start getting a check."[24] LaBruzzo was incredulous when asked if his concerns were ultimately issues of poverty or issues of race. He asserts that he will no longer bow to political correctness and that he would state aloud what he believes we can all see. He went on to proclaim that poorer Whites in rural Louisiana work hard to maintain a two parent household and to convey appropriate morals and values to their children. While these same morals, values, and work ethic, in his estimation, do not exist in poorer Black urban communities. According to LaBruzzo, the poorer Black and now, since Katrina, Latino populations in Louisiana, continue to grow in numbers and generate myriad institutional problems, including: welfare fraud; young girls having babies because, "they want to get a check"; welfare being an incentive to keep having babies; failure of Black families to teach, "values morals and a system of achieving"; and Blacks' refusal to value education.

LaBruzzo reports that his assertions are clearly evidenced by the current condition of urban Blacks in New Orleans. As such, though that specific sterilization plan has been scrapped for the time being, he further reports that he still has every intention of introducing as many as five (5) pieces of legislation to address his concerns about Black women on welfare in Louisiana. As representative to the nearly all-White district 81, LaBruzzo asserts that he has heard from his constituency and there is overwhelming support for him to take action.[25]

January 6, 2009—Ann Coulter releases, *Guilty: Liberal Victims and Their Assault on America.* The professed purpose of the book is to expose the ways in which some members of society portray themselves as victims in order to access opportunities; while, according to Coulter, actually victimizing the rest of America. To prove her point, Coulter attacks Black politicians; Black actors; Black musicians; and the Black proletariat. The release of the book, though cloaked in questionable statistics and controversy, serves as an effort to sabotage the proudest moment in U.S. history to date—the inauguration of the nation's first Black president.[26] Included within this text is a racist condemnation of the new president. Claiming that she is critiquing political, economic, and social issues, she in fact adds to the frenzy of negative social rhetoric about Blacks in the United States. Invoking every fear middle class White America has ever held about successful Blacks while simultaneously reifying every concern middle America has about poorer struggling Blacks.

In one chapter of the book, "Victim of a Crime? Thank A Single Mother"; Coulter highlights the social impacts of single motherhood. In this discussion Coulter makes outright claims that single mothers raise children who become the nation's criminals—often even while still juveniles. On a January 12, 2009 appearance on the talk show, *The View*, Coulter insists her critique of single mothers is not a race-specific assault. However, at best, the assertions of her book are misogynistic and classist; and at worst, they are both misogynist; classist; *and* racist. Her references to *some people* and *single mothers* who are the parents of so-called criminals is typical of double speak employed to thinly disguise overt racism. Coulter's book only serves to breathe new life into the old notion that the social crises: of the prison industrial complex; sexual exploitation; drug addiction; and violent crimes, can all be blamed on the failures of single Black mothers. As Black men occupy the largest single population held in custody, and nearly half of the more than one and a half million children with a father in prison are Black; her reference to single mothers whose children end up in prison clearly connotes Black women.[27]

Whether for political gain; for book sales; or in the supposed best interest of Black women, the propaganda forwarded by the Ann Coulter's and the John LaBruzzo's of this society only serve to mire us deeper in the negative social rhetoric that has brought us to where we are today. This social rhetoric has proven devastating to Blacks in general, but specifically impact Black women.

Summary

In summary, the data show that Black labor becomes even less profitable in the latter years of the twentieth century, due to technological advancements that exclude the unskilled worker and allow access to a global labor force. The policy period between 1975 and 1995 sees the nation experience cycles of expansion, contraction, and recession. While the policy period between 1996 and 2009 sees expansion persist for the wealthiest and contraction for the poorest. Technology continues to be at an all time high throughout both policy periods allowing access to a global labor force. No longer in need of Black women's reproduction, the state harnesses new reproductive technologies, sponsoring a number of programs that attempt to reform Black women and control reproduction. These previously restrictive and controlling policies become proactively coercive, in the neoliberal period (1996–2009), resulting in even stricter regulations on Black reproduction and leading to shockingly high rates of female surgical sterilization among Black women in the United States.

Further Readings

Abramovitz, Mimi. *Regulating the Lives of Women: Social Welfare Policy from Colonial Times to the Present*, revised edition. Cambridge, MA: South End Press, 1996.

Albiston, Catherine. "The Social Meaning of the Norplant Condition: Constitutional Considerations of Race, Class, and Gender." In *The Reproductive Rights Reader: Law, Medicine, and the Construction of Motherhood*, ed. Nancy Ehrenreich, pp. 275–287, New York: New York University Press, 2008.

Anderson, Elijah. *Against the Wall: Poor, Young, Black, and Male (The City in the Twenty-first Century)*. Philadelphia: University of Pennsylvania Press, 2008.

Brinkley, Douglas. *The Great Deluge: Hurricane Katrina, New Orleans, and the Mississippi Gulf Coast*. New York: Harper Perennial, 2006.

Brown, Michael K. *Race, Money, and the American Welfare State*. Ithaca, NY: Cornell University Press, 1999.

Cassidy, John. *Dot.con: How America Lost Its Mind and Its Money in the Internet Era*. New York: HarperCollins, 2002.

Chandra A. 1998. "Surgical Sterilization in the United States: Prevalence and Characteristics, 1965–95." *National Center for Health Statistics. Vital Health Stat* 23(20). http://www.cdc.gov/reproductivehealth/WomensRH/PDF/sr23_20.pdf/.

Clarke, Richard. *Against All Enemies: Inside America's War on Terror*. New York: Free Press, 2004.

Gordon L. "The Long Struggle for Reproductive Rights." In *Radical America* 15: pp. 75–88, 1981.

Grown. Caren, Elissa Braunstein, and Anju Malhotra. *Trading Women's Health & Rights? Trade Liberalization and Reproductive Health in Developing Economies*. New York: Zed Books, 1997.

Holleran, Andrew. *Chronicle of a Plague, Revisited: AIDS and Its Aftermath*. Philadelphia, PA: Da Capo Press, 2008.

Hull, N.E.H. and Peter Charles Hoffer. Roe v. Wade: *The Abortion Rights Controversy in American History (Landmark Law Cases and American Society)*. Lawrence: University Press of Kansas, 2001.

Joffe Carole. *The Regulation of Sexuality. Health, Society, and Policy*. Philadelphia, PA: Temple University Press, 1986.

Jones, Jacqueline. *American Work: Four Centuries of Black and White Labor*. New York: W.W. Norton, 1998.

Katz, Michael B. *The Undeserving Poor: From the War on Poverty to the War on Welfare*. New York: Pantheon Books, 1989.

Kindleberger, Charles P. *Manias, Panics, and Crashes: A History of Financial Crises*, fifth edition. New York: Wiley, 2005.

Lawson Annette and Deborah L. Rhode (Eds.). *The Politics of Pregnancy. Adolescent Sexuality and Public Policy*. New Haven, CT: Yale University Press, 1995.

Lewis, Oscar. "The Culture of Poverty." *Society* 35(2): pp. 7–9, 2008.

McLaren, Angus. *Twentieth-Century Sexuality: A History (Family, Sexuality and Social Relations in Past Times)*. Malden, MA: Blackwell, 1999.

Mink, Gwendolyn. *Whose Welfare?* Ithaca, NY: Cornell University Press, 1999.

Noble, Charles. *Welfare as We Knew It: A Political History of the American Welfare State*. New York: Oxford University Press, 1997.

Quadagno, Jill. *The Color of Welfare: How Racism Undermined the War on Poverty*. New York: Oxford University Press, 1994.

Rifkin , Joel. *The Age of Access: The New Culture of Hypercapitalism, Where All of Life Is a Paid For Experience*. New York,: Tarcher, 2001.

Roberts, Dorothy. "Making Reproduction a Crime." In *The Reproductive Rights Reader: Law, Medicine, and the Construction of Motherhood*, ed. Nancy Ehrenreich, pp. 368–386, New York: New York University Press, 2008.

Smith, Robert C. *Racism in the Post–Civil Rights Era: Now You See It, Now You Don't*. New York: State University of New York Press, 1995.

The Pew Center on the States. "One in 100: Behind Bars in America 2008." Washington, DC: Pew Charitable Trusts, February 2008.

Tudge, Colin. *The Impact of the Gene: From Mendel's Peas to Designer Babies*. New York: Hill and Wang, 2002.

Williams, Lucy A. "The Ideology of Division: Behavior Modification Welfare Reform Proposals." In *The Reproductive Rights Reader: Law, Medicine, and the Construction of Motherhood*, ed. Nancy Ehrenreich, pp. 288–295, New York: New York University Press, 2008.

Wilson, William Julius. *When Work Disappears: The World of the New Urban Poor*. New York: Vintage Books, 1997.

Woodward, Bob. *Bush at War*. New York: Simon & Schuster, 2002.

Woody, Bette. *Black Women in the Workplace: Impacts of Structural Change in the Economy*. Westport, CT: Greenwood Press,1992.

Zucchino, David. *The Myth of the Welfare Queen*. New York: Touchstone, 1997.

PART 5

Commodifying Black Reproduction

CHAPTER FIFTEEN

Rationalizing Commodification

Though program names have changed and government language has evolved the rights of citizens who have endured the harshest struggles of American society continue to be attacked. Throughout history Black women have often been relegated to the lowest economic and social positions, as the State has made purposeful efforts to maintain an economic and social divide between Black women and the rest of American society.[1] Weakened by poverty, drug addiction, lack of access to education, and wealth-building opportunities, poorer Black women remain the victims of sterilization abuse and other forms of neoliberal oppressions.

And though a significant Black middle class has developed in the United States, this does not negate the effectiveness of the determined efforts of the State to rationalize its ongoing exploitation, restriction, control, and manipulation of Black women. Consider the disgraceful circumstances under which any such sterilization program, as described in the previous chapter, could be implemented. Regardless of who the organization targets: Whites; men; criminals—should it matter? Wrenching away control of someone else's most base right—to reproduce—is misogynistic patriarchal tyranny and no matter how you spin it, is fundamentally discriminatory at its core. To presume that any one group within any given society should or even *can* determine which among us is fit to reproduce; is absolutely appalling and would never be tolerated in the reverse. Imagine, for a moment, a traveling band of Black women, fed up with White society and all its flaws. Sick of the: climbing divorce rate; teen pregnancies; sexually transmitted diseases; drug and alcohol addiction; unemployment; homelessness; and persistent poverty, they are determined to sterilize as many *White* women as possible. Or policies that would have White women so afraid of being forcibly sterilized that they refuse to visit a doctor, no matter how gravely ill. The nation would have never supported such drastic and inhumane notions had they been devoted to higher class White populations. Such things would be unheard of.

So why the double standard; why are Black women's rights so cavalierly up for debate? Why do we think it is even worth consideration? Why aren't we all, Black; White; male; female, devastated by the premise? The answer is clearly exposed by the latent and overt stereotypes that persist about Blacks and other nonwhite peoples that serve to marginalize certain populations. This social rhetoric succeeds in slandering their character and reducing them to little more than social problems and statistics. Thus, rationalizing the reduction of their humanity to economic loss or profit. There is no other plausible reason that would make such treatment viable.

At this point, it should go without saying that that such programming must be fought and extinguished at all costs. However, the presence of such policy only offers one more example in a case study of a much larger problem. And its termination, while meaningful and necessary, will hardly suffice in resolving the longstanding deeply ingrained pathology of American society. The real persistent crisis is far greater than the simple act of ending these crimes against humanity, for more critical lingering issues remain. Consider America's reaction to Nazi Germany. The legacy of the eugenics history discussed within this volume lays the very foundation for the meticulous planning and implementation of the tragic Nazi assault on humanity during World War II.[2] Was it enough to close the camps? To censure and condemn the monsters who implemented the heinous crimes, and then look forward in silence? No. There are entire university centers devoted to the study of the Holocaust. The evidence of these events is enshrined in museums around the world. This is done to face this tragic past; to remember the victims and to honor the survivors; and to ensure that it never happens again.

While the tragedies that have befallen Black America are enshrouded in a conspicuous and deafening silence. This denial and dismissal of history coupled with the ongoing rationalization of ongoing abuses reveals that these crises evolve over time and continue. This research explores some of these challenging and painful realities that have historically plagued Black women and others which continue to persist today. Exploring the role of media; government initiatives; and national sentiment, this research contextualizes these histories within American culture.

CHAPTER SIXTEEN

Justifying Commodification

In failing to examine historic and material forces that affect Black women's reproduction in the United States, much of the existing research overlooks the fundamental elements of hegemonic control. This text explores this level of domination by identifying ways in which images of Black women's reproduction are manipulated in order to justify ongoing exploitation and repression of Black labor-biological, reproductive, and manual. Then purposefully links the hegemonic regulation and dominance of each policy period to the status of the forces of production that impact the political economy. This in turn, determines the role of Black reproduction in the United States. In making these connections this research has provided a context for examining policy as an expression of hegemonic control and media as a hegemonic tool of oppression, revealing the ways in which Black women's reproduction in the United States relates to tools, technology, and labor.[1]

Ideological Hegemony

In analyzing reproductive policy that disproportionately affects Black women, this study examines the role of media image in the development of policy. By exploring ongoing social rhetoric on Black women's reproduction in the United States, this study discovers that Marx's assertions about the various means by which the ruling class controls the masses is valid. Marx contends that the ruling class must maintain its power, not only through force, but through coercion and promotion of a false consciousness as well. The acceptance and perpetuation of this false consciousness reinforces the power of the ruling class and even thrusts the oppressed classes into actively assisting in their own exploitation.[2]

As mentioned throughout this study, Black women's labor—productive, reproductive, and biological—has proven central to the development and ongoing success of capitalism in the United States. But no amount of labor has proven as critical as the role Black women have played in their own domination as described by Antonio Gramsci's ideological hegemony:

> In his doctrine of "hegemony," Gramsci saw that the dominant class did not have to rely solely on the coercive power of the State or even its direct economic power to rule; rather, through its hegemony, expressed in the civil society and the State, the ruled could be persuaded to accept the system of beliefs of the ruling class and to share its social, cultural, and moral values.[3]

Ironically this nation, so dependent on the varied strengths and talents of Black women, has not only controlled her from her first days in the United States, but has—through various apparatuses of the ruling class—managed to actively engage her in her own oppressions.

Media

One of the most powerful apparatus employed to manipulate the masses has historically been the media. There is a fundamental link between media, of all types, and the capitalist owning class who are in turn the dominating controllers of the State.[4] For example, the major media in the United States is owned by major corporations; some traceable to a single capitalist mogul, consider Rupert Murdoch. Murdoch is chairman, CEO, and founder of a major worldwide media conglomerate that holds countless media assets worldwide. These holdings include such varied media outlet as: *HarperCollins* publishing; *The New York Post* and *The Wall Street Journal* newspapers; *Fox News* television network; even *Parents* magazine.[5] This is simply one example of the ways in which mass media is owned and controlled by the interests of industry, rather than the interests of the people. Several other prime examples of this present themselves as well: Viacom owns CBS; General Electric owns NBC; Disney owns ABC; and Time Warner owns controlling interest in CNN.[6] As such, the media cannot be trusted as an independent source of information. Instead, as Marx argues, the media should be taken as the voice of the ruling class that must incessantly promote its own interests. Unfortunately, however, due to an acceptance of propaganda images in lieu of factual evidence, Americans do tend to rely heavily on media to lead the way in forming public opinion:

> The mass media encourages us to look up the economic ladder and fantasize about and identify with the superrich, while unscrupulous politicians encourage people to direct their blame and anger toward people one or two rungs down the economic ladder. The scapegoats for the polarized economy include women on welfare and new immigrants.[7]

As a result, for all the generations of organizing and for all of the civil rights gained, today—as one hundred years ago—Black women are still being coerced into sterilizing themselves through cash incentives; threats to welfare benefits; and pressure from health care facilities. Yet, due to social rhetoric propagated by media, American society believes that Black women *need* this manipulation. Therefore, instead of an assault on humanity, the nation perceives itself as answering a call to arms. As long as society continues to lack the collective class consciousness to sift through the media images presented to the masses, this hegemonic control will continue to be perpetuated and internalized.

Tools of Oppression

In serving as an apparatus of hegemonic control by the ruling class, the media becomes a tool of oppression rather than the instrument of liberation as it is touted. The support and acceptance of dominant negative social rhetoric surrounding Black women's reproduction perpetuates the exploitation and oppression of Black women's labor-reproductive, productive, and biological.

These tools of oppression are disseminated through various media; pseudoscientific "research," and political stratagem employed by the ruling class, creating images internalized by the masses,

> ...seems like a national campaign to "dumb us down." Politicians have become experts in squeezing the complexity out of issues to produce compressed, thirteen-second sound bites. Think-tank publicists bombard us with out-of-context snippets of information sometimes called "factoids."...[L]ittle fragments of data, broken

off from their original planetary moorings zinging merrily through space...that's very much how the mass media deliver information. News outlets, every bit as much as advertising agencies, need to trumpet their wares...[8]

Film, television, radio, news, popular literature, political platforms, popular research, and even our textbooks are subject to the political and intellectual influence and control of the ruling class, as they alone possess the economic strength to contribute so significantly to society. These contentions are supported by the ongoing strength of the White male elite in the United States, as the owners of mass media, they control: production companies, newspapers, television stations, and publishing firms. Beyond media influence, the power of the white male elite is further evidenced as we continue to witness glaring racial disparities in the United States' education system. The lack of equal education for all populations leads to the development of racial disparities within scientific communities and among the political powers. Given the history of the methods of control and ongoing strength of the elite, this study can assume that the owners have specific agendas that will not go ignored in a society where they maintain inordinate control. Thus, indoctrination efforts exist in every facet of capitalist society-entertainment, news, politics, education, and more.

False Consciousness

It is important to note here, that in the vein of Gramsci's discussion of ideological hegemony, this study does not contend that the current viewpoint espoused by popular social rhetoric surrounding Black women's reproduction is an ongoing conscious effort to sabotage the Black woman. Instead, this study proposes a far more complex argument. As a result of the dominant hegemony, the masses themselves have taken up the creation of the images previously painted by the elite, to control itself *on behalf of* its oppressors. The oppressed "exist in a dialectical relationship to the oppressor, as his antithesis—that without them the oppressor could not exist...."[9]

As a result of the acceptance of this false consciousness, society—comprised of workers of all levels—has labeled Black women as (a) savage slaves; (b) needy surplus labor; (c) pathological matriarchs; (d) and irresponsible welfare queens, depending on what *society* feels is needed of Black women's labor at the time. What society needs is based on the demands of the political economy, which is based on the modes of production. With the working class so focused on the *needs* of the economy, instead of class struggle and revolution, society sees institutionalized racism replaced with internalized racism. This concept illustrated by Freire, asserts that, "because of their identification with the oppressor, they [the oppressed] have no consciousness of themselves as persons or as members of an oppressed class...the oppressed find in the oppressor their model of 'manhood.'"[10]

The concept of Black women identifying with the oppressor in regards to her reproduction is plainly illustrated by the current statistics of Black women's surgical sterilization. Just as eugenics ideology finally begins to lose some credibility and legalized forced sterilizations ended, ironically, Black women themselves began to embrace sterilization in consistently high numbers. This absolute compliance of the masses strengthens the oppressors hold on the collective society as well as on the psyche of the Black woman. The "tranquility [of the oppressors] rests on how well people fit the world the oppressors have created, and how little they question it."[11]

[handwritten note: Not blind acceptance → coercion, incentives pressure, even just wanting it]

CHAPTER SEVENTEEN

Critiquing Commodification: Connecting to Historical Womanism

Historical womanism has been developed as the theoretical base of this study because this meta-analysis offers relevant investigation of the following key elements of the analysis of Black women's labor: bureaucracy; institutionalized racism; the political economy; tools and technology; Black women as a unique laboring class; the intersections of oppressions that impact Black women; universality; plurality; and consciousness, vision, and strategy. Though some elements of this analysis have been developed specifically for the purposes of this research, much of it is gleaned from previously existing theories, including: historical materialism; womanism; Black feminism; critical race theory; and material feminism. In synthesizing these related, but at times disparate, perspectives and infusing key original approaches specific to Black women's labor, historical womanism emerges as a meaningful theoretical perspective.

Historical womanist theory, like dialectical and historical materialism, offers an analysis of the structural role of the State. The theory recognizes that, "the emergence of the state coincided with the emergence of social classes and class struggles resulting from the transition from a primitive communal to more advanced modes of production when an economic surplus was first generated."[2] Historical womanist theory, like critical race theory, further acknowledges the permanent role of the State bureaucracy in regulating lives of the working classes within a Capitalist structure.

Historical womanist theory, informed by dialectical and historical materialism, acknowledges the role of the State in ruling the working neoliberalism

classes. The theory recognizes that under capitalism, as under all previous modes of production, except primitive communism, the State is an instrument of the ruling class' exploitation and domination. As such this theory, like both dialectical and historical materialism and critical race theory, acknowledges an institutionalized system of domination established in the interests of the State for the purposes of regulating working classes, that is, social, political, economic, educational, and legal structures.

Historical womanism further links the commodification of Black women's various forms of labor to the status of the political economy in the tradition of dialectical and historical materialism. Racist, misogynist, and anti-labor ideologies fundamentally link Black women to the ebb and flow of the capitalist economy. As such, adequate analysis of Black women can only develop from analyses of the political economy. Black women having entered the United States as instruments of production, remain a bought, sold, and traded commodity, if no longer literally, as a vital labor force in the U.S. capitalist system.

Historical womanism locates Black women's labor within the context of developing tools and technology. In examining the role of Black women's labor, the theory examines the effects of technological advancement on Black women's labor in the United States from slavery to present, locating Black women's reproduction as a key element of the manipulable labor force within the capitalist structure.

As material feminism recognizes working class *women* as a unique laboring class, historical womanism recognizes Black women as a distinct laboring class. The exploitation and manipulation of Black women's labor has been unique from that of Black men and other non-Black labor. This is primarily attributable to a history of exploitation and control that has made Black women's various forms of labor: productive; reproductive; and biological, vital to the success of U.S. capitalist structure.

When exploring any social phenomena impacting Black women, adequate research cannot consist solely of a strict race analysis, or of a strict gender interpretation. Instead, as asserted by intersectional theory, research on Black women should include an analysis of the complex interplay between race, class, gender, and sexual oppressions. Further, no comprehensive analysis of Black women can exist without an analysis of her historical relationship with racial; gender; economic; and sexual oppressions.

As Blacks have historically been oppressed as both a race and as a class the assumptions presumed within historical womanist theory are theoretically universal, and in a sense, relevant to Blacks of all genders.

Rooted in the womanist ideology of universality, historical womanist theory notes that just as Black women exist in a unique laboring class, so do Black men. Emasculated within a patriarchal system, they have historically held a unique space as a feared necessity. Like Black women, Black men have suffered from various forms of exploitations and oppressions for economic profit that have not been exclusive to slave and wage labor. Promoted by social rhetoric designed to portray Black men as everything from stud animal to the American pimp, in the current neoliberal era, the American Black man has been caged like a wild animal and exploited for profit, within the context of the prison industrial complex. Dismissed as a gangster, yet, through the clever application of ongoing racist and misogynist social rhetoric—that is, ironically, even embraced by much of Black America—he is lauded as the epitome of masculinity, in the most primal sense of the term. As with Black women, given Black men's historical relationship with the political economy, the only manner in which to fully explore Black men is to locate the research within the context of the intersections of: labor; race; class; gender; and sexuality oppression and exploitation. This; however, is not to imply that there should be a historical womanist analysis of Black men's labor. Instead, a theory should be created and applied that offers an analysis specific to the Black male experience, as historical womanism highlights Black women's experiences.

Patricia Hill Collins asserts that Alice Walker's womanism has some roots in a nationalist tradition that privileges Black experiences of oppression above any given White agenda—in this case feminism. In response to this critique of womanism, historical womanist theory asserts that each labor group has its own distinct class characterized by that group's unique history with the political economy. As such, the historical womanist analysis of Black women's relationship to the economy is by no means a privileging of Black women's labor experience above Black men or other laboring classes. Instead it is a theory that highlights Black women as a labor class.

The final key element to historical womanist theory is informed by perhaps the most significant element of dialectical and historical materialism—resolution. Historical womanist theory, like historical materialist theory, asserts that the only means by which to liberate Black women from historical exploitation; restriction; control; and coercion by the State is through the development of a collective consciousness of their position as a distinct class; a re-visioning of an egalitarian system free of racist, sexist, and classist oppressions; and collectively strategizing the reorganization of the structure.[3]

Given the elements of this theory described above, historical womanism places Black women's reproduction within the context of commodified labor. As such, historical womanism perceives the shifts in Black reproduction as a response to shifts in the forces of production that affect the capitalist superstructure throughout its various economic stages, rather than as isolated phenomena that can be explained by middle range analysis.[4] Middle range theories don't show how a problem fits into the broad conceptual framework of capitalism. In order to wholly comprehend the problem of the commodification of Black reproduction over a chosen period of time, one would have to look at the system base of capitalism for adequate analysis of the problem.

Understanding that historical womanist theory assumes that capitalist structure is predicated upon competition and inequity, we see how relevant this theory is to the long history of exploitation and abuse borne by Black women in the United States.[5] Marx recognizes the economic system as the most essential element of a society's foundation. He claims this is illustrated by the economic structure's influence over society's most substantial and valued institutions. The institution of family, for instance, is a critical aspect of society as well as a profoundly private structure. However it continually evolves depending upon the needs of the ruling class.[6] In a similar fashion, sexuality, in the form of sexual norms; social attitudes; and reproductive policies, is dictated considerably by the shifts in the demands of the political economy.[7] As the political economy is ruled by the forces of production, arguably, the forces of production—at least to some extent—dictate social life. As such, it is evident that the most appropriate framework for this analysis is the historical womanist conceptualization. This research places the ongoing commodification of Black women's reproduction in the United States within a historical context that considers the impact of the economic structure.

As such, historical womanist theory locates Black women as a unique laboring class within the capitalist structure. As the dialectical and historical materialism from which historical womanism is born offers in depth analysis of the political economy, the role of the State and ideology, along with an analysis of social agency and revolutionary social change that culminates in profound social and historical transformation.

This transformation will occur when the most oppressed classes of the exploitative structure, that is, capitalism, demand a reorganization of the structure that considers the interests of these exploited classes. Dialectical and historical materialism asserts this revolutionary transformation occurs through a process of consciousness, vision, and strategy.[8]

In becoming self aware of their shared social and political position as a unique laboring class, Black women can achieve a sense of consciousness. In determining a structure that will work in their best interests, rather than exploit, manipulate, and oppress them, Black women will develop a vision of a society that they as a collective can support. Formulating a plan that encourages Black women's agency, according to historical womanism, will be the strategy to revolutionize the oppressive structure that exists and replace it with an egalitarian system chosen by the people.

Thus, this historical womanist research advances a theory of Black women's reproduction that asserts four major points. First, that Black women exist in a unique laboring class tapped for biological, reproductive, and physical labor by the capitalist owning class. Second, that racist, misogynist, and anti-labor ideologies fundamentally link Black women's reproduction to the ebb and flow of the capitalist economy. Third, that racist and misogynist ideologies are employed as tools to justify economic assaults on Black womanhood by the capitalist owning class. And finally that, the U.S. mass media is employed as a tool of oppression in its dissemination of social rhetoric that supports reproductive policies that disproportionately affect Black women in the United States.

CHAPTER EIGHTEEN

Understanding Commodification

This chapter reiterates that there is a significant relationship between key reproductive policies that have disproportionately affected Black women in the United States and the status of the national economy. The status of the nation's need for Black labor has directly affected the image promulgated by United States media and the State. Public image and opinion of Black reproduction is shaped by state-sponsored propaganda; which is determined by the needs of the economy and disseminated by various forms of media, significantly impact on these reproductive policies. This ever-changing narrative of the sexuality and reproduction of Black women continues to "justify" the United States' policy decisions that assist in the ongoing commodification of Black women's reproduction.

In summary, the historical descriptive data have drawn important links between the national economy and Black labor forces. This research has examined Black women's reproduction in the United States in four policy periods dated: 1845–1865; 1929–1954; 1975–1995; and 1996–2009. These periods occur over three economic eras: the agricultural era (1619–1865), the industrial age (1896–1950), and the era of global capitalism in the electronic age (1975–2009). Analysis of the four policy stages, reproductive exploitation; forced sterilization; vilification of Black reproduction; and coercive contraception, respectively, relates the shifts in the United States political economy to the sociopolitical and economic conditions of Black women in the United States.

The needs of the national economy during the policy period between 1845 and 1865 are clearly links to the passage of exploitative policies as they relate to enslaved Black women in the United States. In this period the U.S. economy is in a state of expansion with low technology and high labor demand. Black reproduction is depended upon as the primary source of labor.

The State has historically justified the commodification of this labor source, with particular emphasis on various forms of media representations of Black women as savages needing their sexual energies channeled. A pseudo-paternalistic social response develops *justifying* the enslavement of Black women. As a result of this paternalistic social climate and the reliance of the White owners on the institution of slavery as a system of controlling a cheap manipulable labor force, exploitative types of policies and protocols are developed that dehumanize the Black mother and maximize the profits of the White owners.

The policy period between 1929 and 1954 reveals the extent to which the status of the political economy impacts upon Black women's labor. In this period, the nation experiences economic moments of both contraction and expansion. The period also undergoes an explosion of technology, which is fundamental in leading to the obsolescence of Black women's labor—both productive and reproductive. Black reproduction is no longer directly linked to the forces of production, as it had been during slavery. Black reproduction, previously encouraged for profit, becomes problematized in the social consciousness. The new demands of the industrial forces of production in the United States render Black women's labor superfluous and push Black women's production and reproduction to the periphery of society. Policies in this period are restrictive. National efforts are implemented to maintain distance from Blacks who are freely migrating across the country and to stem concerns of Black overpopulation.

Black labor becomes even less profitable in the latter years of the twentieth century, due to technological advancements that exclude the unskilled worker and allow access to a global labor force. The policy period between 1975 and 1995 sees the nation experience cycles of expansion, contraction, and recession. While the policy period between 1996 and 2009 sees expansion persist for the wealthiest and increasing contraction for the poorest. Technology continues to be at an all time high throughout both policy periods allowing access to a global labor force. Black women's reproduction is manipulated and curbed when no longer needed for labor.

Throughout this period and into the next, various efforts and initiatives are employed and endorsed by the state, in order to harnesses new reproductive technologies. These efforts include sponsoring a number

Table 18.1 Commodification of Black reproduction

Policy Period	Nature of Economy	Social Rhetoric	Social Response	Types of Policies	Affect on Black Women's Reproduction
1845–1865 Slave Era	• Expansion • Low technology • Hi labor demand • Black reproduction is primary labor source	Animalistic • Sexual savage	Paternalistic • Tame savage behavior	Exploitative laws and de facto protocol to maximize profit	• Raped • Mated like animals • Punished for not reproducing • Forced to trade their biological reproduction for minimal incentives • Lose autonomy over their own offspring • Worth is reduced to her reproductive capabilities
1930–1950 Era of the Negro Project	• Contraction • Expansion • Hi Technology • Surplus labor supply • Broad unskilled labor force	Parasitic • Needy Surplus Labor	Separatist • Curtail danger of overpopulation and intermingling of races	Restrictive laws and policies to minimize expenditure	• Criminalized for undesirable heredity, i.e., race, gender • Criminalized for undesirable characteristics, i.e., poverty, perceived intelligence, chastity • Criminalized for undesirable status, i.e., race, woman
1975–1995 Post-Civil Rights Era	• Expansion • Contraction • Recession • Hi technology • Low labor demand • Global labor force	Pathological • Pathological Matriarch	Reformist • Heal sickness of Black women	Controlling policies to minimize expenditure	• Subjected to State control of her sexuality and reproduction • Sexuality is criminalized • Endures medical trials and ensuing illnesses from test contraceptives • Stigmatized for needing public assistance • Stigmatized as lazy, conniving, and amoral
1996–2009 Welfare Reform Era	• Expansion for wealthier • Contraction for poorer • Hi technology • Low labor demand • Global labor force	Conniving • Irresponsible Welfare Queen	Punitive • Punish manipulative Black women	Coercive policies to minimize expenditure	• Subjected to sterilization abuses • Stigmatized as lazy, conniving, and amoral • Stigmatized for needing public assistance • Left without a safety net

of programs that attempt to reform Black women and control reproduction. Previously restrictive and controlling policies become proactively coercive. The latter part of the neoliberal period between 1996 and 2009, reveals even stricter regulations on Black reproduction. These policies, procedures, and initiatives lead to shockingly high rates of female surgical sterilization among Black women in the United States. In restricting the reproductive freedom of Black women throughout the final two policy periods, Black reproduction is increasingly vilified and effectively criminalized.

Other than the period of forced reproduction for profit during the reproductively exploitative slave era, the literature repeatedly points to images of Black women's reproduction as detrimental to the U.S. political economy. History shows that regulatory reproductive policies result in periods of negative social rhetoric related to Black women's reproduction in the United States. This negative social rhetoric is disseminated when Black women's labor becomes unnecessary for the success of the U.S. political economy. As such, it is necessary to examine the use of media as a tool to convey this message and to influence and control the masses.

Further, there is an evident and ongoing historical trend toward perfecting technological methods of controlling Black reproduction. As such, in order to fully comprehend the commodification of Black women's labor, it is necessary to explore various ways in which reproductive technologies have influenced reproductive policies that disproportionately affect Black women. This analysis reveals that the tools and technologies of each economic stage directly affect the status of all laboring classes. Thus, impacting on Black women, who occupy a position as a unique laboring class. A class which both, produces goods and services for the capitalist class as well as reproduces the labor pool.

In sum, as outlined in table 18.1, there is a significant and ongoing relationship between the needs of the United States political economy and Black women's reproduction. Social rhetoric significantly affects reproductive policy and is directly impacted by the nature of the economy.

Further Readings

Brown G.F. and E.H. Moskowitz. "Moral and Policy Issues in Long-Acting Contraception." In *Annual Review of Public Health* 18: pp. 379–400, 1997.

Byrd, Rudolph P. and Beverly Guy-Sheftall. *Traps: African American Men on Gender and Sexuality.* Bloomington: Indiana University Press, 2001.

Collins, Patricia Hill. *Black Sexual Politics: African Americans, Gender, and the New Racism.* New York: Routledge, 2004.

Davis, Angela. "Racism, Birth Control, and Reproductive Rights." In *The Reproductive Rights Reader: Law, Medicine, and the Construction of Motherhood,* ed. Nancy Ehrenreich, pp. 86–93, New York: New York University Press, 2008.

Ehrenreich, Barbara. "The Colonization of the Womb." In *The Reproductive Rights Reader: Law, Medicine, and the Construction of Motherhood,* ed. Nancy Ehrenreich, pp. 391–401, New York: New York University Press, 2008.

Gill, Stephen and David Law. "Global Hegemony and the Structural Power of Capital." In *Gramsci, Historical Materialism and International Relations,* ed. Stephen Gill, pp. 93–126. New York: Cambridge University Press, 1993.

Gordon Linda. *The Moral Property of Women: A History of Birth Control Politics in America.* Urbana: University of Illinois Press, 2007.

———. "The New Feminist Scholarship on the Welfare State." In *Women, the State, and Welfare,* ed. Linda Gordon, pp. 9–35. Madison: University of Wisconsin Press, 1990.

Myers, Nick J. *Black Hearts: The Development of Black Sexuality in America.* Victoria, Canada: Trafford, 2006.

Staples, Robert. *Exploring Black Sexuality.* Lanham, MD: Rowman & Littlefield, 2006.

Weitz, Rose. *The Politics of Women's Bodies: Sexuality, Appearance, and Behavior.* New York: Oxford University Press, 2003.

PART 6

Liberation

CHAPTER NINETEEN

Finding Freedom

How can we prevent future reproductive policies from continuing to satisfy historically racist and economically exploitative ideologies? We have already begun to examine and compare the histories of Black reproduction and Black labor demands in the United States, as well as link these trends to social and economic shifts in the national economy. However, many questions remain. How does the nation begin to link the historical exploitation of Black women's reproduction to her current status? How can the people of the nation resist exploitative reproductive policies? How do we reconceptualize Black women's reproduction as a human rights issue, rather than as a valid response to economic crises? How can the nation envision itself surviving economic and social shifts without exploiting Black labor?

We can begin to address these issues with the development of analytical knowledge of this theory on the commodification of Black women's reproduction in four steps. This first step is to develop a conceptualization of regulatory reproductive policies that disproportionately affect Black women's reproduction, as racist and misogynist tools to carry out economic attacks, rather than strictly institutionalized racism. The second step is to socially locate Black women's reproductive needs and freedoms within the context of the ongoing broader struggle for reproductive rights. The third step is to establish a firmer grasp of economic, political, and social trends that vitally affect Black reproduction. And the final step is to develop a public philosophy that links social rhetoric, moral discourse, and political and economic changes to the development of reproductive policy.

The Future of Black Women in
the United States?

Fundamentally, how does one fully gauge the racism, misogyny, systematic discrimination, sexism, physical, psychosexual, emotional, and psychological abuses of a people? Even in an effort such as this work, that attempts to look back over four centuries of such exploitation, subjugation, oppression, and suppression that have so impacted who, not only African Americans, are today, but Black women living in America, it is near impossible to explore every nuance of every policy, every national moment, and each of its outcomes. That said, no task is more urgent. In a society that has historically prided itself on independence, patriotism, and justice for all, that finds itself embroiled once again in a fundamental internal controversy over race relations when a Black man runs for president.

Though Obama did actually win the election, we have seen the basest foulest responses flood our media outlets, both traditionally and electronically. Television played a gargantuan role in the 2008 presidential election, whether through news programming, talk shows, or even situation comedies. The Obama campaign spent more on advertising than any other candidate in U.S. history. Perhaps to combat the social rhetoric surrounding the Black man and the Black family so deeply entrenched in our national psyche. But, just as the 2008 election year saw nonviolent revolutionary action taken by the masses in the form of a monumental upswing in political participation, including: voter registration; campaign volunteering; and monetary donations, there was also a surge in new age nonviolent guerilla tactics meant to destroy the resolve of this *revolution*. Internet blogs, mass text messages, mudslinging commercials, talk radio, it came from all sides. Never have we seen such a prime example of the significance of the media in this nation.

Black women have been instrumental in the ongoing struggles for liberation, access, and autonomy. Imagined as angry, manipulative, and emasculating, Black women have historically borne the brunt of the so-called failings of Black society. Labeled everything from mammy to welfare queen, Black women have scarcely been considered much more than a problem when visioning our political landscape. As we settle into the twenty-first century are we seeing the dawn of a new era for Black women? As we proudly watched Barack Obama and Hillary Clinton vie for a presidency that had never before been within reach of anyone nonwhite or non-male. Are we glimpsing the evolution of our society? Never having been fully included in women's movements and equally relegated to a second tier among Black struggles, do we dare see ourselves in these candidates? Do we have the audacity to hope for the day when the woman running for president is not White or the Black candidate is a woman? In imagining this future, there must be some reevaluation of the impact of Black histories. With that perhaps there can be a reinvigoration of Black consciousness that can assist in the development of an inclusive re-visioning of a Black community that can effectively strategize movement towards a more perfect nation.

Further Readings

Ertman, Martha, M. "What's Wrong with a Parenthood Market? A New and Improved Theory of Commodification." In *The Reproductive Rights Reader: Law, Medicine, and the Construction of Motherhood,* ed. Nancy Ehrenreich, pp. 299–307, New York: New York University Press, 2008.

Fairclough, Adam. *Better Day Coming: Blacks and Equality, 1890–2000.* New York: Penguin Books, 2002.

hooks, bell. *Black Looks: Race and Representation.* Boston, MA: South End Press, 1992.

James, Joy. *Resisting State Violence: Radicalism, Gender, and Race in U.S. Culture.* Minneapolis: University of Minnesota Press, 1996.

Sterling, Dorothy. *Black Foremothers: Three Lives,* second edition. New York: Feminist Press at The City University of New York, 1988.

Wyatt, Gail. *Stolen Women: Reclaiming Our Sexuality, Taking Back Our Lives.* New York: John Wiley & Sons, 1997.

NOTES

Introduction

1. For specific definition of the *political economy*, see Key Concepts and Definitions.
2. For further discussion on the enduring significance of labor roles for Blacks in America see Cox, *Caste Class and Race*; for further discussion on the relationship of Blacks to the capitalist structure see: Cox, *Capitalism as a System*.
3. For further conceptualization of the *stages of capitalism* highlighted within this research, see Key Concepts and Definitions.
4. For specific definition of *instrument of production*, see Key Concepts and Definitions; as reproductive labor has historically been a contentious term amongst various feminist factions, it is imperative that it be defined specifically in terms of this research study. Historically reproductive labor has been a reference to what is commonly known as "women's work." For the purposes of this study, "reproductive labor includes activities such as purchasing household goods, preparing and serving food, laundering and repairing clothes, maintaining furnishings and appliances, socializing children, providing care and emotional support for adults, and maintaining kin and community ties" see Glenn, "From Servitude to Service Work," 405. As demonstrated in Evelyn Nakano Glenn's definition, the physical action of biological reproduction has been (seemingly) purposefully excluded, presumably to accentuate the human-made gendered division of labor (see Marx and Engels, *Selected Works*); for further conceptualization of the three types of Black women's *labor* highlighted within this research, see Key Concepts and Definitions.
5. For further conceptualization of *policy* as applied in this research, see Key Concepts and Definitions.
6. For further conceptualization of *social rhetoric* highlighted within this research, see Key Concepts and Definitions.
7. Please note that this particular volume focuses on the exploitation and abuse of Black women's labor and reproduction; however, this is not to imply that other populations do not experience similar and unique oppressions related to these issues. Throughout the text it will be noted when appropriate that Latin; Native American; and poorer populations of various genders and racial and ethnic backgrounds have experienced these and other oppressions. However, this text will focus primarily on the experiences of Black women.
8. For further conceptualization of *commodification* within this research, see Key Concepts and Definitions; for more literature with a historical, political, and economic analysis of Black women in the United States, see: Firestone, *The Dialectic of Sex*; Mies, *Patriarchy and Accumulation on a World Scale*; Solinger, *Wake Up Little Susie*; Roberts, *Killing the Black Body*; and Ross, *African-American Women and Abortion*.

9. For further discussion on Marx and Engels' dialectical and historical materialism, see: Fishman, Gomes, and Scott, "Materialism"; Marx and Engels, *Selected Works*; and Marx and Engels, *The Communist Manifesto*. Also see part 1's Further Readings.

10. Though this book does discuss the status of the political economy 2006–2009, the primary focus of the data analysis will be on the previous eras ending in 2006. Given the profundity of the economic contraction that exploded between 2006 and 2009, that some actually deem an economic depression, more data analysis as well as hindsight would be required to accurately explore its social impact.

11. hooks, *Ain't I a Woman*.

12. For further discussion see Ross, *African-American Women and Abortion*; see also Hine and Thompson, *A Shining Thread of Hope*.

13. hooks, *Ain't I a Woman*.

14. Although as you read this book you will discover that the period of legally sanctioned forced sterilizations certainly began well before 1929 and continued into the 1980s, and for some populations even persist today, please note that the decision to focus on this particular time period (1929–1954) is due to the exceptionally virulent efforts aimed at specifically sterilizing Blacks in this historical moment, as well as the status of the economy, as the nation experiences economic: contraction, depression, and expansion during this twenty-five year period; for further conceptualization of the *forces of production*, see Key Concepts and Definitions.

15. For more information see Kline, *Building a Better Race*; see also Luker, *Dubious Conceptions*.

16. Roberts, *Killing the Black Body*.

17. For more information see Reagan, *When Abortion Was a Crime*; see also Asbell, *The Pill*.

18. For more information see Solinger, *Abortion Wars*; see also Davis, *Women, Race, & Class*; Roberts, *Killing the Black Body*; and Ross, *African-American Women and Abortion*.

19. For further discussion of the impacts of new technologies on the labor forced see Rifkin, *The End of Work*; for further discussion of the relationship of capitalist development to the obsolescence of a population, see Dickerson and Rousseau, "Black Senior Women and Sexuality"; see also, Dickerson and Rousseau, Ageism through Omission."

20. Hill, *The Strengths of Black Families*; cf. D.P. Moynihan, "The Negro Family." A study commissioned by the United States government, conducted by the U.S. Department of Labor's Office of Policy Planning and Research. Known as The Moynihan Report, this study on the status of Blacks in the United States argued that Blacks failed to thrive in the United States and instead developing a pathology that bound them in a cycle of poverty that would destroy the race.

21. For more on impact of derogatory stereotypes of Black mothers see: Roberts, *Killing the Black Body* and Williams, *The Constraint of Race*.

22. For further conceptualization of *neoliberalism*, see Key Concepts and Definitions.

23. U.S. Government, National Center for Health Statistics, 2004, "Health, United States, 2004 with Chartbook on Trends in the Health of Americans," In *Centers for Disease Control and Prevention, National Center for Health Statistics, National Survey of Family Growth*. Hyattsville, MD: National Center for Health Statistics.

One   On Historical Womanist Theory

1. For further discussion see Kerlinger, *Foundations of Behavioral Research*.

2. For more information see unpublished dissertation, Nicole Rousseau, "A Historical Materialist Analysis of the Commodification of Black Women's Biological Reproduction in the United States."

3. For further conceptualization of *modes of production*, see Key Concepts and Definitions.

4. For further discussion see Marx, *The Grundrisse* and Fishman, Gomes, and Scott, "Materialism."

5. Quoted in Marx, *The Grundrisse*, 205–206.

6. For further conceptualization of *means of production* within this research, see Key Concepts and Definitions; for further discussion of inequality and its role in capitalist structure, see Marx and Engels, *The Communist Manifesto*.

7. For further conceptualization of *alienation* within this research, see Key Concepts and Definitions; for further discussion of the exploitation of the working class within capitalist structure, see Marx and Engels, *The Communist Manifesto*; and Berberoglu, *An Introduction to Classical and Contemporary Social Theory*.

8. Berberoglu, *An Introduction to Classical and Contemporary Social Theory*; for further conceptualization of the *relations of production*, see Key Concepts and Definitions.

9. Quoted in Marx and Engels, *The Communist Manifesto*, 9.

10. For further discussion on global village; globalization; and neoliberal era see: Harvey, *A Brief History of Neoliberalism*; Kiely, *The Clash of Globalisations*; see also Rupert and Smith, *Historical Materialism and Globalisation*. For further discussion see part 1's Further Readings.

11. Berberoglu, *An Introduction to Classical and Contemporary Social Theory*, 13.

12. Berberoglu, *An Introduction to Classical and Contemporary Social Theory*, 62.

13. Berberoglu, *An Introduction to Classical and Contemporary Social Theory*, 62.

14. Berberoglu, *An Introduction to Classical and Contemporary Social Theory*, 15.

15. Quoted in Berberoglu, *An Introduction to Classical and Contemporary Social Theory*, 62.

16. Quoted in Berberoglu, An introduction to classical and contemporary social theory, 62–63; for further discussion of Gramsci's conceptualization of ideological hegemony see Morton, *Unravelling Gramsci*.

17. For further discussion on class consciousness and revolution see: Marx and Engels, *The Communist Manifesto*; and Fishman, Gomes, and Scott, "Materialism."

18. Quoted in Berberoglu, *An Introduction to Classical and Contemporary Social Theory*, 63.

19. Quoted in Freire, *Pedagogy of the Oppressed*, 29

20. For further discussion see Marx and Engels, *The Communist Manifesto*.

21. Berberoglu, *An Introduction to Classical and Contemporary Social Theory*.

22. Quoted in Berberoglu, *An Introduction to Classical and Contemporary Sociology*, 16.

23. Marx and Engels, *The Communist Manifesto*, 25.

24. For further discussion see Sernau, *Global Problems*.

25. Sernau, *Global Problems*.

26. For further discussion on impact of capitalism on wage laborer, see Marx and Engels, *The Communist Manifesto*.

27. For further discussion on the capitalist exploitation of women in the working class, see Kollontai, "Towards a History of the Working Women's Movement in Russia."

28. For further discussion see Kollontai, "Sexual Relations and the Class Struggle."

29. For further discussion see Davis, *Women, Race, & Class*.

30. For further discussion see hooks, *Ain't I a Woman*.

31. For further discussion of the exploitation of Black women's reproductive labor see Roberts, *Killing the Black Body*; Jones, *Labor of Love, Labor of Sorrow*; Davis, "Surrogates and Outcast Mothers."

32. Although the works of significant theorists who do achieve this level of analysis, such as Davis and hooks, make noteworthy contributions to the analysis of Black women and the State, many of their works on the topic were published in the 1970s and 1980s and are no longer current and now require considerable updating.

33. For more on the impact of the state on women's bodies, see: Brewer et al., "Women Confronting Terror"; Dickerson and Rousseau, "Black Senior Women and Sexuality"; Dickerson and Rousseau, "Ageism through Omission."

34. For more on Alice Walker's conceptualization of *womanism*, see Walker, "Coming Apart"; Walker, *In Search of Our Mother's Gardens*; and Phillips, "Womanism: On Its Own." For interdisciplinary analyses of womanist perspective see Phillips, *The Womanist Reader.* Also see part 1's Further Readings.

35. Intersectionality theory is a term coined by Kimberle Williams Crenshaw, it is now closely associated Patricia Hill Collins' conceptualization of Black feminism. For further discussion of intersectionality theory see Crenshaw, "Mapping the Margins"; for further discussion of Black feminism, see Collins, *Black Feminist Thought.*

36. For further discussion of the links between Black feminism and womanism see Collins, "What's in a Name?"

37. For further discussion of womanism see Collins, "What's in a Name?"

38. For further discussion of critical race theory and its relationship to dialectical and historical materialism, see Edghill, "Historical Patterns of Institutional Diversity"; for further discussion of critical race theory see, Crenshaw et al., *Critical Race Theory*; for more on critical race theory see part 1's Further Readings.

39. For further discussion on institutional racism see Crenshaw et al., *Critical Race Theory.*

40. For further discussion of U.S. Civil War see Conniff and Davis, *Africans in the Americas.*

41. Quoted in Collins and Yeskel, *Economic Apartheid in America*, 107.

42. Quoted in Collins and Yeskel, *Economic Apartheid in America*, 106.

43. Quoted in Collins and Yeskel, *Economic Apartheid in America*, 107.

44. Quoted in Brewer et al., "Women Confronting Terror," 102–103.

45. Quoted in Brewer et al., "Women Confronting Terror," 104.

46. For further discussion of the role of Black woman as biological laborers see Davis, "Surrogates and Outcast Mothers."

47. Quoted in Jones, *Labor of Love, Labor of Sorrow*, 196.

48. Quoted in Shulman, *The Betrayal of Work*, 69.

49. For further discussion see Shulman, *The Betrayal of Work.*

50. For further discussion see: hooks, *Ain't I a Woman*; Mies, *Patriarchy and Accumulation on a World Scale*; and Roberts, *Killing the Black Body.*

51. Quoted in Zeitlin, *Ideology and the Development of Sociological Theory*, 63.

Two   On Historical Materialist Method

1. Quoted in Marx and Engels, *Selected Works*, 18.

2. Quoted in Marx and Engels, *Selected Works*, 18.

3. Quoted in Code, *How Do We Know?* 15.

4. Quoted in Goode and Hatt, *Methods in Social Research*, 314.

5. Quoted in Goode and Hatt, *Methods in Social Research*, 313.

6. Quoted in Goode and Hatt, *Methods in Social Research.*

7. For further discussion see Barret, *Women's Oppression Today*; Glenn, "Racial Ethnic Women's Labor"; and Glenn, "From Servitude to Service Work."

8. Quoted in Goode and Hatt, *Methods in Social Research*, 331.

9. For further discussion see Neumann, *Social Research Methods.*

Three   The Significance of Social Rhetoric

1. For further discussion of the role of the media in the initiation of the *war on terror* see Kuypers, *Bush's War.*

2. According to the *American Civil Liberties Union* (ACLU) the Patriot Act passed October 26, 2001, offers unprecedented powers the Executive Branch of the U.S. government. The Patriot Act allowed the government rights to the medical records; tax records; and school records of American citizens. Reminiscent of the McCarthy period of the 1950s, it allowed for the covert investigation of political and religious organizations and even allowed the government to monitor book purchases and library loans! Under the auspices f the Patriot Act, individuals have been detained for months with no charges filed and no access to legal representation. These sweeping powers fundamentally threatened six Constitutional amendments:

- **First Amendment**—Freedom of religion, speech, assembly, and the press.
- **Fourth Amendment**—Freedom from unreasonable searches and seizures.
- **Fifth Amendment**—No person to be deprived of life, liberty, or property without due process of law.
- **Sixth Amendment**—Right to a speedy public trial by an impartial jury, right to be informed of the facts of the accusation, right to confront witnesses and have the assistance of counsel.
- **Eighth Amendment**—No excessive bail or cruel and unusual punishment shall be imposed.
- **Fourteenth Amendment**—All persons (citizens and noncitizens) within the United States are entitled to due process and the equal protection of the laws.

3. In 2004 the media began reporting a story of devastating abuse perpetrated by American soldiers on prisoners in the Iraqi detention center, Abu Graib. The media released searing photos that clearly show prisoners being physically, psychologically, and sexually tortured, humiliated, and degraded. See part 1's Further Readings for more on Abu Graib scandal and government abuse of social rhetoric.

4. For further discussion on persuasion see, Aristotle, *The Rhetoric, Book I [1354a]*.

5. Fred Hampton was a cutting edge African American activist assassinated by the FBI and a team of Chicago police officers at the age of twenty one and all but forgotten by our history books. Part of a dynamic nationwide team of young African Americans who were on the ground fighting the battle against racism, inequality, and poverty, Hampton, along with other prominent members of the Black Panther party, were relentlessly pursued by J. Edgar Hoover's FBI as well as the local police. Though personally responsible for bringing a truce to warring gangs in the Chicagoland area, setting up a Chicago branch of a program to feed inner city children breakfast before school, and an active college student, the government's notorious counterintelligence program, commonly known as COINTELPRO, designated Hampton as an enemy of the state. For this, he and his fellow activists endured an onslaught of assaults that culminated in his and Mark Clark's assassination. Mark Clark was twenty two at the time of his assassination. For more on disinformation campaigns and government abuse of social rhetoric, see part 1's Further Readings.

6. For further discussion see: Dickerson and Rousseau, "Black Senior Women and Sexuality"; Dickerson and Rousseau, "Ageism through Omission."

7. Quote in Collins, *Black Feminist Thought*, 68.

8. For further discussion see Collins, *Black Feminist Thought*. For more on the impact of social rhetoric on Black women see, Dickerson and Rousseau, "Black Senior Women and Sexuality"; Dickerson and Rousseau, "Ageism through Omission."

9. Quoted in Collins, *Black Feminist Thought*, 68.

10. Quoted in Collins, *Black Feminist Thought*, 69. For more on the impact of controlling propaganda images of Black Women see, Dickerson and Rousseau, "Black Senior Women and Sexuality"; Dickerson and Rousseau, "Ageism through Omission."

11. Quoted in Collins, *Black Feminist Thought*, 69.

12. Quoted in Solinger, *Wake Up Little Susie*, 344. For more on the disparity between Black and White women's sexuality see, Dickerson and Rousseau, "Black Senior Women and Sexuality"; Dickerson and Rousseau, "Ageism through Omission."
13. For further discussion see Solinger, *Wake Up Little Susie*. For more on racial disparities in reproductive policies see Roberts, *Killing the Black Body*; Solinger, *Pregnancy and Power*; and Solinger, *Abortion Wars*. Also see part 1's Further Readings for more on the long struggle for reproductive rights.
14. For further discussion see: Ross, *African-American Women and Abortion*; Dickerson, "Ethnic Identity and Feminism; Dickerson and Rousseau, "Ageism through Omission."
15. Quoted in Sharpley-Whiting, *Black Venus*, 71.
16. African women constituted only eleven of the 12,707 registered prostitutes in France in 1831. Quoted in Sharpley-Whiting, *Black Venus*, 71–72.
17. For further discussion of Reconstruction era social rhetoric surrounding Black women see Lerner, *Black Women, White America*.
18. Quoted in White, *Too Heavy a Load*, 217.
19. For further discussion see: Dickerson and Rousseau, "Black Senior Women and Sexuality"; Dickerson and Rousseau, "Ageism through Omission."
20. See Moynihan, The Negro family for more on the "pathology" that was argued to have been engrained by the Black single parent household, by Black mothers who, according to the study, could neither discipline nor educate Black male children (how to successfully fit into the role of an American man).
21. For further discussion see: Dickerson and Rousseau, "Black Senior Women and Sexuality"; Dickerson and Rousseau, "Ageism through Omission."

Four   Becoming Instruments of Production

1. The American-Indian Wars, though punctuated by several well-known historically significant battles, are generally considered to have been an ongoing struggle fought in a series of skirmishes, conflicts, treaties, and policies between 1622 and 1898. See Nabokov, *Native American Testimony*.
2. For more information on revolutionary period see Coffin and Stacey, *Western Civilizations*. The revolutionary period began immediately following the French and Indian War—1754–1763 (see Note 3). The Revolutionary War was 1775–1783.
3. Coffin and Stacey, *Western Civilizations*. Unpopular taxes were levied in the New World to recoup some of the losses caused by the Seven Years War and to fund their protection. These taxes, along with severe trade restrictions on American products passing through British ports, were imposed without representation or consent by the colonists and were perceived as an attack on the New World economy.
4. Stearns et al., *World Civilizations*. North America maintained an insignificant population, only 3 million, compared to Latin America.
5. For more information on the experiences of Blacks in the diaspora see Conniff and Davis, *Africans in the Americas*. By mid-eighteenth century 20.2% of the colonies were comprised of people of African descent. According to census data, South Carolina actually had a majority Black population at 60.9% in 1750, while Virginia was at nearly half, with 43.9% Black.
6. For further discussion on slavery in the colonies, see Conniff and Davis, *Africans in the Americas*. Between the settlement at Jamestown, VA, in 1607 and approximately 1619, other means of labor are exclusively employed by the colonists. However, the first recorded slavery trafficking transaction of 1619 implies the growth of employing Africans for labor in the Colonies.

7. See Stearns et al., *World Civilizations*. Not only were the numbers sparse in terms of a viable labor force, settlers were often in search of religious freedom and/or financial success and therefore did not seek agricultural work.
8. For further discussion see Hine and Thompson, *A Shining Thread of Hope*.
9. Hine and Thompson, *A Shining Thread of Hope*, 15.
10. See Conniff and Davis, *Africans in the Americas*. Survivors of the Middle Passage, that could last anywhere from two weeks to more than twenty, experienced a degradation, the depths of which are unimaginable. Stripped naked; systematically raped; psychological and physically abused; often sick from the unsanitary conditions; all the while confused about what has happened to them and where they are even going. Only to arrive on foreign shores surrounded by Whites who speak unintelligible words, to be treated with insurmountable cruelty.
11. Quoted in hooks, *Ain't I a Woman*, 23.
12. Conniff and Davis, *Africans in the Americas*. Importing only 5% of Africans traded in the Americas for slave labor, the Black population in the United States grows to be the largest in the Americas. A little over a century into the slave trade, the majority of Blacks in the United States are American-born.
13. Quoted in hooks, *Ain't I a Woman*, 17.
14. Quoted in hooks, *Ain't I a Woman*, 16.
15. Quoted in hooks, *Ain't I a Woman*, 85.
16. Quoted in hooks, *Ain't I a Woman*, 18.
17. For further discussion see Zeitlin, *Ideology and the Development of Sociological Theory*.
18. For further discussion see Lenin, *The State and Revolution*.
19. For further discussion see: Browne, *Autobiography of a Female Slave*; Bullough, Shelton, and Slavin, *The Subordinated Sex*; Bynum, *Unruly Women*; and hooks, *Ain't I a Woman*.
20. For further discussion see: hooks, *Ain't I a Woman*; Jacobs, *Incidents in the Life of a Slave Girl*; Reiss, *The Showman and the Slave*.
21. For further discussion see hooks, *Ain't I a Woman*.
22. Quoted in hooks, *Ain't I a Woman*, 15.
23. Quoted in hooks, *Ain't I a Woman*, 15.
24. For further discussion see hooks, *Ain't I a Woman*.
25. Quoted in hooks, *Ain't I a Woman*, 16.
26. For further discussion of the impact of the severing of enslaved Black women's sovereign rights to her children see Davis, "Surrogates and Outcast Mothers."
27. Quoted in hooks, *Ain't I a Woman*, 39.
28. Quoted in hooks, *Ain't I a Woman*, 39; for further discussion of the coerced and forced breeding of enslaved Black women see Davis, "Surrogates and Outcast Motehrs."
29. For further discussion of forced breeding of enslaved Black women see hooks, *Ain't I a Woman*.
30. Quoted in hooks, *Ain't I a Woman*, 33.
31. See Hine and Thompson, *A Shining Thread of Hope*; for more on other slave revolts in the US and in the Americas, see Conniff and Davis, *Africans in the Americas*.
32. For further discussion see Hine and Thompson, *A Shining Thread of Hope*.
33. Quoted in Hine and Thompson, *A Shining Thread of Hope*, 100.
34. For further discussion on enslaved Black women's organized collective resistance see Hine and Thompson, *A Shining Thread of Hope*.
35. Quoted in Hine and Thompson, *A Shining Thread of Hope*, 99.
36. Quoted in Hine and Thompson, *A Shining Thread of Hope*, 100.
37. Quoted in Ross, *African-American Women and Abortion*, 145.
38. For more information see Brodie, *Contraception and Abortion*.

Five   Is This the White Man's Burden—Or Ours?

1. For further discussion see Brewer et al., "Women Confronting Terror"; and Dickerson and Rousseau, "Black Senior Women and Sexuality."
2. The actual term "White Man's Burden" is adapted from an 1899 Rudyard Kipling poem of the same name, which discusses the role of the White race in civilized society; however, the concept lived as long as enslaving of Black Africans had existed.
3. White man's burden" ideology is furthered through myriad forms of media. Including advertising: "The first step towards lightening The White Man's Burden is through teaching the virtues of cleanliness. Pears' Soap is a potent factor in brightening the dark corners of the earth as civilization advances, while amongst the cultured of all nations it holds the highest place—it is the ideal toilet soap." Published on the inside front cover of the October 1899 issue of *McClure's Magazine*. Public domain.
4. Quoted in Jewell, *From Mammy to Miss America and Beyond*, 37; For further discussion see Jacobs, *Incidents in the Life of a Slave Girl*; hooks, *Ain't I a Woman*.
5. Quoted in Giddings, *When and Where I Enter*, 47.
6. Quoted in Giddings, *When and Where I Enter*, 47.
7. Quoted in Giddings, *When and Where I Enter*, 47.
8. Quoted in Giddings, *When and Where I Enter*, 46.
9. For further discussion of silence around enslaved black women giving birth to biracial children see Davis, "Surrogates and Outcast Mothers."

Six   Age Old Pimpin': Exploitative Reproductive Policies

1. For further discussion of forced breeding of enslaved Black women see: hooks, *Ain't I a Woman*; Ross, "Black Women and Abortion"; and Hine and Thompson, *A Shining Thread of Hope*.
2. Quoted in Hine and Thompson, *A Shining Thread of Hope*, 15.
3. For further discussion of exclusionary laws see Gomes and Williams, *From Exclusion to Inclusion*.
4. Quoted in Hine and Thompson, *A Shining Thread of Hope*, 45.
5. Quoted in Hine and Thompson, *A Shining Thread of Hope*, 50.
6. For further discussion of relationships between: enslaved Blacks; Indian laborers; and White laborers, see Conniff and Davis, *Africans in the Americas*. In the generations between 1680 and 1720, when indentured servants and Indian laborers overlapped with the onset of Black slave labor, often times Whites and Native Americans found themselves living and working in similar conditions.
7. Quoted in Hine and Thompson, *A Shining Thread of Hope*, 15.
8. For further discussion on the legislating slavery in Colonial America, see Conniff and Davis, *Africans in the Americas*. During the long, tedious, and arduous process of systematizing the institution of slavery, it was established early that White's could not legally be enslaved; quoted in Hine and Thompson, *A Shining Thread of Hope*, 16.
9. Quoted in Hine and Thompson, *A Shining Thread of Hope*, 16.
10. For further discussion see: Hine and Thompson, *A Shining Thread of Hope*; Conniff and Davis, *Africans in the Americas*.
11. For further discussion of the devastating impacts of slavery on motherhood, see: Hine and Thompson, *A Shining Thread of Hope*; hooks, *Ain't I a Woman*.
12. For further discussion see hooks, *Ain't I a Woman*.

13. For further discussion see Solinger, *Pregnancy and Power*.
14. Quoted in Davis, "Unfinished Lecture on Liberation—II, 53."
15. Quoted in Gomes and Williams, *From Exclusion to Inclusion*, 21.
16. For further discussion see Gomes and Williams, *From Exclusion to Inclusion*, 28.

Seven   Labor in the Industrial Age

1. Quoted in Giddings, *When and Where I Enter*, 47.
2. According to the 1860 U.S. Census, there were 3,933,587 slaves in the United States in 1860. Utilizing the method employed by the census to estimate population increase of slaves (at 21.9% for every ten years), an estimated 4,278,169 slaves, could have been freed by 1863. This number is excluding the expected increase in mortality rates due to the Civil War as well as the number of elderly, children, and infirmed who would not join the labor force.
3. Zeitlin, *Ideology and the Development of Sociological Theory*, 170.
4. Statistics cited from Jones, *Labor of Love, Labor of Sorrow*. For further discussion of Black women's economic position in the years following Emancipation see Jones, *Labor of Love, Labor of Sorrow*; for further discussion of the impact of the economy and social policy on Black women's reproduction see Roberts, *Killing the Black Body*.
5. Statistics on Black women's labor cited from Christian, "Introduction"; for further discussion of Black women's labor in early to mid-twentieth century see part 3's Further Readings.
6. For further discussion see Collins, *Black Feminist Thought*, Giddings, *When and Where I Enter*; hooks, *Ending Female Sexual Oppression*.

Eight   Becoming a Social Problem

1. Quoted in Foner, *A Short History of Reconstruction*, 145.
2. For more information of Sir Francis Galton (1822–1911), see: The Image Archives, "The American Eugenics Movement," Dolan Springs DNA Learning Center at the Cold Spring Harbor, Lab: http://webgiant.sdf1.org/carnivale/eugenics.html (accessed January 19, 2009); and Galton.org, "Francis Galton as Eugenicist," http://galton.org/ (accessed January 19, 2009).
3. For further discussion on the conception of Galtonian eugenics cf. Galton, *Inquiries into Human Faculty and Its Development*. For further discussion of the history of eugenics and its impact on racial inequality, see Ewan and Ewan, *Typecasting*.
4. For further discussion of the links between eugenics ideologies and compulsory sterilization programs see For further discussion of the links between eugenics ideologies and Nazi Germany see: Allen, "The ideology of Elimination"; and Black, *War Against the Weak*.
5. Quoted in Kline, *Building a Better Race*, 2.
6. Quoted in Kline, *Building a Better Race*, 3.
7. See Kline, *Building a Better Race*.
8. Quoted in Kline, *Building a Better Race*, 2.
9. Quoted in Kline, *Building a Better Race*, 2.
10. Quoted in Luker, *Dubious Conceptions*. 43.
11. Quoted in Luker, *Dubious Conceptions*. 43.
12. Quoted in Luker, *Dubious Conceptions*. 44.
13. Quoted in Davis, *Women, Race, & Class*, 213. For further discussion on famous eugenicists and financial contributors to eugenics movement see Black, *War Against the Weak*.

14. See Marx, *The Grundrisse*.
15. Quoted in Zeitlin, *Ideology and the Development of Sociological Theory*, 162.
16. Quoted in hooks, *Ain't I a Woman*, 23.
17. Positive eugenics encourages the reproduction of the so-called superior of the human race; while negative eugenics discourages the reproduction of the undesirables of the species. The distinction is significant, as negative eugenics has historically been used as a stepping stone towards scientific racism and genocide. For more on the history of eugenics see part 3's Further Readings.
18. Advertisers, carnivals, state fairs, schools, and more hold "fitter family" competitions, to determine who the healthiest families are. Eugenical health is only considered a characteristic of certain members of society.
19. Quoted in Coontz, *The Way We Really Are*, 39.
20. Dates are specified per the U.S. Census Bureau; the term *baby boom* is coined by a *New York Times* columnist in 1951: Sylvia Porter, "Babies Equal Boom," *New York Times*, May 4, 1951; the years of the so-called baby boom vary depending on perspective; as some assert that the era produced two distinct generations: Baby Boomers and Generation Jones. For more on these differing perspectives see: Noveck. "Welcome Obama, Bye-Bye Boomers"; Alter, "Twilight of the Baby Boom"; Wastell, "Generation Jones Comes of Age"; and Generation Jones, "Homepage."
21. As per the Postal Store. "Celebrate the Century. 1940s," United States Post Office, http://shop.usps.com/webapp/wcs/stores/servlet/ProductDisplay?catalogId=10152&storeId=10001&productId=16915&langId=-1&parent_category_rn=13382, (accessed September 14, 2008).
22. For more on the reimagining of the 1950s era see Coontz, *The Way We Never Were*.
23. Quoted in Coontz, *The Way We Really Are*, 36.
24. For more on the changes on the invention of the nuclear family and the encouragement of consumerism in the 1950s, see: Coontz, *The Way We Never Were* and Coontz, *The Way We Really Are*.
25. Quoted in Coontz, *The Way We Really Are*, 36.
26. Quoted in Coontz, *The Way We Really Are*, 39.
27. For more on social; political; and economic distinctions between White middle class reproduction and Black reproduction in the postwar period, see Solinger, *Wake Up Little Susie*.
28. For further discussion of race riots see Christian, "Introduction"; and Massey and Denton, *American Apartheid*.
29. Per the Bureau of Labor Statistics, "Economic News Release: Employment Situation Summary," U.S. Department of Labor, http://www.bls.gov/news.release/empsit.nr0.htm by December 2008 the national unemployment rate had risen from 6.7% in November 2008 to 7.2% in December. Per the Bureau of Labor Statistics, "Local Area Unemployment Statistics: Current Unemployment Rates for States and Historic Highs/Lows," U.S. Department of Labor, http://www.bls.gov/web/lauhsthl.htm, though some states are quickly approaching it, no states have reached their individual unemployment peaks, nor has the nation reached the 25% unemployment rate experienced at the height of the Great Depression; these rates remain the highest the majority of these states have seen in twenty five years or more. Over half of the states in the nation have unemployment rates above 6%; with some states, such as Rhode Island and Michigan above 9%. The national underemployment rate is at 12.5%. For further discussion of the historical context of the 2008 recession see Kristina Cowan's comment on "Unemployment during the Great Depression: Are We Getting Close?" The Salary Reporter Blog, comment posted December 18, 2008, http://blogs.payscale.com/salary_report_kris_cowan/2008/12/unemployment-during-the-great-depression-are-we-getting-close.html (accessed January 12, 2009); the subprime lending market is generally accepted as a significant factor in the late 2000s recession. It

is further commonly understood that the recipients of said loans are poorer working-class and "minority" borrowers. Many media reports, too numerous to cite here, have openly asserted that these *types* of people should never have been given loans in the first place and that their loans are responsible for the housing market crisis; Note—I typically refrain from the use of the term "minority"; as it is marginalizing and offensive. The term is utilized here as a representation of the language employed within the media.

Nine   Morons, Mental Defectives, Prostitutes, and Dope Fiends: Restrictive Reproductive Policies

1. The Hayes-Tilden compromise also known as the Compromise of 1877 is a reference to a political agreement between Samuel J. Tilden and Rutherford B. Hayes that decides the hotly contested 1876 presidential election. In an effort to win the election, Rutherford B. Hayes conceals an agreement with southern states to withdraw troops from the South if he is elected. This ends federal initiatives to establish civil rights for Blacks in the South and thus ends Reconstruction; for further discussion see: Gomes and Williams, *From Exclusion to Inclusion*; and Foner, *A Short History of Reconstruction*.
2. Statistical information in Gomes and Williams, *From Exclusion to Inclusion*.
3. Quoted in Foner, *A Short History of Reconstruction*, 137. For further discussions on reconstruction era, including differing views on the legacies of Reconstruction and the time frame of the era see part 3's Further Readings.
4. For further discussion on inequality and institutional exclusion see Gomes and Williams, *From Exclusion to Inclusion*. Though it is true that Black political participation has significantly suffered in the generations following Reconstruction, it should be noted that the landmark 2008 presidential campaign sees record Black participation. Barack Obama's victory sees the first Black man gain the democratic nomination and then successfully win the presidency in U.S. history, 131 years after the end of Reconstruction; 143 years after Emancipation; and 389 years after the first Blacks are sold at Jamestown.
5. See Foner, *A Short History of Reconstruction*; see also, Gomes and Williams, *From Exclusion to Inclusion*.
6. Quoted in Giddings, *When and Where I Enter*, 79.
7. Quoted in Gomes and Williams, *From Exclusion to Inclusion*, 24.
8. Foner, *A Short History of Reconstruction*, 146.
9. Foner, *A Short History of Reconstruction*, 146.
10. Foner, *A Short History of Reconstruction*.
11. See *Plessy v. Ferguson*, 163 U.S. 537 (1896); for further discussion of *Plessy v. Ferguson* see Rousseau, "Passing."
12. For further discussion see Gomes and Williams, *From Exclusion to Inclusion*.
13. For further discussion of the Black migration and labor see Rifkin, *The End of Work*.
14. Quoted in Giddings, *When and Where I Enter*, 79–80.
15. For further discussion of the changes in Black labor with the onset of industrialization see Rifkin, *The End of Work*.
16. Though compulsory sterilizations had begun twenty years before, the language cited here is the language used by Supreme Court justice Oliver Wendell Holmes, Jr., in the landmark decision *Buck v. Bell* that upholds eugenics-based compulsory sterilizations in the United States in 1927. This Supreme Court decision will underscore thousands upon thousands of compulsory sterilizations before the individual state laws are finally repealed. The final compulsory sterilizations are performed well into the 1980s. For further discussion see: Ewan and Ewan, *Typecasting*; and Black, *War against the Weak*.

17. Conceptualization of eugenics is illustrated through tree metaphor used as the logo at the Second International Congress of Eugenics in 1921. For image see, Image Archives of the American Eugenics Movement, "Eugenics Tree," Dolan Springs DNA Learning Center at the Cold Spring Harbor Lab, http://pirate.shu.edu/~vigorimi/genealogy/eugenics_tree. htm (accessed January 13, 2009); Quotation cited by right of public domain.

18. For further discussion of the overt racism exhibited by eugenics organizations in the United States see Black, *War against the Weak*.

19. Quoted in Davis, *Women, Race, & Class*, 214.

20. See Lombardo, "Eugenics Sterilization Laws." For map that illustrates proliferation of Eugenics-based sterilization laws in the United States in 1935, see, The Image Archives of the American Eugenics Movement, "Eugenics Map," Dolan Springs DNA Learning Center at the Cold Spring Harbor Lab, http://people.clarkson.edu/~postnl/HP201/Pictures%20 on%20Webpage/States%20with%20eugenics%20laws.jpg (accessed January 13, 2009).

21. For further discussion see Black, *War against the Weak*.

22. Quoted in Sanger, *Pivot of Civilization*, Appendix.

23. For further discussion see Davis, *Women, Race, & Class*.

24. Davis, *Women, Race, & Class*, 214.

25. For further discussion see Davis, *Women, Race, & Class*; Lombardo, "Eugenics Sterilization Laws."

26. For further discussion on impact of sterilization abuses on Latina women, see: Davis, *Women, Race, & Class*; Briggs, *Reproducing Empire*; and Findlay and Gilbert, *Imposing Decency*.

27. See Davis, *Women, Race, & Class*.

28. See Davis, *Women, Race, & Class*.

29. For further discussion see Green, *The Negro Project*.

30. For further discussion on Black women as sexually deviants see: Giddings, *When and Where I Enter*; Green, *The Negro Project*, Sharpley-Whiting, *Black Venus*; Simson, *The Afro-American Female*.

31. Quoted in Giddings, *When and Where I Enter*, 183.

32. Quoted in Davis, *Women, Race, & Class*, 217.

33. Quoted in Davis, *Women, Race, & Class*, 217.

34. For further discussion of sterilization abuse against Black girls and women in the twentieth century see Davis, *Women, Race, & Class*.

35. For further discussion of Margaret Sanger and her role in perpetuating coercive sterilization programs see Davis, *Women, Race, & Class*.

36. Quoted in Asbell, *The Pill*, 326.

37. For further discussion see Green, *The Negro Project*.

38. For further discussion of Sanger's views on exterminating Blacks see Davis, *Women, Race & Class*; for further discussion of Sanger's relationship to Black media see, Chesler, *Woman of Valor*.

Ten   Global Capitalism in the Electronic Age

1. For further discussion of the Great Migration and the labor pool see Rifkin, *The End of Work*.

2. For further discussion of the varied impacts of technology on unskilled labor, see Rifkin, *The End of Work*.

3. For further discussion of neoliberalism, see: Kiely, *The Clash of Globalisations; see also,* Harvey, *A Brief History of Neoliberalism*. For further discussion of the history of the U.S. economy see part 4's Further Readings.

4. For further discussion of neoliberalism and globalization, see: Harvey, *A Brief History of Neoliberalism*; see also Rupert and Smith, *Historical Materialism and Globalisation*; see also, Kiely, *The Clash of Globalisations*.
5. For further discussion of *war on terror* see part 4's Further Readings.
6. For further discussion of the events of Hurricane Katrina see part 4's Further Readings.

Eleven   Pathologizing the Black Woman

1. Quoted in White, *Too Heavy a Load*, 217.
2. For further discussion of so-called Black pathology see Moynihan, *The Negro Family*.
3. Quoted in White, *Too Heavy a Load*, 217.
4. Quoted in hooks, *Ain't I a Woman*, 59.
5. Quoted in Reagan, When *Abortion Was a Crime*, 230.
6. Quoted in Reagan, When *Abortion Was a Crime*, 230.
7. For further discussion see Reagan, *When Abortion Was a Crime*.
8. Quoted in Reagan, When *Abortion Was a Crime*, 230–231.
9. The Negro Project is a government funded program run by Margaret Sanger, cofounder of Planned Parenthood, that encouraged rural Black women and men to be sterilized in.
10. Quoted in Asbell, *The Pill*, 236.
11. Quoted in Asbell, *The Pill*, 236.
12. Quoted in Asbell, *The Pill*, 237.
13. For further discussion on the evolution of contraception see Asbell, *The Pill*; and Reagan, *When Abortion Was a Crime*. For more on the histories of contraception and reproductive rights in the United States see part 4's Further Readings.
14. Quoted in Ross, *African-American Women and Abortion*, 148.
15. Quoted in Ross, *African-American Women and Abortion*, 143.
16. Quoted in Ross, *African-American Women and Abortion*, 143.
17. For more information see documentary film Chana Gazit (Producer, Director, and Writer), *The Pill*.
18. For further discussion on *the underclass* see Wilson, *The Truly Disadvantaged*; for further discussion on the *culture of poverty* and the development of the underclass see part 4's Further Readings.
19. For further discussion of the impact of welfare and welfare reform on Black mothers, see: Roberts, *Killing the Black Body*; Solinger, *Wake Up Little Susie*; Albelda and Withorn, *Lost Ground*; and Neubeck, *Welfare Racism*; for more on the development of the child welfare industry see: Reich, *Fixing Families*.

Twelve   She's Out of Control:
Controlling Reproductive Policies

1. Quoted in Davis, *Women, Race, & Class*, 216.
2. Quoted in Davis, *Women, Race, & Class*, 216.
3. Quoted in Davis, *Women, Race, & Class*, 216.
4. These statistics are highly contestable, as though data was kept on the performed surgeries, as one might anticipate forced and coerced procedures are not recorded as such. There is effectively no way to determine for certain how many people were forcibly sterilized over the course of the twentieth century. For more information on statistics related to

court-mandated sterilizations see Roberts, *Killing the Black Body*; see also Chase, *The Legacy of Malthus*. For more on eugenics philosophies; Malthusian theories; and compulsory sterilization programs, see part 4's Further Readings.

5. Quoted in Solinger, *Wake Up Little Susie*, 57.
6. Quoted in Solinger, *Wake Up Little Susie*, 57.
7. For full text see Women's Liberation Movement: An On-line Archival Collection. "Poor Black Women," Special Collections Library, Duke University, http://scriptorium.lib.duke. edu/wlm/poor/ (accessed January 13, 2009).
8. Oral contraceptives had been approved for other uses by the FDA in 1957. The same drug is approved for contraceptive use in 1960; but not marketed as such until 1961. The use of oral contraceptives does not become accessible to married women in every state until the landmark legal case *Griswold v. Connecticut* in 1965; and remains inaccessible to all unmar-ried women until after the groundbreaking *Eisenstadt v. Baird* in 1972. See *Griswold v. Connecticut*, 381 U.S. 479 (1965); and *Eisenstadt v. Baird*, 405 U.S. 438 (1972); for further information on the decriminalization of abortion see *Roe v. Wade*, 410 U.S. 113 (1973).
9. Retrieved from Planned Parenthood Web site: http://www.plannedparenthood.org/pp2/ portal/medicalinfo/birthcontrol/.
10. For further discussion on contraception and population control see: Blank, *Fertility Control*; David and Sanderson, "Rudimentary Contraceptive Methods"; and Diepenbrock, *Gynecology and Textuality*.
11. For further discussion of abuses against women receiving welfare benefits, see: Solinger, *Wake Up Little Susie*; and Neubeck, *Welfare Racism*.
12. Quoted in Solinger, *Wake Up Little Susie*, 52.
13. Quoted in Solinger, *Wake Up Little Susie*, 53.
14. Quoted in Solinger, *Wake Up Little Susie*, 52.
15. For further discussion see Inciardi, Suratt, and Saum, *Cocaine-Exposed Infants*.
16. For further critical analysis of the child welfare industry see Roberts, *Killing the Black Body*; and Roberts, *Shattered Bonds*.
17. Child welfare statistics cited from Roberts, *Shattered Bonds*.

Thirteen   Vilifying Black Motherhood

1. For further critical analysis of the Black matriarchy thesis see Davis, "Reflections on the Black Woman's Role in the Community of Slaves."
2. For further discussion of the "underclass," see: Massey and Denton, *American Apartheid*; William Julius Wilson, *The Truly Disadvantaged*; see also, Lewis, "The Culture of Poverty. For a variety of perspectives on the creation of the underclass in the United States see part 4's Further Readings.
3. Controversial genetic testing of fetuses that in the future may allow parents to screen out undesirable traits. Geneticists could potentially bioengineer future generations made to order, with parents choosing eye and hair color, sex, even possibly height, weight, sexual orientation, and more. For more on genetic technologies see part 4's Further Readings.
4. Quoted in Roberts, *Killing the Black Body*, 3.
5. Quoted in Roberts, *Killing the Black Body*, 3; For more information see also Brewer et al., "Women Confronting Terror."
6. White, *Too Heavy a Load*, 237.
7. The cited statistics are taken from United States Department of Justice, "Prison and Jail Inmates at Midyear 2006"; for more on historical incarceration trends and on 2008 incar-ceration rates see part 4's Further Readings.

8. For further discussion of the role of racism in the prison industrial complex, see Davis, "Race and Criminalization."

9. For further discussion of the significance of technology in the prison industrial complex, see Davis, "Race and Criminalization."

Fourteen   Gettin' Your Tubes Tied: Coercive Reproductive Policies

1. For further discussion see White, *Too Heavy a Load*.
2. Davis, *Women, Race, & Class*, 204.
3. For further discussion of the welfare reform debate, see: Roberts, *Killing the Black Body*; and Albelda and Withorn, *Lost Ground*; and Neubeck, *Welfare Racism*. See also part 4's Further Readings.
4. For further discussion of welfare reform, see: Block et al., "The Compassion Gap in American Poverty Policy"; and Corcoran et al., "How Welfare Reform Is Affecting Women's Work."
5. For data on welfare participation see: Block et al., "The Compassion Gap in American Poverty Policy"; and Corcoran et al., "How Welfare Reform Is Affecting Women's Work."
6. Sterilization statistics are per the National Center for Disease Control and Prevention, "National Survey of Family Growth."
7. Sterilization statistics are per the National Center for Disease Control and Prevention, "National Survey of Family Growth"; demographic statistics are per the 2004 U.S. Census.
8. National Center for Health Statistics, "Use of Contraception."
9. For full Web site see Dominic Marchiano, M.D., "Sterilization," www.saludchicago.com (accessed January 18, 2009).
10. For further discussion see: Grubb et al., "Regret after Decision to Have a Tubal Sterilization"; and Wilcox, Chu, Eaker, Zeger, and Peterson, "Risk factors for Regret after Tubal Sterilization."
11. For further discussion of characteristics associated with remorse after sterilization procedure, see: Grubb et al., "Regret after Decision to Have a Tubal Sterilization"; Allyn et al., "Presterilization Counseling and Women's Regret about Having Been Sterilized"; and Wilcox et al., "Risk Factors for Regret after Tubal Sterilization."
12. Project C.R.A.C.K. (Children Requiring a Caring Kommunity) ; as of July 25, 2008, the organization reports paying 2,546 clients for the following: long term chemical sterilization (approximately 42%) i.e., Depo-Provera; long term implantation devices (approximately 3%), i.e., Implanon and Norplant; contraceptive barriers (approximately 17%), i.e., Intrauterine Device (IUD); as well as permanent surgical sterilization (approximately 37%), i.e., vasectomy and tubal ligation.
13. Quoted at www.projectprevention.org.
14. According to their Web site, Project Prevention, "Objectives," Project Prevention, http://www.projectprevention.org/cause/objectives.html:
   …Project Prevention seeks to reduce the burden of this social problem on taxpayers, trim social worker caseloads, and alleviate from our clients the burden of having children that will potentially be taken away. Unlike incarceration, Project Prevention [is] extremely cost effective and does not punish the participants.
15. Approximately 1% of paid clients were male from 1997 to July 25, 2008. These 29 clients all received permanent surgical sterilization—vasectomies.

16. As of fall 2008, per their Web site, Project Prevention, "Home Page," Project Prevention, www.projectprevention.org, Project C.R.A.C.K. now refers to itself as Project Prevention: Children Requiring a Caring Community. However, after more than a decade as Project C.R.A.C.K., this change only appears on their Web site—all media references, documentation, and organizational propaganda still references *Project CRACK.*

17. As evidenced by FAQ #3 posted on their Web site, Project Prevention, "Frequently Asked Questions," Project Prevention, http://www.projectprevention.org/program/faqs.html:
    3. Are you targeting blacks? It is racist, or at least ignorant, for someone to learn about Project Prevention and assume that only black addicts (or minorities) will be calling us. The reality is, not all drug addicts are black. Project Prevention targets a behavior not a racial demographic.

18. Statistics are from Office of Applied Studies, "National Survey on Drug Use and Health Report," Substance Abuse and Mental Health Services Administration.

19. Of Project CRACK's 2,546 paid clients, 42.5% were Caucasian; 28.5% were African American; 12.75% were Hispanic; and 16.25% were listed as other ethnic backgrounds. This 16.25% listed as other is of particular interest. As a category already exists for "white," it is evident that the 16.25% "other" are nonwhite; changing the statistics significantly, making nearly 60% of their clients People of Color.

20. According to WGAL out of Harrisburg, PA, "Group Offers Addicts Cash For Sterilization," July 13, 2007, http://www.wgal.com/news/13679726/detail.html (accessed September 26, 2008).

21. For further discussion of LaBruzzo's tentative sterilization plan see: Waller, "LaBruzzo: Sterilization Plan Fights Poverty."; Webster, "Metairie Lawmaker Considers Bill to Fund Sterilizations"; and Baram "Pol Suggests Paying Poor Women to Tie Tubes."

22. David Duke, previous Grand Wizard of the Ku Klux Klan, was the elected representative of Metairie, LA, from 1989 to 1992. His bill was eventually defeated.

23. As per a telephone interview with the author that took place November 19, 2008; throughout the interview, LaBruzzo made repeated references to "us," "them," and "these people." When questioned about who "these people" are, he scoffs, claiming this interviewer is clear about who "they" are. It is this interviewer's understanding that LaBruzzo attempts to delineate between a working, middle, and upper class population, considered moderately to extremely successful, by capitalistic standards and a poorer class, reliant on public assistance. Though he insists that this is a purely economic division, his comments repeatedly reinforce racial stereotypes.

24. During the November interview, LaBruzzo recounted tales of Black women on welfare, colleagues of his had allegedly encountered. One woman supposedly claimed that she was teaching her young daughter the welfare process because she was expected to get pregnant soon and would therefore need the services. LaBruzzo also spoke at length of young girls getting pregnant to help their families financially. He surmised that having a baby for "people like us," means reevaluating our budget, while having a baby for "these people," means an increase in household income. LaBruzzo insists that this potential increase of only $50–$200 per month is enough incentive for girls and women to actually plan unwed teen pregnancies and have babies strictly for the money.

25. According to LaBruzzo his district is "3 percent minority," however, other statistics report that District 81 is 85% White, rather than 97%.

26. Countless media sources have questioned the application of facts in Coulter's works over the years. For more on Ann Coulter's misapplication of data and use of dubious statistical sources in her writings see: Scherer and Secules, "Books: How Slippery Is *Slander?*"; see also, Nyhan, comment on "Screed,"; for more on Ann Coulter's denial of racist foundations of *Guilty* cf.: Ann Coulter, comment on "Answering My Critics"; cf. *The View.*

27. Statistics cited from U.S. Department of Justice, "Prisoners at Midyear 2007"; and U.S. Department of Justice, "Parents in Prison and Their Minor Children."

Fifteen   Rationalizing Commodification

1. For further discussion of Black middle class see Feagin and Sikes, *Living With Racism*; Frazier, *Black Bourgeoisie*; and Pattillo-McCoy, *Black Picket Fences*. As the subject of this book is primarily Black women's labor, I have opted not to focus directly on the Black middle class, but instead to examine the poorer and working class experience. I do, however, contend that class status does not exclude the Black middle class from labor exploitation and abuse. No manner of class, status, or power can overcome the forces of production; social rhetoric; and reproductive policies that plague Black women of all classes.

2. For further discussion of the links between Nazi genocide programs and American eugenics see: Allen, "The ideology of Elimination"; and Black, *War against the Weak*.

Sixteen   Justifying Commodification

1. The term *tool of oppression* is both an homage and a reference to Audre Lorde's sharp and insightful analysis of the manipulation and control of Black women through assaults on reproductive freedoms, i.e. lack of access to abortion and compulsory sterilization, being employed as a tool of oppression against Black women. Lorde likened this abuse to rape. Within this text the use of the term is specifically related to media, which I believe has played a significant role in applying the tools of oppression referred to by Lorde. For further discussion of *Tools of Oppression* concept, see Lorde, *Sister Outsider*.

2. Marx and Engels, *The Communist Manifesto*.

3. Quoted in Berberoglu, *An Introduction to Classical and Contemporary Sociology*, 63.

4. For further discussion see Hack, *Clash of the Titans*.

5. For further discussion see Wolff, *The Man Who Owns the News*; and Greenwald and Kitty, *Outfoxed*.

6. For more information see Collins and Yeskel, *Economic Apartheid in America*.

7. Collins and Yeskel, *Economic Apartheid in America*, 4

8. Quoted in Coontz, *The Way We Really Are*, 26–27.

9. Quoted in Freire, *Pedagogy of the Oppressed*, 31.

10. Quoted in Freire, *Pedagogy of the Oppressed*, 28.

11. Quoted in Freire, *Pedagogy of the Oppressed*, 28.

Seventeen   Critiquing Commodification:
Connecting to Historical Womanism

1. The conceptualization of *consciousness, vision, and strategy* is well defined in Fishman, Gomes, and Scott, "Materialism." For further discussion of dialectical and historical materialist theories, see Further Readings.

2. Quoted in Berberoglu, *An Introduction to Classical and Contemporary Social Theory*, 15–16.

3. See Fishman, Gomes, and Scott, "Materialism."

4. For specific definition of *superstructure*, see Key Concepts and Definitions.
5. For further discussion see Marx, *Capital*. For more on the impact of capitalism on Black women's sexuality see Dickerson and Rousseau, "Black Senior Women and Sexuality"; Dickerson and Rousseau, "Ageism through Omission."
6. For further discussion see Zaretsky, *Capitalism, the Family, and Personal Life*.
7. For more on the impact of social policy on private life, see: Dickerson and Rousseau, "Black Senior Women and Sexuality"; Dickerson and Rousseau, "Ageism through Omission."
8. For further discussion of *consciousness, vision, and strategy, see* Fishman, Gomes, and Scott, "Materialism."

KEY CONCEPTS AND
DEFINITIONS

This research utilizes several major theoretical concepts at various points of the analysis. The following is a list of definitions of these theoretical terms and concepts.

Alienation: As Marx contends that the system of capitalism dehumanizes the wage laborer; he further asserts that the wage laborer is alienated from his/her very humanity by being forced to trade his/her labor for survival, and in the process reduced to an *instrument of production,* rather than an active member of the production process.

Commodification: This research conceptualizes commodification as the process of objectifying and compartmentalizing a given variable, in this case, Black women's labor, for the purposes of maximizing profit. Any element that is established as a means by which to gain money, capital, or power through its exploitation, control, and/or manipulation is commodified. This term does not solely reference making money. As, once identified as a means to maximize profit, i.e., objectified as *ownable* property that can be bought, sold, or traded, e.g., Black labor; the element forever remains commodified—even if it loses economic value.

Labor: This research acknowledges three types of labor in reference to Black women in the United States: Biological; Physical (or Manual); and Reproductive.

Biological Labor. Reference to the act of propagation. By reproducing Blacks, Black women also reproduce a significant percentage of the American wage labor pool.

Physical or Manual Labor. Reference to the dialectical and historical materialist definition of "labor," as the production of the worker—of the subjugated class—forced to trade his/her productivity for sub-sistence level pay (such as field labor and factory labor)—though in the case of Black women in the United States, as an enslaved people forced to work, their labor went uncompensated.

Reproductive Labor: Historically a reference to what is commonly known as "women's work." For the purposes of this book, "repro-ductive labor includes activities such as purchasing household goods, preparing and serving food, laundering and repairing clothes, main-taining furnishings and appliances, socializing children, providing care and emotional support for adults, and maintaining kin and community ties."[1] As demonstrated in Glenn's definition, the physi-cal action of biological reproduction has been (seemingly) purpose-fully excluded, presumably to accentuate the human-made gendered division of labor.[2]

Neoliberalism: A set of economic philosophies that favor as little government as possible within a free market economy. Neoliberal policies are pro-capitalist and favor deregulation/privatization poli-cies. Neoliberalism fundamentally opposes government intervention. *Neoliberalism* is reinvention of the liberal capitalism of early America, and has re-emerged as a backlash to the brief period of New Deal reform policies and bottom up popular movements that empower the working classes and impact capitalist profit.

Policy: For the purposes of this research, the term policy is to be loosely defined as both local, city, state, and federal legislation; as well as common practice and procedure. For example, children born to enslaved Black women are relegated to "follow the condition of the mother" in Virginia in 1662. This is a clear legal policy instituted by state government. An example of a more loosely defined policy of the period would be the common practice of demanding more money for the sale of women of childbearing age.

Political Economy: The social, political, and economic variables related to the superstructure.

Production Elements:

Means of Production. The means by which production occurs, "the land, forests, waters, mineral resources, raw materials, instruments of production, production premises, means of transportation and com-munication, etc."[3]

Instrument of Production. The means by which products are created—tools, technology, as well as human and animal labor.

Forces of Production. This term is a historical reference to the labor process at the point of production, i.e. the factory, further defined by Berberoglu, "Through time, humans created and developed tools, skills, knowledge, and work habits—in short, *the forces of production*—to an extent that permitted, for the first time, the accumulation of surplus."[4] In short, the technology behind the production of goods and services.

Relations of Production. "With the development of social classes and class inequality, there emerged historically specific social *relations of production,* or class relations, between those who produced surplus and those who claimed ownership and control of that surplus of that surplus (e.g., slaves vs. masters; serfs vs. landlords; wage laborers vs. capitalists)."[5]

Modes of Production. "Marx and Engels pointed out that the forces of production (including the labor process at the point of production) and the social relations of production (class relations) together constitute a society's *mode of production,* or its social-economic foundation, defined as the way in which a society's wealth is produced and distributed—in short, the social-economic system (e.g., slavery, feudalism, capitalism)."[6]

Social Rhetoric: This term is a negative application of an externally produced narrative concerning a population. Often this rhetorical narrative is created with little to no input from members of the given group, yet comes to define the group. More salient than a stereotype in that it does not simply exaggerate specific fantastical characteristics of the population, rather it is used to define, explain, and understand the group. Typically not rooted in fact, but in justifying the mistreatment of a population, social rhetoric is purposefully employed to control the group it alludes to and to manipulate the masses it is directed toward. As Aristotle critiqued the establishment of social rhetoric in a given population, "The arousing of prejudice, pity, anger, and similar emotions has nothing to do with the essential facts, but is merely a personal appeal to the man who is judging the case."[7] Social rhetoric is disseminated throughout society by various far reaching methods. Some means of distribution include: educational institutions; music; television; films; comic strips; novels; advertising; as well as oral traditions.

This social rhetoric can lead to an unearned national identity. This identity is dynamic as it changes as the narrative does.

Stages of Capitalism in the United States:

Agricultural. From the 1500s to 1865, this stage is characterized by the development of the southern plantation economy that exploited Black (African) slave labor. Upon the dissolution of slavery in 1863, and the consequent emancipation proclamation of 1865, the South—and in turn the United States—struggled for over ten years to rebuild the southern region and integrate Blacks into United States society (Reconstruction) in the aftermath of the Civil War.

Industrial. The earliest stages of the Industrial era began in the last decades of the Agricultural era, as the efforts to increase agricultural production is a great incentive to technological advancement. The efforts to increase agricultural production lead to the development of Eli Whitney's *Cotton Gin* in 1793. Credited by some historians as facilitating the birth of the *Industrial Revolution* in the United States; according to the Smithsonian National Museum of American History, Whitney's Cotton Gin increases cotton production from 187,000 pounds in 1793 to a staggering six million pounds in 1795. Over the next few years Whitney continues to improve upon his original design by incorporating the use of steam power. The mechanization of cotton production in the South then leads to the establishment of factories throughout New England in the early 1800s. The Industrial Age continues as technological advancement leads to even more inventions over the next century, including: the Mechanical Spinner, Power Loom, and the Cotton Picking machine. The United States establishes itself as a world superpower during the Industrial Age as the nation corners the market on various types of production, including textiles and raw materials, such as rice, grain, tobacco, and lumber and steel used to rebuild the infrastructure and superstructure of Europe after the devastation of World War II.

Electronic. From the 1970s to the present, this stage is characterized by the onset of the use of the computer chip for mass production. "The global integration of the economy; the high technology revolution; the downsizing of corporations, the government, and social institutions; and deregulation and privatization...."[8]

Superstructure. The superstructure is comprised of the State, economic and political institutions, and the bureaucratic structures that support them.[9] "Once a class society emerges—in which the production process is firmly established, a surplus is generated, and social classes have developed—the relations of production (or class relations) become the decisive element defining the nature of the dominant mode of production, which in turn gives rise to the political *superstructure*, including first and foremost the State, as well as other political and ideological institutions that serve the interests of the propertied classes in society. Thus the superstructure arises from and becomes a reflection of the dominant mode of production, which reinforces the existing social order..."[10]

Notes

1. Quoted in Glenn, "Racial Ethnic Women's," 405.
2. For further discussion see Marx and Engels, *Selected Works*.
3. Quoted in Stalin, *History of the Communist Party*, 32–33.
4. Quoted in Berberoglu, *An Introduction to Classical and Contemporary Social Theory*, 11.
5. Quoted in Berberoglu, *An Introduction to Classical and Contemporary Social Theory*, 12.
6. Quoted in Berberoglu, *An Introduction to Classical and Contemporary Social Theory*, 12.
7. Quoted in Aristotle, *The Rhetoric, Book I [1354a]*.
8. Quoted in Scott and Katz-Fishman, *The South and the Black Radical Tradition*, 74.
9. For further discussion see Berberoglu, *An Introduction to Classical and Contemporary Social Theory*.
10. Quoted in Berberoglu, *An Introduction to Classical and Contemporary Social Theory*, 13.

REFERENCES

Albelda, Randy and Ann Withorn (Eds.). *Lost Ground: Welfare Reform, Poverty, and Beyond.* Cambridge, MA: South End Press, 2002.

Allen, Garland E. "The Ideology of Elimination: American und German Eugenics, 1900–1945." In *Medicine and Medical Ethics in Nazi Germany: Origins, Practices, Legacies,* ed. Francis R. Nicosia, pp. 13–39. New York: Berghahn Books, 2002.

Allyn, D.P., D.A. Leton, N.A. Westcott, and R.W. Hale, "Presterilization Counseling and Women's Regret About Having Been Sterilized." In *Journal of Reproductive Medicine* 11: pp. 1027–1032, November 1986.

Alter, Jonathan. "Twilight of the Baby Boom: A Generational Struggle Is Underway. What's So Unusual Is It's Taking Place in a Single Generation." *Newsweek,* February 11, 2008.

Aristotle. *Nicomachean Ethics (Book I: 1095A, 1095B, 1096A, 1143B).*

Aronowitz, Stanley and William DiFazio. *The Jobless Future: Sci-Tech and the Dogma of Work.* Minneapolis: University of Minnesota Press, 1994.

Asbell, Bernard. *The Pill: A Biography of the Drug that Changed the World.* New York: Random House, 1995.

Baram, Marcus. "Pol Suggests Paying Poor Women to Tie Tubes." *ABC News,* September 25, 2008. Online edition, http://abcnews.go.com/US/story?id=5886592&page=1 (accessed September 26, 2008).

Barret, Michéle. *Women's Oppression Today: Problems in Marxist Feminist Analysis.* London: Verso, 1980.

Bennett, Gwendolyn B. "To a Dark Girl." In *Black Sister: Poetry by Black American Women, 1746–1980,* ed. Erlene Stetson, p. 76. Bloomington: Indiana University Press, 1981.

Berberoglu, Berch. *An Introduction to Classical and Contemporary Social Theory: A Critical Perspective.* New York: General Hall, 1998.

Black, Edwin. *War against the Weak: Eugenics and America's Campaign to Create a Master Race.* New York: Four Walls Eight Windows, 2003.

Blank, Robert H. *Fertility Control: New Techniques, New Policy Issues.* New York: Greenwood Press, 1991.

Block, Fred, Anna C. Korteweg, Kerry Woodward, Zack Schiller, and Imrul Mazid. "The Compassion Gap in American Poverty Policy." In *Contexts,* 5(2): pp. 14–20, 2006.

Briggs, Laura. *Reproducing Empire: Race Sex, Science, and U.S. Imperialism in Puerto Rico.* Berekley: University of California Press, 2002.

Brewer, Rose, Walda M. Katz-Fishman, Bahati Kuumba, and Nicole Rousseau. "Women Confronting Terror: Land, Labor, Power, and Our Bodies." In *The Roots of Terror,* second ed. Atlanta, GA: Project South: Institute for the Elimination of Poverty and Genocide, 2004.

Brodie, Janet Farrell. *Contraception and Abortion in Nineteenth-Century America*. Ithaca, NY: Cornell University Press, 1994.

Browne, Martha. *Autobiography of a Female Slave*. Miami, FL: Mnemosyne, 1969.

Bullough, Vern L., Brenda Shelton, and Sarah Slavin. *The Subordinated Sex: A History of Attitudes toward Women*. Athens: University of Georgia Press, 1988.

Bureau of Labor Statistics. "Economic News Release: Employment Situation Summary," U.S. Department of Labor, http://www.bls.gov/news.release/empsit.nr0.htm (accessed January 12, 2009).

———. "Local Area Unemployment Statistics: Current Unemployment Rates for States and Historic Highs/Lows," U.S. Department of Labor, http://www.bls.gov/web/lauhsthl.htm. (accessed January 12, 2009).

Bynum, Victoria. *Unruly Women: The Politics of Social and Sexual Control in the Old South*. Chapel Hill: University of North Carolina Press, 1992.

Chase, Allen. *The Legacy of Malthus: The Social Costs of the New Scientific Racism*. New York: Knopf, 1977.

Chesler, Ellen. *Woman of Valor: Margaret Sanger and the Birth Control Movement in America*. New York: Simon and Schuster, 1992.

Christian, Barbara. "Introduction." In *Black Foremothers: Three Lives*, second edition, ed. Dorothy Sterling, xxi–xliii New York: Feminist Press at The City University of New York, 1988.

Code, Lorraine. "How Do We Know? Questions of Method in Feminist Practice." In *Changing Methods: Feminists Transforming Practice*, ed. Sandra Burt and Lorraine Code, pp. 13–44. Orchard Park, NY: Broadview Press, 1995.

Coffin, Judith and Robert Stacey. *Western Civilizations: Their History & Their Culture*. New York: W.W. Norton, 2005.

Collins, Chuck and Felice Yeskel, with United for a Fair Economy and Class Action. *Economic Apartheid in America: A Primer on Economic Inequality and Insecurity*, revised and updated edition. New York: New Press, 2005.

Collins, Patricia Hill. "What's in a Name? Womanism, Black Feminism, and Beyond." In *The Womanist Reader*, ed. Layli Phillips, pp. 57–68. New York: Taylor & Francis, 2006 [1996].

———. *Black Feminist Thought: Knowledge, Consciousness, and the Politics of Empowerment*. New York: Routledge Press, 1990.

Conniff, Michael L. and Thomas J. Davis. *Africans in the Americas: A History of the Black Diaspora*. New York: St. Martin's Press, 1994.

Coontz, Stephanie. *The Way We Really Are: Coming to Terms with America's Changing Families*. New York: Basic Books, 1997.

———. *The Way We Never Were: American Families and the Nostalgia Trap*. New York: Basic Books, 1992.

Corcoran, Mary, Sandra Danziger, Ariel Kalil, and Kristin S. Seefeldt. "How Welfare Reform is Affecting Women's Work." In *Annual Review of Sociology* 26: pp. 241–269, 2000.

Cox, Oliver. *Caste Class and Race*. New York: Monthly Review Press, 1959.

———. *Capitalism as a System*. New York: Monthly Review Press, 1964.

Crenshaw, Kimberle Williams. "Mapping the Margins: Intersectionality, Identity Politics, and Violence Against Women of Color." In *Critical Race Theory: The Key Writings that Formed the Movement*, ed. Kimberle Williams Crenshaw, Neil Gotanda, Garry Peller, and Kendall Thomas, pp. 357–383. New York: New Press, 1996.

Crenshaw, Kimberle Williams, Neil Gotanda, Garry Peller, and Kendall Thomas (Eds.). *Critical Race Theory: The Key Writings that Formed the Movement*. New York: New Press 1996.

Darwin, Charles. *The Origin of Species: By Means of Natural Selection or the Preservation of Favoured Races in the Struggle for Life*. New York: NAL Penguin Books, 1958.

David, Paul A. and Warren C. Sanderson. "Rudimentary Contraceptive Methods and the American Transition to Marital Fertility Control." In *Long Term Factors in American Economic Growth*, ed. Stanley L. Engerman and Robert E. Gallman, pp. 307–390. Chicago, IL: University of Chicago Press, 1986.

Davis, Angela Y. "Race and Criminalization: Black Americans and the Punishment Industry." In *The Angela Y. Davis Reader*, ed. Joy James, pp. 60–73. Malden, MA: Blackwell, 1998.

———. "Surrogates and Outcast Mothers: Racism and Reproductive Politics in the Nineties." In *The Angela Y. Davis Reader*, ed. Joy James, pp. 210–221. Malden, MA: Blackwell, 1998.

———. "Women and Capitalism: Dialectics of Oppression and Liberation." In *The Angela Y. Davis Reader*, ed. Joy James, pp. 161–192. Malden, MA: Blackwell, 1998.

———. "Reflections on the Black Woman's Role in the Community of Slaves." In *The Angela Y. Davis Reader*, ed. Joy James, pp. 111–128. Malden, MA: Blackwell, 1998.

———. "Unfinished Lecture on Liberation—II." In *The Angela Y. Davis Reader*, ed. Joy James, pp. 53–60. Malden, MA: Blackwell, 1998.

———. *Women, Race, & Class*. New York: Vintage Books, 1983.

Dickerson, Bette J. and Nicole Rousseau. "Black Senior Women and Sexuality." In *Black Sexualities: Probing Powers, Passions, Practices, and Policies*, ed. Sandra Barnes and Juan Battle. Piscataway, NJ: Rutgers University Press, Forthcoming.

———. "Ageism through Omission: The Obsolescence of Black Women's Sexuality." In *Journal of African American Studies*, ed. Anthony Lemelle, Forthcoming.

Diepenbrock, Chloé. *Gynecology and Textuality: Popular Representations of Reproductive Technology*. New York: Garland, 1998.

Edghill, V. "Historical Patterns of Institutional Diversity: Black Women in Race-Specific Positions on Predominantly White College Campuses." Ph.D. diss., Howard University, 2007.

Ewan, Elizabeth and Stuart Ewan. *Typecasting: On the Arts & Sciences of Human Inequality*. New York: Seven Stories Press, 2008.

Feagin, Joe R. and Melvin P. Sikes. *Living with Racism: The Black Middle Class Experience*. Boston, MA: Beacon Press Books, 1994.

Findlay, Eileen and Joseph Gilbert. *Imposing Decency: The Politics of Sexuality and Race in Puerto Rico, 1870–1920 (American Encounters/Global Interactions)*. Durham, NC: Duke University Press, 1999.

Firestone, Shulamith. *The Dialectic of Sex: The Case for Feminist Revolution*. New York: William Morrow, 1970.

Fishman, Walda Katz, Ralph C. Gomes, and Jerome Scott. "Materialism." In *Blackwell Encyclopedia of Sociology*, second edition, ed. George Ritzer, Vol. VI, pp. 2836–2839. Oxford: Blackwell, 2006.

Foner, Eric. *A Short History of Reconstruction, 1863–1877*. New York: Harper & Row, 1990.

Frazier, E. Franklin. *Black Bourgeoisie: The Book that Brought the Shock of Self-Revelation to Middle-Class Blacks in America*. New York: Free Press, 1957.

Freire, Paulo. *Pedagogy of the Oppressed*, new revised edition. New York: Continuum, 1998.

Galton, Francis. *Inquiries in Human Faculty and Its Development*. London: MacMillan, 1883.

Galton.org. "Francis Galton as Eugenicist," http://galton.org/. Accessed May 27, 2009.

Generation Jones, "Homepage," Generation Jones, http://generationjones.com/2008election.html (accessed January 13, 2009).

Giddings, Paula. *When and Where I Enter: The Impact of Black Women on Race and Sex in America*. New York: Perennial, 2001.

Gillham, Nicholas Wright. "Sir Francis Galton and the Birth of Eugenics." In *Annual Review of Genetics* 35: pp. 83–101, 2001.

Gillham, Nicholas Wright. *A Life of Sir Francis Galton: From African Exploration to the Birth of Eugenics.* New York: Oxford University Press, 2001.

Glenn, Evelyn Nakano. "Racial Ethnic Women's Labor: The Intersection of Race, Gender and Class Oppression." In *Review of Radical Political Economy* 17: pp. 86–108, 1985.

————. "From Servitude to Service Work: Historical Continuities in the Racial Division of Paid Reproductive Labor." In *Unequal Sisters: A Multicultural Reader in U.S. Women's History,* second edition., ed. Vicki L. Ruiz and Ellen Carol Dubois, pp. 405–435. New York: Routledge Press, 1994.

Gomes, Ralph C. and Linda F. Williams (Eds). *From Exclusion to Inclusion: The Long Struggle for African American Political Power.* Westport, CT: Praeger, 1995.

Goode, William Josiah and Paul K. Hatt. *Methods in Social Research.* New York: McGraw-Hill, 1952.

Green, Tanya L. "The Negro Project: Margaret Sanger's Eugenic Plan for Black Americans." Fayetteville, NC: Life Education and Resource Network, 2004.

Greenwald, Robert and Alexandra Kitty. *Outfoxed: Rupert Murdoch's War on Journalism.* New York: Disinformation, 2005.

Grubb, G.S., H.B. Peterson, P.M. Layde, and G.L. Rubin, "Regret after Decision to Have a Tubal Sterilization." In *Fertility and Sterility* 44 (2): pp. 248–253, August 1985.

Hack, Richard. *Clash of the Titans: How the Unbridled Ambition of Ted Turner and Rupert Murdoch Has Created Global Empires that Control What We Read and Watch.* Leeds, NY: New Millennium, 2003.

Hancock, Ange-Marie. *The Politics of Disgust: The Public Identity of the Welfare Queen.* New York: New York University Press, 2004.

Harvey, David. *A Brief History of Neoliberalism.* New York: Oxford University Press, 2007.

Hill, Robert B. *The Strengths of Black Families.* New York: Astoria Press, 1972.

Hine, Darlene Clark and Kathleen Thompson. *A Shining Thread of Hope: The History of Black Women in America.* New York: Broadway Books, 1998.

hooks, bell. *Ain't I a Woman: Black Women and Feminism.* Boston, MA: South End Press, 1981.

————. "Ending Female Sexual Oppression." In *Feminist Theory: From the Margin to Center,* pp. 147–156. Boston, MA: South End Press, 1984.

Image Archives, The. "The American Eugenics Movement," Dolan Springs DNA Learning Center at the Cold Spring Harbor, Lab: http://webgiant.sdf1.org/carnivale/eugenics.html. Accessed May 27, 2009.

Inciardi, James, Hilary L. Surratt, and Christine Saum. *Cocaine-Exposed Infants: Social, Legal, and Public Health Issues.* Thousand Oaks, CA: Sage, 1997.

Jacobs, Harriet. *Incidents in the Life of a Slave Girl: Written by Herself.* Cambridge, MA: Harvard University Press, 1987.

Jewell, K. Sue. *From Mammy to Miss America and Beyond: Cultural Images and the Shaping of US Social Policy.* New York: Routledge, 1993.

Jewish World Review: News and Opinion Blog, The. http://www.jewishworldreview.com/. Accessed May 27, 2009.

Jones, Jacqueline. *Labor of Love, Labor of Sorrow: Black Women, Work and the Family, from Slavery to Present,* second edition. New York: Vintage Books, 1995.

Kerlinger, Fred N. *Foundations of Behavioral Research,* third edition. New York: Holt, Rinehart & Winston, 1986.

Kiely, Ray. *The Clash of Globalisations: Neo-liberalism, the Third Way and Anti-Globalisation.* Leiden, The Netherlands: Martinus Nijhoff and VSP, 2005.

Kline, Wendy. *Building a Better Race: Gender, Sexuality, and Eugenics from the Turn of the Century to the Baby Boom.* Berkeley, CA: Berkeley University Press, 2001.

Kollontai, Alexandra. *Sexual Relations and the Class Struggle*, translated by Alix Holt. New York: Falling Wall Press, 1972 [1921].

———. "Towards a History of the Working Women's Movement in Russia," in *Selected Writings of Alexandra Kollontai*, trans. and ed. Alix Holt. London: Allison and Busby, 1977.

Kuypers, Jim A. *Bush's War: Media Bias and Justifications for War in a Terrorist Age.* Rowman & Littlefield, 2006.

Lenin, Vladimir I. *The State and Revolution.* Whitefish, MT: Kessinger. 2004 [1918].

Lerner, Gerda. *Black Women in White America: A Documentary History.* New York: Vintage Books, 1972.

Lombardo, Paul. "Eugenics Sterilization Laws." In *Image Archive on the American Eugenics Movement.* Cold Spring Harbor, NY: DDLCCSH Laboratory, 2005.

Lorde, Audre. *Sister Outsider.* Berkeley, CA: Crossing Press, 2007 [1984].

Luker, Kristin. *Dubious Conceptions: The Politics of Teenage Pregnancy.* Cambridge, MA: Harvard University Press, 1996.

Marx, Karl. *Capital: A Critique of Political Economy.* Germany: Charles H. Kerr, 1906.

———. *The Grundrisse.* Ed. and trans. David McLellan. New York: Harper and Row, 1971.

Marx, Karl, and Friedrich Engels. *Selected Works*, Vol. 1. Moscow: Progress, 1969.

———. *The Communist Manifesto.* New York: Bantam Books, 1992.

Massey, Doug and Nancy Denton. *American Apartheid: Segregation and the Making of the Underclass.* Cambridge, MA: Harvard University Press, 1998.

Mies, Maria. *Patriarchy and Accumulation on a World Scale: Women in the International Division of Labour.* New York: Zed Books, 1998.

Moynihan, Daniel P. *"The Negro Family: The Case for National Action."* Washington, DC: U.S. Department of Labor, 1965.

Nabokov, Peter (Ed.). *Native American Testimony: A Chronicle of Indian-White Relations from Prophecy to the Present, 1492–1992.* New York: Penguin Books, 1992.

Nagel, Joane. *Race, Ethnicity, and Sexuality: Intimate Intersections, Forbidden Frontiers.* New York: Oxford University Press, 2004.

National Center for Health Statistics. "Use of Contraception and Use of Family Planning Service in the United States: 1982–2002". Hyattsville, MD: National Center for Health Statistics, 2002.

———. "Health, United States, with Chartbook on Trends in the Health of Americans." In *Centers for Disease Control and Prevention, National Center for Health Statistics, National Survey of Family Growth.* Hyattsville, MD: National Center for Health Statistics, 2004.

Neubeck, Kenneth. *Welfare Racism: Playing the Race Card against America's Poor.* New York: Rutledge Press, 2001.

Neumann, William Lawrence. *Social Research Methods.* Needham Heights, MA: Allyn and Bacon, 1991.

Noveck, Jocelyn. "Welcome Obama, Bye-Bye Boomers: With a New Administration, Many See an End to an Era." *The Chicago Tribune*, January 11, 2009, Online edition, http://www.chicagotribune.com/news/politics/sns-ap-obama-bye-bye-boomers,0,2932352.story (accessed January 13, 2009).

Office of Applied Studies, Substance Abuse and Mental Health Services Administration. "National Survey on Drug Use and Health Report." October 2007.

Pattillo-McCoy, Mary. *Black Picket Fences: Privilege and Peril among the Black Middle Class.* Chicago, IL: University of Chicago Press, 1999.

Phillips, Layli. "Womanism: On Its Own." In *The Womanist Reader*, ed. Layli Phillips, xix–lv. New York: Taylor & Francis, 2006.

——— (Ed.). *The Womanist Reader.* New York: Taylor & Francis, 2006.

Porter, Sylvia. "Babies Equal Boom." *New York Post*, May 4, 1951.

Project Prevention. "Frequently Asked Questions," Project Prevention, http://www.projectprevention.org/program/faqs.html (accessed January 12, 2009).

———. "Objectives," Project Prevention, http://www.projectprevention.org/cause/objectives.html (accessed January 12, 2009).

———. "Home Page," Project Prevention, http://www.projectprevention.org (accessed November 19, 2009).

Reagan, Leslie J. *When Abortion Was a Crime: Women, Medicine, and Law in the United States, 1867–1973.* Berkeley: University of California Press, 1997.

Reich, Jennifer, A. *Fixing Families: Parents, Power, and the Child Welfare System.* New York: Taylor & Francis, 2005.

Reiss, Benjamin. *The Showman and the Slave: Race, Death, and Memory in Barnum's America.* Cambridge, MA: Harvard University Press, 2001.

Rifkin, Jeremy. *The End of Work: The Decline of the Global Labor Force and the Dawn of the Post-Market Era.* New York: G. P. Putnam's Sons, 1995.

Roberts, Dorothy. *Shattered Bonds: The Color of Child Welfare.* New York: Basic Civitas Books, 2002.

———. *Killing the Black Body: Race, Reproduction, and the Meaning of Liberty.* New York: Vintage Books, 1997.

Ross, Loretta J. "African-American Women and Abortion: 1880–1970." In *Theorizing Black Feminisms: The Visionary Pragmatism of Black Women,* ed. Stanley M. James and Abeena P.A. Busia, pp. 141–159. New York: Routledge, 1993.

Rousseau, N. "A Historical Materialist Analysis of the Commodification of Black Women's Biological Reproduction in the United States." Ph.D. diss., Howard University, 2006.

———. "Passing." In *Blackwell Encyclopedia of Sociology*, second edition, ed. George Ritzer, vol. 7 pp. 3368–3370. Oxford, England: Blackwell, 2007.

Rupert, Mark and Hazel Smith (Eds.). *Historical Materialism and Globalisation: Essays on Continuity and Change.* London: Routledge, 2002.

Salary Reporter Blog, The. http://blogs.payscale.com/. Accessed May 27, 2009.

Scherer, Michael and Sarah Secules. "Books: How Slippery Is *Slander?*" In *Columbia Journalism Review* 4, p. 14: November/December, 2002.

Scott, Jerome and Walda Katz-Fishman. "The South and the Black Radical Tradition: Slave Institutions to Anti-Globalization Movements." In *The Roots of Terror*, second edition. Atlanta, GA: Project South: Institute for the Elimination of Poverty and Genocide, 2004.

Sernau, Scott. *Global Problems: The Search for Equity, Peace, and Sustainability.* Boston, MA: Allyn and Bacon, 2006.

Sharpley-Whiting, T. Denean. *Black Venus: Sexualized Savages, Primal Fears, and Primitive Narratives in French.* Durham, NC: Duke University Press, 1999.

Shulman, Beth. *The Betrayal of Work: How Low-Wage Jobs Fail 30 Million Americans and Their Families.* New York: The New Press, 2005.

Simson, Rennie. "The Afro-American Female: The Historical Context of the Construction of Sexual Identity." In *Powers of Desire: The Politics of Sexuality*, ed. Anita Snitow, Christine Stansell, and Sharon Thompson. New York: Monthly Review Press, 1983.

Solinger, Rickie (Ed.). *Abortion Wars: A Half Century of Struggle, 1950–2000.* Berkeley: University of California Press, 1998.

———. *Wake Up Little Susie: Single Pregnancy and Race Before Roe v. Wade.* New York: Routledge, 2000.

———. *Pregnancy and Power: A Short History of Reproductive Politics.* New York: New York University Press, 2005.

Spinsanity Blog, The. http://www.spinsanity.com/. Accessed January 19, 2009.

Stalin, Josef. *History of the Communist Party, Soviet Union.* San Francisco, CA: Proletarian, 1976.

Stearns, Peter, Michael Adas, Stuart B. Schwartz, and Marc J. Gilbert. *World Civilizations: The Global Experience.* New York: Longman Press, 2001.

U.S. Census Bureau. "Preliminary Report on the Eighth Census." Washington, DC: U.S. Department of the Interior, 1862.

U.S. Department of Justice. "Prison and Jail Inmates at Midyear 2007." Washington, DC: Bureau of Justice Statistics, June 2007.

————. "Parents in Prison and Their Minor Children." Washington, DC: Bureau of Justice Statistics, August 2008.

————. "Prison and Jail Inmates at Midyear 2006." Washington, DC: Bureau of Justice Statistics, June 2007.

Walker, Alice. "Coming Apart." In *The Womanist Reader,* ed. Layli Phillips, pp. 3–11. New York: Taylor & Francis, 2006 [1979].

————. *In Search of Our Mother's Gardens: Womanist Prose.* Orlando, FL: Harcourt Books, 1983.

Waller, Mark. "LaBruzzo: Sterilization Plan Fights Poverty." *The Times-Picayune,* September 24, 2008. Online edition, http://www.nola.com/news/t-p/capital/index.ssf?/base/news-6/122223371288730.xml&coll=1 (accessed September 26, 2008).

Wastell, David. "Generation Jones Comes of Age in Time for the Election." *The Telegraph,* June 19, 2001.

Webster, Richard A. "Metairie Lawmaker Considers Bill to Fund Sterilizations." *New Orleans City Business,* September 23, 2008. Online edition, http://www.neworleanscitybusiness.com/UpToTheMinute.cfm?recID=20404 (accessed September 26, 2008).

White, Deborah G. *Too Heavy a Load: Black Women in Defense of Themselves: 1894–1994.* New York: W. W. Norton, 2000.

Wilcox, L.S., S.Y. Chu, E.D. Eaker, S.L. Zeger, and H.B. Peterson, "Risk Factors for Regret after Tubal Sterilization: 5 Years of Follow-Up in a Prospective Study," in *Fertility and Sterility* 55(5): pp. 927–933, May 1991.

Williams, Linda Faye. *The Constraint of Race: Legacies of White Skin Privilege in America.* University Park, PA: Pennsylvania University Press, 2004.

Wilson, William Julius. *The Truly Disadvantaged: The Inner City, the Underclass, and Public Policy.* Chicago, IL: University of Chicago Press, 1987.

Wolff, Michael. *The Man Who Owns the News: Inside the Secret World of Rupert Murdoch.* New York: Broadway Books, 2008.

Women's Liberation Movement: An On-line Archival Collection. "Poor Black Women," Special Collections Library, Duke University, http://scriptorium.lib.duke.edu/wlm/poor/.

Zaretsky, Eli. *Capitalism, the Family, and Personal Life.* New York: Harper & Row, 1976.

Zeitlin, Irving M. *Ideology and the Development of Sociological Theory,* sixth edition. Englewood Cliffs, NJ: Prentice-Hall, 2001.

INDEX